Holiday Stories from Prince Edward Island

Snow Softly Falling

edited by *Richard Lemm*

P.O. Box 22024
Charlottetown, Prince Edward Island
C1A 9J2
acornpresscanada.com

Printed in Canada
Copy edit by Laurie Brinklow
Cover photo by Lee Ellen Pottie
Cover and interior design by Matt Reid

Library and Archives Canada Cataloguing in Publication

Snow softly falling : holiday stories from Prince Edward Island
/ Richard Lemm.

ISBN 978-1-927502-45-7 (paperback)

1. Christmas stories, Canadian (English)--Prince Edward Island.
2. Canadian fiction (English)--21st century. I. Lemm, Richard, 1946-,
editor

PS8237.C57S66 2015   C813'.0108334   C2015-904411-1

Canada   Canada Council Conseil des Arts
for the Arts du Canada

The publisher acknowledges the support of the Government of Canada through the Canada Book Fund of the Department of Canadian Heritage, the Canada Council of the Arts Block Grant Program and the support of the Province of Prince Edward Island.

Holiday Stories from Prince Edward Island

Snow Softly Falling

edited by *Richard Lemm*

The Acorn Press
Charlottetown
2015

Contents

Introduction:
Feast, Embrace, Endure

❄ Richard Lemm ❄

I hadn't been home for Christmas with my family in five years. I'd seen them just once, when my mother, Gloria, travelled with Uncle Curt, her only sibling, and Aunt Fern from their suburban Seattle home to my cottage on Tsawwassen Beach, south of Vancouver. A local tourism promoter had told me that *tsawwassen* in the North Salish language meant "facing the shining sea." The "shining" part was a booster's invention, but the sun did sparkle on the waters that Fourth of July for this bittersweet reunion.

My uncle had worked at Boeing Aircraft since leaving the U.S. Navy at the end of the Second World War. His domain was commercial airliners, not the B-52s of the Strategic Air Command or the more recent cruise missile production, which helped keep Boeing afloat during lean civilian aircraft contract times. A cheerful and never obnoxious patriot, he was spending this secularly sacred holiday with his draft dodger and pacifist nephew, a fugitive from justice wanted by the FBI, in my Canadian home. My apolitical mother, lodged permanently in a retirement-nursing home as a result of a "nervous breakdown" when I was a baby, electro-convulsive therapy, and potent medications, was simply overjoyed to see her only child for a few sun-blessed hours on a deck overlooking the sea, islands, and mountains. Her mind largely stuck back in the age of Frank Sinatra and Ella Fitzgerald, Presidents Roosevelt and Truman, and *Casablanca* and *High Noon*, she had almost no comprehension of the Vietnam War and war resistance. What she knew piercingly, as we hugged farewell late that American holiday afternoon, was that she might not see her son for a long time, or ever again.

I was aware that Uncle Curt had voted for Richard Nixon for president in 1968. Whatever he and Aunt Fern had thought about

1

my war resistance and emigration to Canada—disloyalty, cowardice, betrayal—they had moved enough beyond or suppressed on that holiday. They treated me with the love and warmth I'd known throughout my childhood, when they were a second family for me. Raised by Curt's mother after Gloria's breakdown, I was a kind of younger brother as well as nephew. Thus, when we hugged goodbye, all disapproval was set aside, and I knew he was tearful.

"I should have voted for George McGovern," he said. The most startling and unexpected words from his mouth and his heart. He was referring to the Democratic candidate's promise to end the war, which would have made it possible, he thought, for draft dodgers in Canada, for his nephew, to return home.

A year later, I learned that criminal charges had quietly been dropped against me and many other draft dodgers. Indeed, in October 1973, a month after I became a Canadian citizen, I received an official letter from the U.S. government stating that I had been "improperly denied Conscientious Objector status." My first thought: I can go home for Christmas.

As I entered my uncle and aunt's home on Lake Ballinger that Christmas morning, I anticipated an updated but approximate version of my childhood Christmases.

My grandmother, Aileen, and stepgrandfather, Harry, adhered to familiar traditions. My grandmother and I decorated the tree a week in advance to the dulcet sound of Bing Crosby's "White Christmas" and carols by the Mormon Tabernacle Choir, while Grandpa watched us and sipped his bourbon. Grandma paused to rest her feet and sip from her own glass. They liked their whiskey neat. On Christmas Eve and morning, Grandpa, a bartender by profession, would make Tom and Jerrys, a variant on eggnog, with brandy or rum, devised by a British journalist in the 1820s, and popular in America. My mug would be booze-free. I loved decorating the tree, except for the tinsel icicles: draping them on branches was a tedious task. As working-class survivors of the Great Depression, my grandparents saved almost everything, and one of my post-Christmas chores was to remove the icicles one by one and carefully place them in their box. Glass bulbs, too, were to be handled with reverence bred of both frugality and sentimental attachment.

Grandma played our upright piano agreeably and sang with a strong, lovely voice, which became more animated with each glass of bourbon or mug of Tom and Jerry. She knew most carols by

2

heart, but would spread open her songbooks and sheet music in case I forgot the lyrics. During the week before Christmas, I would sit beside her on the piano bench, matching the variations in her voice with mine. Grandma infused every song with chromatic feeling. In any season, and especially during Christmas, her emotional canvas quivered with a rich palette. Grandpa, on the sofa half-listening while reading Zane Grey or Mickey Spillane, was a landscape painting just before sunrise or after sunset.

The Christmas gifts would accumulate night by night under the tree. I would study them, pick them up when I was alone, to determine if I was getting a new baseball glove or football helmet, a Sorry or Monopoly game. At school, I compared expectations and under-the-tree evidence with friends. With my wealthier Jewish friends, I envied their Hanukkah: eight lavish days of gifts. With much less affluent Jewish kids, I sympathized with their longing for Christmas largesse. On Christmas Eve, I tore myself away from the tree and served as an altar boy for midnight mass at St. Clement's, which transformed, with the arrival of a new priest when I was eleven, from a Protestant Episcopal church to an Anglo-Catholic parish. Swinging the thurible with its frankincense burning, I briefly forgot about presents and was suffused with the fragrance of the saviour's birth. As the priest intoned nativity passages from the King James Bible, and hymns arose from the organ and choir and congregation, in my imagination the wise men and angel figurines on our piano top were no longer decorations, but embodiments of the divine presence on earth. For nearly two hours I had no need of Santa, filled as I was with holiness.

Returning home, I found my sleepy grandparents sitting on the dining room sofa, whiskey glasses empty, gazing at the flames in our fireplace, Christmas tree lights illuminating the living room and gifts. Grandma, a lapsed Methodist, and Grandpa, a lapsed Lutheran, patiently listened to my glowing account of the sacred wonders revealed unto their grandson. Then I climbed the stairs to my bedroom, left them to their mysterious reflections, forgot about Jesus, and fell asleep with visions of baseball gloves dancing in my head.

Before I was eleven, Christmas mornings were an untarnished joy, followed by afternoons with Curt and Fern and their two children in their home. By my eleventh year, however, Grandma and Grandpa's nightly drinking had intensified. So, too, had their frequent and often bitter quarreling. Christmas morning still began sweetly. But by midmorning, after almost all the presents were opened and they had consumed several Tom and Jerrys, the Christmas mood began to darken. The clouds had been forming beyond the horizon for weeks, after they promised each other not to spend serious money on each other's major gift. I knew about this promise. So when Grandpa announced that he had one more gift for Grandma, I heard thunderclaps too close for comfort. He handed her a small package, which she unwrapped with, it seemed, unsuspecting delight. But when she saw the diamond ring, she scowled and declared, joylessly, that she would have to ask for a refund on the wood-turning lathe she had bought him for his basement workshop.

"What lathe?" he asked, upset. "We can't afford a lathe."

"Well, I don't need another diamond ring. And you promised not to waste money we don't have on some extravagance I don't need."

"Seems to me you promised the same thing."

And the battle was on, smouldering at first, then heating up from the broken promises to incandescent recriminations making a scorched earth of their marriage and licking at the heels of their "spoiled, ungrateful" grandson as he fled to his room with his arms full of games and toys.

The next two Christmases, I knew what was coming. I managed to suppress my dread enough during the first half of the morning to enjoy the gift opening. Then came those "last little presents." Whoever definitively identifies the causal factors for repetitive disastrous behaviour, for failure to gain insight from catastrophes and to change, will be a trillionaire and multiple Nobel Prize–winner. Before the battle royale came close to its crescendo, I was a block away in the cheerful home and sanctuary of Leonard and Emma Gayton, an African-American couple. Lynn, their second-oldest child, was one of my best friends, and the oldest, Tomás, would become an athletic, intellectual, and social mentor in high school. They, too, were altar boys at the Anglo-Catholic church situated midway between our homes, and had attended midnight mass with me, while the parents attended the Christmas morning service at the First African Methodist Episcopal Church. After church, Mrs. Gayton cooked up one of her legendary breakfast feasts of waffles, bacon, scrambled eggs, and cornbread and honey.

The Gaytons belonged to one of Seattle's pioneer African-American families. Tomás became a civil rights and liberties lawyer, activist, and poet, and chronicled his family history in a memoir that delves back to slavery in Mississippi, touches on Leonard's early adult career as a jazz musician, and celebrates his parents' dignity and pride as a working-class Black family. On Christmas afternoon, their home resonated with gratitude, love, playfulness, and generosity. Whatever sorrows, insults, and hardships Leonard and his wife Emma had endured were channeled through the sounds of Billie Holiday and Duke Ellington on their phonograph, and not, as in my home during my grandmother's final few years, through inebriated disappointment and rancor. Forgotten for a few hours in the Gaytons' abode were my gloomy home and the two people sullen and sulking, licking their wounds, gathering themselves for the visit to Curt and Fern's.

On one of those Christmas afternoons, Grandma swayed on her high heels on Curt and Fern's living room carpet in their suburban home, Tom and Jerry mug in her hand, singing a jolly Christmas tune. Sitting on a sofa with Grandpa, I could tell that Curt was uncomfortable and Fern sternly disapproving. My usual enjoyment of Grandma's performances faded into nervous embarrassment. Then she teetered and spilled her drink on the carpet. Fern rose to her feet.

"You're drunk," my aunt said haughtily, adding that my grandmother was a common lush, or something to that horrifying effect. Curt remained sitting, downcast, suspended between his wife's disdain and his mother's mortification.

I sensed that Fern's reaction involved more than disgruntlement over my grandmother's intoxicated behaviour. Curt had risen at Boeing from a blue-collar worker to management status, still on the assembly line floor, but as a supervisor. My uncle and aunt's lifestyle had altered accordingly, with a ranch house, new furniture, and a classy station wagon. My grandmother and grandfather were content to remain lower middle-class. Indeed, in spite of his bartender's white shirt and tie, Grandpa insisted proudly on his working-class identity, and instilled class consciousness in me. Grandma was both pleased with her son and daughter-in-law's success and sensitive to what she and Grandpa felt was their newly superior gaze. Grandma liked to point out, when she felt judged, that Fern was from Idaho, which to many Seattleites then was a synonym for "sticks" and "hicks." Thus, frozen on the sofa, my head swirling with both chagrin and indignation, I knew that the tension in the

room was about more than Grandma drinking too much and stain-
ing the carpet. Christmas day, I realized, could also be a battleground
of people's values, identities, and relative standing in society. I
didn't, of course, think in those sophisticated terms, but I knew as
sharply as we know such things from our earliest experiences at
school or church, on neighbourhood streets and playgrounds, at
family holiday gatherings.

Grandpa rose, told me to get up, and took Grandma's hand.

"We're leaving," he said to my uncle and aunt, "and never coming
back."

And we didn't. Both to my great disappointment and with full
support for my grandparents and our way of living. I assumed that
the ice would eventually melt and we'd gather before each other's
Christmas trees once more. Then Grandma died in the summer of
my fourteenth year, and I've ever after had to see through that
afternoon in their suburban living room to the many joyous holidays
with Curt and Fern and my cousins before the damage of booze
and class ambition, pride, and resentment.

I have no recollection of how I spent Christmas after my grandmother's death and before my desire to celebrate a winter holiday
revived, during my early twenties, in secular or pagan forms. Childhood memories of Christmas powerfully remain, as they do for
countless people in North American society, where Christmas has
morphed from a dominant cultural and spiritual tradition into an
overwhelming, weeks-long rite of economic necessity, a cultural
orgy of production, consumption, and financial transactions.

Every Christmas I revel in visions of my grandparents and me
cheerful around the gifts and tree, and lament the bitter words that
drove me from the house. I know from a lifetime of friendships and
storytellers that holidays—Hanukkah, Eid, Deepavali, Chinese
New Year, and Canadian and American Thanksgiving, as well as
Christmas—are for many people, and perhaps for most, a time of
conflicting emotions, bright and dark memories, felicity and distress,
euphoria and pain. I know people for whom their holiday season
is an Elysian field of cherished, unsullied memories, and others
whose harsh recollections won't let them go within a country mile
of a Christmas or Hanukkah gathering. Most people, I suspect,
have a bittersweet relationship with their holidays, the weight of
the sweet and the bitter varying, depending on one's experience and
psyche. On the alchemy of those holiday memories: dross and gold.

My earliest reliable memory is of a Christmas Eve when I was three. I lived with my grandparents in an apartment across from Garfield High School, where my mother, uncle, and Jimi Hendrix had gone to school. A wet snowfall that day and evening had brought magic to the otherwise dreary inner-city streetscape, and left the pavement slick. I was sitting at our small kitchen table when we heard a loud crash. We hurried to the living room window, and saw two cars smashed hood-to-hood together. I was told not to look, as my grandparents donned shoes and coats and went outside. But I kept watching as other cars stopped, a driver emerged from one wrecked car, and people, including my grandparents, peered through the windows of the other car. And as a police car arrived with that usually exciting but now ominous siren.

My memory goes blank until my grandparents return with two children, a brother and sister, a couple years older than me. My grandmother is between them, a hand on each shoulder, guiding them toward the kitchen. My grandfather holds a large cake box, half-smushed. He quietly tells me to wait in the hallway with him, while my grandmother helps the children take off their coats and sits them down at the table.

"Their parents have been killed," Grandpa says softly, in his taciturn, no-nonsense way. "Be nice to them."

My grandmother sets three saucers, forks, and glasses on the table. Pours milk, cuts three large slices of cake from the good side. A white cake with vanilla icing, the kind you buy at the Woolworth's bakery. And green and red ribbons and bells.

We eat silently. How can they eat cake, I think, when their parents have just died? Why aren't they crying? The cake is delicious. I want another piece, but know enough not to ask. My father's death in a car crash when I was nine months old, inaccessible for now, waits in my brain's wiring to be a memory switched on, an absence at Christmas to be later rued, as I will bemoan my mother's absence during the holidays, in her mental-hospital room.

The children's grandparents arrive, wait in the hallway, thank mine. Drape their arms around the boy and girl. They are gone.

I choose to believe that those two children were raised, as I was, by lovingly devoted grandparents, who made their winter season holidays a time of warmth and delight, gratitude and joy. There would have been heartaches and tensions, too, disappointments and losses, embedded in those holidays and later memories. For this is our bitter-and-sweet fate as humans and our calling as storytellers and audience. Think of the great Christmas stories: Dickens' *A Christmas Carol* with Scrooge and his ghosts and Tiny Tim's disability and impoverished family; *How the Grinch Stole Christmas*; James Stewart in *It's a Wonderful Life*, who requires the intervention of a guardian angel to dissuade him from suicide on Christmas Eve; the abandoned child besieged by burglars, and the lonely older man estranged from his children, in *Home Alone*; the destitute, starving, freezing children of Europe in "The Little Match Girl" by Hans Christian Andersen; even poor Rudolph, mocked and shunned by all the other reindeer.

Hanukkah celebrates the rededication of the Holy Temple in Jerusalem during the Maccabean Revolt against the Seleucid Empire during the second century BCE. A joyous occasion, for sure, but an outcome of oppression, suffering, armed revolt. In T.S. Eliot's famous poem "Journey of the Magi," the magi asks, "were we led all that way for / Birth or Death?" Eliot stresses that the nativity is extraordinary because it is the prelude to the main event, the crucifixion, the sacrifice, and the resurrection. This is a richer, more complex, more fully human vision than the narrowly cheerful pleasure of "Away in a Manger" and solemn grandeur of "O Holy Night." Eid may be a day of fabulous feasting, when one is obliged to show happiness, but it ends the month of Ramadan fasting, and the Eid sermon includes a supplication asking for Allah's forgiveness and mercy.

In North America, and on Prince Edward Island, the religious content of the winter holiday has greatly diminished, and vanished altogether for many people, apart from its vestiges in carols and other traditions. Our temples of shopping—the dominant places of worship and promised redemption in modern culture—in the Christmas season look increasingly like the decorated lobby of the hotel where I stay while teaching in Cairo in December: Santas, elves, reindeer, and festooned trees. The clientele, mostly Muslim, dwell comfortably among these commercial icons, humming along with "Jingle Bell Rock." Yet, these symbols, largely devoid of spiritual significance, are powerfully mythic. And myths bind us together, potently shape our identities, and fuel our individual and communal actions.

I was stuck for hours in legendary Cairo gridlock a few years ago on the first day of Eid. Millions of Cairenes heading for shopping malls and restaurants, the famous Khan el-Kalili bazaar downtown, country homes and ancestral villages, the airport for seaside resorts. Within the organized chaos of this holiday weekend, familiar to any modern cosmopolitan dweller, were the mythic forces of a people's ancient heritage: fasting and feasting, penitence and praise. The community's renewal.

In 1973, I drove south, crossing the border for the first time in five years, crawling in bumper-to-bumper traffic on Seattle's freeways, and took the exit for Lake Ballinger and my uncle and aunt's home. In their living room was a spectacular pine tree. Entirely sprayed with fake snow. The piles of gifts, if you lay down with your head on the carpet, as I did to stretch from the long drive, looked like the Manhattan skyline. My cousins and their families were there. The opening of gifts revealed the miracle of America's economic bonanza and swelling middle class. Where would my family put all those mirrors, vases, clocks, serving dishes, power and gardening tools, picture frames, towels, and kitschy figurines? As for children's toys and games, my grandparents sometimes said they spoiled me. And it was true that I was given everything I asked for and more. But I was hard done by compared to the loot my cousins' children were acquiring. Christmas wasn't a time for giving, but for swimming in a sea of abundance.

My mother, liberated for the day from her nursing home, watched all this with the non-stop amazement of a child from a remote Pacific island transported to Las Vegas. She was without envy or resentment—by nature and/or electro-shock and medications—and her wistful longing was not for the cornucopia to spill in her lap, but to be more fully part of her family, lodged with them or me, and not in a nursing home. To be more than a guest on Christmas day.

After the skyline was finally levelled, Fern and her daughter served a brunch that matched the gifts: enough food for a football team, I thought, heaping my plate with sausages, bacon, eggs, strawberries the size of billiard balls, and pancakes.

"Ready for Aurora Mall?" my aunt asked me, eagerly, when the table was cleared.

The Aurora Mall, a five-minute drive away, was one of the largest shopping centres in North America, and inspired the kind of rapture in shoppers we rarely feel anymore, jaded as we are with malls and box stores.

"But stores aren't open on Christmas," I ventured uncertainly.

"Now they are. And the sales will be fantastic."

An hour later, strolling among the crowds in the mall, I thought, sardonically, "Welcome to the future."

Then I saw Levi's on sale for half-price and bought two pair.

I returned to Canada, grateful to have been reunited with my family and for their generosity, and dazzled and bemused by the profound cultural transformation in such a relatively short time.

During the 1970s and 1980s, I was in rebellion against the commercialization of Christmas—trivialization and bastardization, I thought—and its theological doctrines. Those were the years of winter solstice parties, sometimes with midwinter rituals of non-Judaeo-Christian cultures—from ancient Egyptian and Celtic to pagan Scandinavian and Amerindian—as well as personal rituals devised by my friends. There were, too, secularized Christmas and Hanukkah celebrations. I appreciated whatever customs and rituals were offered.

Now that I am part of a family with my wife's three children and our proliferating grandchildren, Christmas Day supper transpires in our home. My wife, with her Cape Breton Acadian and Newfoundland outport ancestry, cherishes traditions as much as I do. Perhaps more. Her Catholic father deferred to her Jehovah's Witness mother in the raising of their five children, who were not allowed to celebrate Christmas. We amiably negotiate differing traditions: hers of white Christmas tree lights, mine of multicoloured bulbs; her insistence on a turkey, my plea for baked ham. With family crowded into our living room while opening gifts, and around our dining table, she revels in what she was not permitted as a child. I'm immersed once more in the warm and glowing waters of family treasuring one another, as I once floated in the happier currents flowing through midwinter celebrations in the homes of Grandma and Grandpa, Curt and Fern, Emma and Leonard Gayton.

There will be, on future holidays, tensions, disappointments, misunderstandings, hardships, losses. And those, too, are reasons for midwinter celebrations, secular and religious: bringing us together to celebrate with and honour one another during tough times. Reasons as powerful as our need to rejoice, to give thanks, to give and receive, to feast and embrace, to laugh and sing and dance.

In colder climates for millennia, until rather recently, midwinter celebrations helped our ancestors endure the months when the earth was frozen, the sky dark most of each day, and homes and beds cold. The celebrations also enabled our ancestors to give homage to the beauty and value of the winter months within nature's cycles and the divine or supernatural schemes. With central heating, bright lighting, overflowing supermarkets, and winter clothing, the midwinter celebration transforms into a "holiday," which retains some of its traditional meaning and purpose and imagery, while serving new functions within capitalist societies.

Yet the traditions are exceedingly strong, and our memories of holidays, of Christmases or Hanukkahs or Eids past, are vibrant. We all have ghosts of winter holidays past: many benign, endearing, reaffirming, inspiring; some haunting us uncomfortably, disturbingly, even stopping us in our tracks. In each of us there's a child, hanging ornaments on a tree, lighting a menorah, arranging the Eid table, singing "Auld Lang Syne" with the tipsy, hugging grownups.

The genesis of *Snow Softly Falling: Holiday Stories from Prince Edward Island* was the desire to share with readers a selection of previously unpublished memoirs, poems, and short stories by Island writers about their winter holiday experiences, imaginings, and reflections. The call for submissions stated that writers "should have a significant Prince Edward Island connection," but that there was "no requirement for 'Island' content: stories may be set in any locale." The hope was for a wide range and variety of winter holiday experiences, "with a focus on the Christmas season or comparable celebrations, e.g., Hannukah, Eid, Diwali, Chinese New Year, Kwanzaa." Secular and religious perspectives were both welcome. Fictional stories and poems as well as personal essays based closely on memory would be welcome. In the tradition of holiday classics, and in keeping with the complex emotional rhythms and tones associated with holiday memories—from the high-spirited to the heavyhearted, from the wistful or plaintive to the enraptured or serene, and often a polyphony of moods—it was expected that the anthology would resonate with the richly varied moods evoked by winter holidays. And so it does.

One thing the anthology, sadly, does not do is adequately reflect the varied and changing demographic of Prince Edward Island. In addition to such longstanding communities as Islanders of Lebanese heritage and descendants of Black Loyalists and Black American slaves, there are growing communities of Islanders with Asian, African, Latin American, and South Asian backgrounds. Unfortunately, there were no submissions from these communities, even with repeated calls, personal appeals, and extended deadlines.

There are, however, contributions from two First Nations writers, one from a writer born and raised in Persia, and stories and poetry reflecting Jewish heritage. Other contributions take us to the birthplaces of "Islanders by choice"—Scotland, England, Georgia, British Columbia, Ontario, and elsewhere. And many stories and poems, of course, entice us back to Island holidays in the recent and distant past: from Yuletide during the rationing and apprehensions of the First World War, to the stress of coping with our hypercommodified Christmas and dealing with far-flung family members estranged by the endless busyness of the modern world; from dreams of skating on homemade Island rinks like the Canadian legend Barbara Ann Scott, to a young Japanese visitor landing on the Island in midwinter and learning to bake Christmas cookies.

Readers will find many familiar voices in *Snow Softly Falling*: long-established Island writers such as J.J. Steinfeld, Dianne Hicks Morrow, Elaine Breault Hammond, David Helwig, Laurel Smyth, and Orysia Dawydiak; newer writers making their mark such as Steven Mayoff, Kathleen Hamilton, Beth E. Janzen, Shaun Patterson, Glenna Jenkins, and Julie Pellissier-Lush; and numerous other writers whose names will be recognized for their published work and Island Literary Awards, and for other contributions to Island life and heritage. And there are new voices, whose writing careers are launched in this anthology.

Finally, in the interest of full disclosure, I must declare that I still believe in Santa. When my turn came to arrive home from school crying because kids had mocked me for still believing in Santa, my grandmother assured me that Santa was real. How could that be, I demanded through my sniffles and sobs.

"I'm Santa," she said.

The weeping stopped as if mousetraps had snapped shut on my tear ducts. I ricocheted from disillusion to incredulity.

"You can't be Santa," I protested.

"Yes, I can. And so is your grandpa. So are you. Anybody who gives presents is Santa."

This instantly made perfectly logical sense, and offered safe passage from my disenchantment. I boldly tested this hypothesis at school the next day, and while a few kids were scornful and several others skeptical, it mostly met with approval, enough for me to adopt it as a theory, which has been verified countless times through experiential evidence.

This anthology is further proof. Forty-eight authors, Santas all, have crafted gifts in their writing workshops, and given them to us, their readers, for our enjoyment and enrichment. Tales for our winter days and nights—and for any other time of the year, too.

Long Distances
Christmas 2007

❄ Kathleen Hamilton ❄

Christmas is exactly two weeks away. We've been to the woods to chop down our tree. I've lugged parcels to the village post office in Prince Edward Island, where I live, and mailed them to family members in New Brunswick, Ontario, British Columbia, and the Yukon. We're not close, my family. I haven't been in the same room with my brother for twenty-five years. Still, this year, perhaps for the first time in my life, I feel grateful for people I can call family and send homemade candy to at Christmas.

I confess that in the past I have participated grudgingly. Yes, I have put a smile on my face and I have sent the presents and decorated the tree and cooked six vegetables to go with the turkey, but I never—and this is an embarrassing thing to admit when one is nearing a half-century in age—I never got the *meaning*.

Every year since becoming an adult woman, I have felt overwhelmed with the responsibilities of the season: shop for gifts, make gifts, wrap gifts, prepare parcels for mailing, wait in line at the post office, and then when my duties to family members "away" are complete, I turn to my responsibilities to family members at home: bake, shop for presents, make presents, wrap gifts, decorate the house, decorate the tree, order the turkey, invite the guests, clean my house, cook the dinner, serve the dinner, call family members to say Merry Christmas, clean up. This in addition to raising a child and earning an income. It's a lot of work. And at least part of it is in service to family members I seldom or never see.

It has always *felt* like work. And for what purpose? I could see the charm in thrilling the kiddies with presents, but I could never understand the point of exchanging gifts with adults. I did it, but I resented the compulsory-ness. The pressure, the expectations, the deadlines. And the stakes are high: you must come through or people will feel *unloved*.

During Christmas seasons past, there have been moments when, panicking my way through a mall, too hot in my winter boots and coat, the bags I am lugging weighted with impulse purchases for myself (I don't know what anyone else wants), or awake past midnight affixing bows to presents, I have been known to feel sorry for myself. Why oh why has our culture mandated a make-work project of such colossal proportions?

On Christmas mornings past, as we opened gifts, my tradition was to start drinking my seasonal bottle of Bailey's before my husband even had our morning cappuccino brewed. Bailey's is not booze. It's *liqueur*. The truth is, I felt a huge pressure to be happy on Christmas, and I had no reason to believe I could achieve that without my holiday bottle. Now I'm a good ten years sober, and am learning to be at peace with my feelings no matter what they are and no matter what day it is.

The other day an elderly married man asked me the usual December question: "Are you ready for Christmas?"

It occurred to me to answer with a question of my own.

"What do *you* have to do to get ready for Christmas?" I asked him, keeping my voice neutral, curious. "Nothing," he replied. "Not a thing."

His wife does it all. She even turned down a page in her Avon catalogue so he could pick up the phone and order her gift, a pair of gloves. I didn't ask what he'd do about the wrapping. It's something else that's always peeved me, that Christmas is characterized by a sexual division of labour, with the lion's share done by women.

But this year, I don't feel as resentful and anxious about "the season." Things have changed in my family: two years ago, my uncle Myles died right before Christmas, and then last year, again right before Christmas, we lost Nana, our matriarch. The past two Christmases in my family have been upstaged by funerals and deathbed farewells. And this will be our second Christmas since the death of my husband's mother. As for my own mother, she and I are estranged.

I am without matriarchs. I have just realized this. I have lost the women who until now have hosted the family gatherings, whose homes I could go to and see everyone else, or at least I could phone there and talk to everyone else. Or I could talk to the matriarchs and save myself the need to talk to everyone else. The matriarchs had everyone's news. They were the nucleus.

Scientists have recently realized that the nucleus of a cell is not the command centre. If you remove the nucleus, the cell doesn't die instantly. It functions the same. What the nucleus has is the blueprint of the cell. It is in charge of reproduction. Without it, nothing can be replaced, so eventually the cell dies. Eventually.

That's how it feels in my family right now. I know it's not a perfect analogy. Theoretically, someone else could become the matriarch, someone else could have everyone's news.

Last weekend we went with friends on our annual tree-hunting expedition, on land of theirs in the country. Cuyler, our seven-year-old, asked if he could be the one to chop. My husband handed him the axe and coached him through the job, and in the end our son had chopped the trunk so thin that he was able to push it over, and then proudly helped carry our Christmas tree out of the woods.

He loves to help with the work of Christmas, my son. He tapes down the edges of the wrapping paper, rolls the cookie dough into balls, and painstakingly prints his name on gift tags. He was impressed by the countrywide destinations of our presents, pronounced the eighty-nine dollars charged by Canada Post to deliver them "cheap."

I've been thinking that, too. On Vancouver Island, in Whitehorse, in Guelph, and in Gagetown, our far-flung family members will soon open our modest presents from PEI, taste my husband's chocolate hazelnut toffee made with Kahlúa, and maybe, through the magic of Christmas, if they get the meaning, they will feel, if not loved, then at least claimed.

That's what's occurring to me this year. The value of claiming each other. It doesn't matter that my family members don't always understand and appreciate each other and want to spend our summer vacations together. That estrangements can and do endure for decades. It doesn't matter that we aren't burning up the phone lines the rest of the year, or that I didn't recognize my Aunt Betty-Jean at the funeral two years ago. We are who we are, we live where we live, and we love who we love. We belong perhaps not always with each other, but to each other. We're family. And if waiting in line at the post office at Christmas can help to remind me of that, I'm thankful.

Why I Believe in Santa Claus

❄ Laurel Smyth ❄

When I was six, Santa came to see me. It's true. My mother saw him, too. And I remember…

First, the most wonderful of childhood sleeps, that visions-of-sugar-plums slumber of the innocent who knows she will awaken to Christmas Day in all its glory. Then, my mother's voice quietly speaking my name, "Laurel," her tall black silhouette in a stream of light from the hallway. She bent and placed her face close to mine to see if I was awake in the shadows. I could tell she didn't want to disturb my older sister sleeping beside me in the bed. Why?

On her face I saw a most beautiful expression of tenderness, and some other seldom-seen look of expectancy, or delight. Whatever it was, it sure looked good on her; she was like a dream of herself. But, no, she patted my cheek, she was real. "Wake up, Laurel." Her voice was low.

"Why?" I asked, this time aloud. A little louder than I planned, in fact. I startled us both with my crisp demand for information— it was so at odds with my sleepy six-year-old body. "Why?" I corrected myself in an appropriate whisper. She looked me right in the eye and said in perfect seriousness, "Santa Claus is here and he wants to see you."

My breathing stopped. Time suspended while I struggled with the enormity of the news. What could it mean? In all my devoted studies of Christmas lore, all the legends, poems, movies, fairy tales, carols, and cartoons, I'd never heard of Santa having kids woken up. Maybe I was dreaming, or…

"Why?" I croaked again, a little apprehensively. Mother folded back my half of the covers and expertly swung my feet to the floor 'til I tottered on the edge of the box spring mattress. She put her lips to my ear. I inhaled the scent of her face powder and shivered at the tickle of her sherry-warm breath as she whispered the magic words: "Santa says you've been such a good girl all year, he wants to see you for himself."

HALLELUJAH! Virtue is rewarded right here on Earth—you don't have to wait for Heaven. It pays to be good. Oh, a valuable life lesson, and a lucky one to learn so young. For if ever a child strove to be good in that year of our Lord, 1955, I swear it was me.

You see, I was only five the last time I saw my Grandma Wanless, but I remember that, too. She took my face between her hands, her fingers so thin the nails and pads at the ends seemed too large. "You've always been a good girl for your Grandma, Laurel. You keep on being such a good girl." Then she kissed me goodnight with that warm, dry lip-pursing of hers, and I climbed down from her bed and scampered off to my own.

When my mother brought in a breakfast tray the next morning, she found Grandma all laid out, nice and straight, her arms folded across her breast, her face serene. She'd just… left. I thought a lot about her goodbye to me.

So, I was being good. Good enough for Grandma, and for Santa, too, it seemed. Now, I was to be rewarded beyond imagining. I gave my big sister no more than a backwards glance as we left her sleeping there, for which she'd never forgive us. But she didn't believe in Santa anymore, so why should I worry? I climbed in silent wonder down the steep and shiny stairs, held my mother's hand along the deep red linoleum of the back hallway and into the evergreen living room.

And there, in Dad's big velvet armchair, he waited for me. He was like and unlike any Santa I've seen before or since. The first and most striking thing I noticed was the nimbus of light that surrounded his entire being. He was glowing golden, and brighter than our tree of many colours, the only other light in the room. He didn't smoke a pipe, but he did smell of whiskey. He didn't laugh with a hearty "Ho Ho Ho!" He just chuckled softly, held out his arms, and said in the kindest voice ever, "Hello, Laurel."

I didn't feel any of the hesitation I'd felt in the department store; I knew a good thing when I saw it. I went right on over, climbed in his lap and laid my little head on his big furry chest. Up close, the suit was silky velvet, the fur soft as real, the beard crinkly with the proper whiskery feel; and when I pulled back to look up into that face I'd never seen before but would never forget, I saw the beard springing naturally from his skin. Hey, I may have been starstruck, but I was no dummy, I knew what telltale signs to look for: I'd met many a false Santa in my day.

But then all ability to analyze fell away, the moment he placed his palm on the centre of my back. From that hand radiated an energy so pure, so alive, I felt myself filled from the core with humming light. I hung, speechless, trembling, ecstatic, on that flow of power, able only to nod, dumb and wide-eyed, as Santa rumbled softly, "You keep on being such a good girl, Laurel."

Then he gave me a child-sized broom set that I really liked. The broom had a dustpan tied to its red wooden handle by a big green ribbon. "Merry Christmas!" he laughed again, and broke the spell with a kiss on my forehead. I slid obediently to the floor, clutching my present, and padded to my parents watching by the door. When I looked back, he was still there, halo and all, in the armchair by the tree. "Goodbye, Santa," I think I whispered. I was all choked up; it may not have come out. He nodded to me solemnly, and solemnly off I went.

So, I believe in Santa Claus. Wouldn't you? Oh, as I grew up, the times certainly came when I questioned the truth of even this best of memories, wondering if perhaps it should be filed along with the odd assortment of fey events from my past that did not quite stand up to the brand of logic being promoted in Canadian schools in the early '60s. Things like seeing the great snowy owl down the Etobicoke Creek. Or seeing Grandma Wanless and her old friend strolling arm in arm down her street shortly after she had "passed away." Or the dream of the grass snake that came true the next day; and the one of Jesus and all his angels that hasn't come true... yet. All these terrific experiences, I was discovering, had best be referred to in rational society as "childish imagination," or, better yet, not mentioned at all. The difference with seeing Santa Claus was this: *my mother saw him, too.*

So I asked Mom for her version of the Santa memory as we trimmed the tree for my thirteenth Christmas. That year we had both known tremendous changes. My mother had been widowed; and I had suffered the triple shocks of my father's death, the onslaught of puberty, and a six-month, six-inch growth spurt that had changed me forever from the little girl that I was. Mom was so brave through it all, I loved her more than ever.

It seems that after she and Dad had finished setting out all the presents and stuffing our stockings, they'd slipped over to the corner neighbours' for some Christmas cheer. Around about midnight there came a knock at the door. Mom said Harry Bell, their host, was joking as he went to answer, "I dunno who it could be at this time Christmas Eve, 'cept Santa Claus." From her seat, she saw Harry swing the door open with a flourish; then, as she put it, his chin nearly hit the floor as Santa himself stepped into the hall with a hearty "Merry Christmas!"

She said that at the sight of their shocked faces, Santa laughed so hard he doubled over and slapped his knee, so they all had to have a good laugh, too. He declined the offer of a drink; he said he was jolly enough. He wondered if there were any children in the house they would like him to see. He did this every year, "just for the love of it," Mom remembers him saying. He'd give the kiddies any present their folks had gotten for them; or, if need be, he had some toys in his sack, "just in case." And he winked.

My mother, bless her, said right away that she had just the girl for him to see, a true devotee, and asked him to please come by as soon as the Bells' little girl had had the pleasure. It was Mom who'd bought the broom set for me. Thanks, Mom.

So, my "bestest friend," Iris Bell, saw Santa that night, too, but it didn't seem to make as much of an impression on her. She stopped believing in him the very next Christmas. Things were never really the same with us after that. I believed with utter simplicity until I was twelve years old. Every Christmas Eve the radio would announce, "An unidentified flying object has been tracked by radar moving south from the North Pole. Air Force officials report that it appears to be a sleigh and eight reindeer." And I was hooked again.

I may not believe all radio reports anymore, but I still believe in Santa Claus. I think of him as my patron saint. Because when I think of my mother's explanation of that night, I realize that he didn't say anything that denied his Santa-hood. "Just for the love of it…"

And I remember his light, and the warmth from his hand, and… it doesn't matter. Even if he was pretending, just acting—in that moment, on that Christmas Eve, he *was* Santa for me. I made him Santa Claus if he wasn't already. Faith can work wonders.

And I may not always have been good, but I've always known I can be. So if you're reading this, Santa—*thanks*.

Christmas on Lennox Island First Nation

❄   Julie Pellissier-Lush   ❄

"It is okay to be poor if everyone around you is as poor as you are," said my father, Louis Pellissier, when he talked about our early years in Prince Edward Island.

This still rings true to me as much as it did when I was little, but I must add that this does not include Christmas time. When all the community children were getting excited about the upcoming holiday and making Christmas lists full of hope in the wonderful magic of Christmas, parents would lower their heads as they read the long lists of toys that their children were asking Santa for.

In my community of Lennox Island First Nation, back in the early 1970s, the families were never small, and money was always hard to find, especially when all the fishermen and fisherwomen were off work for the winter months. It was a very hard time for everyone: food usually did not stretch out for the whole season, and many times parents would go without for their children. When you add Christmas to this, it would become heartbreaking for many families on the Island.

To this day, I am not sure who came up with the idea, but some-one did, and one day, just before Christmas, people came around, gathering all the children in the community, and we waited as a group, huddled together with our cheeks turning bright and rosy with the cold December wind blowing hard. Once we were all together in the centre of the community, we soon heard a huge helicopter coming. Many of us had never seen a helicopter up close, but there it was, coming nearer and nearer until it landed. The wind whipped around us from the propellers, but none of us minded as we stared with our mouths open at this huge mechanical bird. After it had safely landed, we were brought on board, and we were so excited to be inside and have a look around the cabin. When we were safely seated, the big doors closed, and up up into the air we went, all the way to Slemon Park in Summerside, about fifty kilometers away. It was not a long flight, but time stood still.

We landed at Slemon Park, and went right from the helicopter to the community hall, where there was a huge Christmas party waiting for us. When we were done with our snacks and drinks, we could hear a loud "Ho ho ho!" Santa came to our party, and he had a big red bag full of gifts. He called out our names, and we took our turns going up and getting a gift from Santa, like a new toy truck for the boys or pretty Barbie Doll for the girls.

Once we had our presents and had put on our snowsuits, hats, mitts, and boots, we went back to the helicopter. I know some of us felt as if we had gone to the North Pole, and had sat with the real Santa. Even the older children hugged their gifts tightly on that short flight home, and all of us were smiling from ear to ear. Our parents were there when we got off the helicopter, and we told them about every minute of that magical day. Everyone went home feeling happy and having a new understanding about the wonderful magic of Christmas. I do not know how many years they did this for the children of Lennox Island, but it gave those who did go a newfound joy in the meaning of Christmas. As adults, we will bring up that day every once in a while, and we talk about the time the helicopter landed in Lennox and took us all to Christmas.

The Night That Randolph Danced

❄ David McCabe ❄

every year
in that time of short
dark december afternoons
the lumbering and measured
learning machinery
of the one-room school
ground down to a crawl
and that spare dry place
of straight lines and
shackled enthusiasms
prepared for the christmas concert

a few fathers contrived a stage
of rough-sided spruce planks
girls thinly disguised the walls
with scattered strings of coloured lights
the ceiling was hung with red
green and white crêpe streamers
that stretched from
the framed photograph of
king george's crowned head
to cadbury's mostly imperial pink
map of the world
and a very young teacher was left
to her talents and designs
to mold the raw material at her disposal
into a performance worthy of expectations

sixty years have passed
and how little I remember of
those starry nights
that flashed
into our dusty village lives
eight years there and
I must have delivered a recitation or two
and once I did appear as the wise man balthazar
draped in my father's crimson bathrobe
propped in princely fashion by
a hockey stick staff
but I remember well the night

randolph danced
a new boy in our school
not of our village
and not one of us
he was black
with secrets about
how he got there
and why

perhaps the simple magic
of a wise and caring teacher
knowing somehow
the bare talents of a lost
and hurting
eleven-year-old boy

he stood uncertain
on the yellow platform
before the blazing wood stove
dressed still in outdoor winter clothing
thick plaid woollen jacket
breeches with leather knee patches
and knee-high black gum rubber boots

out of the heavy
sweaty darkness of that
overburdened room
a fiddle played and randolph
swayed to the strains of the music

his body drank in the rising rhythms
he smiled and shifted his feet
face sparkling in the flickering light
while he danced
to the whistles and claps
and laughed and
danced some more

Persian New Year in Charlottetown

❋ Mersedeh Sayafi ❋

It is March 19, 2014. I am standing in front of the window with a warm cup of tea in my hand. It is still snowing outside, nineteen degrees·Celsius, colder with the wind-chill. In this part of the world, the earth still has its clean, beautiful white dress on. Tomorrow is the first day of spring. The day all Persians celebrate Eid Nowruz, known as the Persian New Year. Just like any other Persians, my family and I celebrate Eid. I started getting ready for this New Year weeks ago. It is exciting that Mother allowed me to decorate this year's *Haft sin* table the way I want.

I put the cup of tea on my desk and walk to the living room to check on the *Haft sin* table. It looks magnificent. My friend Sarah, who is originally Canadian and does not know much about the Persian traditions, also thinks the same. She came to visit two days ago and was curious to know the story behind the things I put on our table in the living room. I explained that for Nowruz, Persians put seven items that start with the letter "س," along with some other objects, on a table in their house. This is what we call *Haft sin*, the literal English translation for which is "Seven S."

Instead of thinking about two days ago and Sarah's visit, I focus on the table again. I have to make sure nothing is missing. The five colourful plates I had bought are there. In one of them, I put three *Sirs* (garlics) and in another there is a green *Sib* (apple). The *Sekke* (coins), and some *Somac* and *Samanoo*, are also in their designated plates. That is five of the seven items for *Haft sin*. I look for the other two; there they are, *Sabzeh* and *Sonbol* (Hyacinth).

I remember the circumstance that I was in two days ago. How hard it was to explain to Sarah what *Somac*, *Samanoo*, and *Sabzeh* are. My best explanation was that *Somac* is a Persian spice, *Samanoo* is a sweet pudding made from wheat, and *Sabzeh* is wheat that has grown in a dish. She asked me lots of questions about *Haft sin* and Nowruz.

- Can you put just anything that starts with the letter "س"on the *Haft sin* table?

- No Sarah, it cannot be anything of your choice. The items are the same in every *Haft sin* in any house. The decoration, such as the plates and their arrangement, as well as the tablecloth, is the only thing that could be different, based on the tastes and creativity of each individual.

- I thought you said there are seven objects on the table. I can see more, though. Why?

- The other things that you see, like the mirror, the painted eggs, the goldfish in the fishbowl, and the candles, do not start with the letter "س" but still have to be there. These are what Persians hundreds of years ago prepared for Nowruz and each is symbolic.

- Well, what does the apple stand for or the eggs?

- The apple represents health and beauty and the eggs represent fertility. *Sabzeh* represents rebirth and *Samanoo* is an indication of sophisticated Persian cooking.

- How about the garlic and, what was its name, *Somac*?

- Yes, *Somac* represents the colour of sunrise. We believe that when the sun appears, good conquers evil. The garlic is there to represent medicine. The coins we put on *Haft sin* table represent prosperity and wealth. The goldfish represents life and movement, and the mirror represents introspection.

Answering all Sarah's questions made me realize how meaningful this tradition is to me. Even after we came to Canada, we continued to celebrate Nowruz, but it does not feel the same way. I can remember the previous Eids we celebrated when we were back home. This time of the year, there was an indescribable joy and happiness among all people. A month before the Eid, people started getting ready by cleaning their houses inside out, or, in other words, Persians deep-clean their house, what we call *Khane tekani*. The streets were extremely busy when it got close to Nowruz time. Tajrish Street, especially, was always loaded with young and old men and women who came out to shop. Everyone bought the items for their *Haft sin*, as well as presents for family members. I miss the busyness of those streets.

The way we celebrate Nowruz here is not comparable to how we celebrated in Iran. I cannot feel the same momentum in the streets in Charlottetown, which, at this time of the year, are full of emptiness. Maybe a few people walking here and there but that is it. I cannot feel that approach of Nowruz when I cannot see the blossoms on trees, when I cannot see the green grass. There is something missing. I am still searching for the lost happiness that is hidden inside *Eid didani*, the tradition of visiting family after the New Year's Day.

How great it was to spend the thirteen days of vacation we had for Eid visiting relatives. Every year, we started the process of *Eid didani* by going to my grandparents' house. In my culture it is necessary to go to the oldest relatives' house first, to show respect for them. I can still remember how warmly my grandparents welcomed my aunt's family and us in their house. We would all then sit on the couch and drink cups of tea together. We planned where to go for Nowruz vacation. Everyone travels to somewhere in Nowruz time, after they are done with *Eid didani*. When we had our trip planned, my grandparents would then invite us to sit around the *Haft sin* table to give us our presents.

Now that I think more, I see that it is not just the *Eid didani* that I miss. We do not celebrate *sizdeh bedar*, the thirteenth and last day of Nowruz vacation, the way we used to. We always went out on a picnic with our family friends on that day. We ate the most delicious Persian foods, *kabab* and *joojeh Kabab*, which is grilled chicken seasoned with saffron. While our parents spoke together, I and my friends played volleyball, badminton, and my favourite game, *vasati*, which is similar to dodgeball. It is too cold in the month of March in Canada to go out and do all these things.

- Do you recognize that you have been sitting at the *Haft sin* for fifteen minutes now? What are you thinking about?

My brother sat down beside me on the couch after asking me this question.

- Nothing. I was just thinking about the previous Eids we celebrated back home.

- I do not remember in great detail, but I believe the Nowruz celebration back home is more complete than the Nowruz celebration here.

He was much younger than me when we moved to Canada, but he now understands how joyful previous Eids were and feels the difference.

When my brother goes into the kitchen, I also leave the living room and go back to my room. My cup of tea is cold now. I do not have the desire to drink the rest of it. I turn on my computer and look at old pictures. I also find some pictures of the last Christmas. Our Christmas tree was decorated beautifully. I remember the gifts I received from my parents. I'd also taken some photos of the street decorations downtown. Everyone was happy and laughing, singing songs, walking and enjoying their time. So were my family and I. We are trying to find a balance between the two cultures. We do not want to forget our traditions but at the same time we respect the new culture we are exposed to, and we try to celebrate special Canadian holidays as best we can. After looking at more pictures while listening to music, I turn off my computer and get ready to sleep.

The next morning I wake up with my mother's voice. I take a shower and wear brand-new clothing. It is a tradition to wear new clothing on the day of Eid. My family and I then gather around the *Haft sin* table. My father goes online with his computer to find a Persian channel. Every Nowruz, special programs are shown on television in Iran. The host of this show is wishing us all a happy New Year. I can see the countdown at the bottom right corner of the TV. Now the host starts reciting the prayer all Persians read when it comes close to the moment the earth finishes turning around the sun one full time. O you, transformer of hearts and spiritual states, make our states the loveliest of states.

The Nativity Set

❄ Sylvia Poirier ❄

Christmas Eve afternoon, 1939. It is their first Christmas together and their worldly goods are few. There will be no Christmas presents tomorrow but there will be Christmas dinner with the relatives. There will be a roast goose, one kept back from the fall raffles, potatoes and turnips and carrots from the cellar, and peas canned from the summer bounty. There will be cranberry sauce and pickles from the preserve cupboard, and plum pudding with brown sugar sauce. The potbellied stove in the dining room will be lit, a treat in itself for a family used to having only the kitchen stove for warmth.

John leads Belle from her warm stall in the barn and harnesses her to a small box sleigh. The little grey mare canters easily through the drifts of snow as she takes John and Beatrice the mile and a half from the farm to St. John the Baptist church in Miscouche. They are going to make their confessions and receive absolution as part of their spiritual preparation for Christmas. Later, Belle will take them back to the church for midnight mass.

They kneel in their pew and complete the traditional penance of prayers dispensed by Father Martin Monaghan. John prays fervently that things will turn around and that there will be a market for the potatoes stored with such hope in the cellar of the old farmhouse.

They make the sign of the cross as they leave the church and walk across the road to DesRoches General Store. Both Frank and Agatha are behind the counter. It is a busy afternoon. The store sells everything from molasses to rope. Beatrice's list is small. She needs brown sugar and tea and she asks if she can add that to their charge account. Agatha wraps the two items in brown paper from the big roll at the end of the counter. She ties the package with a string that comes down from a spool attached to the wooden ceiling.

Then unexpectedly Agatha says, "Beatrice, do you have a nativity set?"

"No," Beatrice replies.

"Well," Agatha says, "We got one in the mail this morning." She takes a box down from the shelf, opens it, and shows the nativity set to Beatrice. It is made of dark pressed cardboard. Straw covers the manger roof that shelters the Infant Jesus, Mary, Joseph, the shepherds, the three wise men, and the animals. It has a single red Christmas light attached to an electric cord. It costs two dollars.

"It is so beautiful," Beatrice says, "but we don't have two dollars. You know how it is, Agatha."

Agatha says, "That's all right Beatrice, you take it. You pay for it whenever you can." She puts the nativity set back in its box, then carefully wraps the box in brown paper, ties it with string, and hands it to Beatrice. "Merry Christmas," she says.

Back at the farm, they gently place their precious gift under the Christmas tree, which John cut down last Sunday from the woods at the back of the farm. The tree is decorated with a few homemade ornaments and strands of silver tinsel. There is no outlet for the electric cord, so no light for the manger. This does not diminish their excitement. It will be sixteen years later that electricity arrives at the farm and they can plug in the cord to shine the light on Bethlehem.

That humble nativity set would become the centre of my parents' Christmas celebration throughout their forty-nine years of marriage. On Christmas Eve they would open the nativity set and place it directly in front of their Christmas tree where they could admire it; in doing so, I imagine, they relived the joy of that first Christmas they were together. My mother often told us children that the Nativity Set was what made Christmas for her. After my father died in 1988, the tradition became even more important for my mother.

When Mom was in her mid-eighties her mobility decreased, so the responsibility of helping her get ready for Christmas fell to me. As I was putting her Christmas decorations away, I noticed that the now sixty-year-old electric cord of the nativity set was frayed, and decided that it should be replaced.

When December 1 of the next year rolled around, I got Mom's Christmas decorations from storage; lo and behold, there was no nativity set. The staff of the Miscouche Villa, now my mother's home, looked everywhere.

My mother said, "Are you sure you put it in the box with the other things?"

31

"Of course I put it in the box, Mom, where else would I put it?"

"Well, Sylvia, you know you can be absentminded."

I looked in every storage spot in my home, thinking that perhaps I had stored it for her with my own decorations, but I could not find it. I expected, though, that the nativity set would turn up at the Villa as the staff continued to search though their various storage rooms. I believed it had been placed with someone else's belongings by mistake.

My mother kept getting more distressed. "It won't be Christmas," she said repeatedly, "if I don't have my nativity set."

Two nights before Christmas, I awoke suddenly from a dead sleep. I sat up in bed and said out loud, "That nativity set is at Burke Electric!"

As soon as Burke Electric opened their doors the next morning I was there. After hunting through shelves and boxes in the back room, the owner, Fred Brown, came back with the much loved and worn nativity set.

"Is this what we are looking for?"

The electric cord had not been replaced.

"You'll have to come back," he said, "because it's Christmas Eve and we're really busy."

I told him the story of the nativity set. Without another word he took it to the back of the shop. He came back shortly and gently handed me the nativity set with its new cord and new red bulb.

"No charge," he said. "Merry Christmas."

I drove immediately to Miscouche. My mother was overjoyed to see her Christmas coming in the door. For me she had some advice.

"Sylvia, you should write things down."

A Buck for the Babe

❋ Paul Vreeland ❋

Hush River is a beautiful place, but tainted. Look into its history: too many suicides and murders for a population numbering in the hundreds. Beautiful, but dark. I have to admit, the village, as I remember it, would be the setting for a Stephen King novel. A strange, out-of-the-way place in the boondocks of western Massachusetts, it's where I envisioned folks closeting their mentally deranged daughters and where the birth of a two-headed calf is not uncommon—the kind of place where Ripley of *Ripley's Believe it or Not* could have gotten his start.

Mom disagrees with me. Says I'm being unfair. Says I'm laying too many embellishments on a paucity of childhood memories. "Think Currier and Ives," she says. You know, a wintery scene with a horse-drawn dray. Dray? What the hell is a dray? Remember that Newhart sitcom where he ran an inn with Tom Poston and a host of other characters who looked like they stepped off the canvasses of Norman Rockwell? "C'mon Jim, be fair," she says.

Hush River is a few miles north of Winsted, a quiet ghost of a once-noisy, once-prosperous New England mill town where I grew up. Back in the days when it was noisy and prosperous, Mom worked for the local newspaper, *The Winsted Evening Citizen*. She suppressed more news than she gave to Bob Haggarty, the editor. The safe stories made it into print, and what was left over she brought home to tell my father over supper—stories my sister and I were not to repeat. We couldn't have, even if we had wanted to, because we were too young to understand much of what she said. We didn't know the precise meanings of words such as "adultery" or "arson" or "incest." I mean, I had ideas, but often the ideas were a bit off.

I understood the story about Chester, however. *The Citizen* had a stringer up in Hush River. I knew what a stringer was—someone who reported the Hush River news whenever something happened, which wasn't very often, and she was paid maybe twenty cents a column inch. I knew what a column inch was, too; it was what was left over after Haggarty got hold of the article. Mom said the Hush River stringer invented news stories just to have some money coming in. One day Mom came home with the story of how the stringer had quit in a huff because Haggarty wouldn't print an obituary she had submitted. Chester's obituary. Chester was a rooster, and after it was killed by a hit-and-run motorist, all the dear folks in Hush River were in mourning. So the stringer claimed. When the story didn't run, she called Haggarty.

"You don't understand," she said. "Chester wasn't your ordinary rooster. He was the village mascot. All the businesses were closed."

Haggarty chewed his cigar and listened to her rant. Finally he said, "If I don't understand, it's because you don't write properly." Haggarty had a reputation for hanging up on people, but the stringer got in the last word.

"I quit," she said, before giving Haggarty the dial tone.

Later he came into the newsroom to make the announcement that *The Citizen* no longer had a reliable source in Hush River. Everyone had a good laugh. Roy Carver doubled over and slapped his thigh. "Businesses were closed? What businesses?"

The story fed my morbid imagination about the village. It probably was big news up there, because, if you read the paper, you knew that nothing happened in Hush River except weekly card parties at the Fire Hall and the occasional benefit dinner hosted by the women's auxiliary at the Grange.

Hush River is on the map of popular consciousness now. In a good way. We remember it today as the origin of a holiday tradition, if fifteen years can make for a tradition. Back then I would have never guessed. Most people wouldn't have.

There were scanners in the newsroom picking up the radio traffic of the town police and fire departments, and the local detachment of the state police, so the reporters usually knew when something was up. How they could listen to the scanners and concentrate on their writing at the same time, I'll never figure out. Day in and day out, what came over the radios was garble of little consequence. Stuff like, "Thirty-four, stop by the deli and pick up a smoked meat on rye for Jolene. She says don't forget the pickle, or she'll have your neck. Ya want to roger me that?"

It's a Monday, ten days 'til Christmas and the newsroom is rather quiet. Haggarty would have been the first one in and picked up the paper scrolling out of the teletype machine with stories from the Associated Press. Who knows, maybe there is news, real news, but when I stop in after school I get the idea that the reporters want it quiet. Haggarty, overwhelmed by the holiday spirit, is not chaining them to the typewriters and I imagine they're more concerned with holiday shopping than tonight's lead. Or maybe that's what I want them to be concerned about. Roy Carver is stirring himself a cup of instant coffee and Ned Bittles is making bird tracks on a draft with a blue pencil. I like Ned because he's been generous with his nickels during the summer afternoons when I'd drop by. "Go down and get me coke from the machine," he'd say. "And get yourself one while you're at it, boy."

Haggarty doesn't mind. When I started hanging around, he said, "Sure kid. If you don't mind going down to the town hall and picking up the court news. This is where real reporters cut their teeth." He also had me doing the police blotter until the editor of *The Torrington Register* called to ask how much he was paying his child labour. Haggarty doesn't ask anymore, but I still do it every once in a while.

Mom doesn't mind me hanging around either. She figures I'll learn something, and she says the guys clean up their language when I'm around. Something I haven't noticed.

At any rate, there's a squawk on one of the scanners and Ned looks around at his colleagues. "A 207 in Hush River. What the hell is that?" The others pause to listen to the radios, while he gets up to check a listing of codes pasted to the side of a file cabinet. He turns with his face all scrunched up, exaggerating another question. "Kidnap?"

Roy is slurping his coffee from a dirty cup. "They don't know how to say that somebody picked up the wrong order at the dry cleaners."

We hear another voice come over like it's talking through a heavy woollen sock.

"They found a note. Twenty-four, what's your twenty?"

"Route 203. South, twelve miles."

"10-4. Bassett's waiting at the church."

"10-4."

"If it's really a 207," says Roy, "we'd better get Haggarty in on this."

Ned heads towards Haggarty's office, moving like the building's on fire.

Mom is working on a weekly column for the entertainment page. I look over at her and she rolls her eyes.

Haggarty comes out of his office chewing on the butt of a cigar. I've never seen him smoke a cigar. I love the smell of cigar smoke and it would be a welcome change from the stench of stale cigarette butts overflowing the ashtrays in the newsroom. But Haggarty never smokes the damn things. Instead, he's got this disgusting chewed-up tobacco salad mess stuck between his lips and teeth. He comes out and looks at Roy, who turns his back to Haggarty and holds up his hands as though he's saying, "Not me boss. I've got other things to do." Haggarty then turns to my mother.

"What are you working on?"

"The compendium column."

"That doesn't run until tomorrow. Get up there and talk to Bassett. Hopefully, the police will still be there. You can do it in twelve minutes, if you give it some gas."

Cripes, he's a real taskmaster, but nobody takes him seriously. Not totally. It's more like twelve minutes for Mom to put on her coat and get down to the car.

She looks at me and rolls her eyes again—a look that tells me I'll have to walk home, and Dad will have to get the supper ready. She gets up, puts on her coat, and takes her purse and keys. Haggarty takes the stump out of his mouth and points to her.

"We won't put the paper to bed until you get back."

If he wants to change the front-page lead, the Linotype operator, the pressman, and my mother will have to work late. I don't go home, but sit at her desk and draw pictures and call my sister to tell her what's up.

Mom drives up to Hush River and comes back with another dilemma: what does she tell Haggarty? And what does she suppress? Nobody looks up when she walks back in the newsroom and takes off her coat. They're waiting for Haggarty to come out of his office and ask, "Whathaveya got?"

And that's exactly what he does.

"The villagers are pretty upset," she tells him. That's what Trooper Bill had told her. "The villagers are pretty upset."

"The villagers are pretty upset," she tells Dad while we're chowing down on his specialty: soft-boiled eggs mixed with crushed Saltina crackers and slivers of raw hot dogs. It's better than that chipped beef on toast he calls shit-on-a-shingle. That's what he gave us the last time she worked late. We're licking our lips while she gives us the lowdown that she didn't give to Haggarty.

Trooper Bill tells her, "The villagers are pretty upset," so she says to the trooper, "What are you going to do to keep them quiet?"

Trooper Bill shakes his head. "They're hungry to be upset. Bored hungry. They haven't had anything to talk about since lightning struck the barber pole and you guys certainly made a sensation of that."

Mom doesn't bother to tell him about the Hush River stringer.

"The note?" she asks.

"Yes. A handwritten note found where the Baby Jesus had lain. '50k for Jesus or no Xmas.' That's what it looked like. Poorly written, illegible except for the mistakes."

"Signed, Santa?"

"Signed, Santa." Bill watches her scribble her notes. "Christ, Reeney," he says. Mom's name is Irene, but everyone calls her Reeney. "Why don't you write up my files for me?"

"C'mon Bill. We know you lazy dogs write up your reports a week late by plagiarizing what you read in the paper."

"Yeah, well, we help you, you help us."

"What else?" she presses him.

"Nothing else," he says.

"Nothing else? What are you going to do about it?" she presses again.

"Between you and me?"

"Off the record."

"Nothing."

She looks at him.

"Hey. It's Christmas," he says. "Staff is skeletal and look, what's it worth? I mean Christ, this is Hush River. You see any political stake in this? No one's in danger. The bored hungry people have got their sensation, and it's like a non-crime. Don't make a big hullabaloo out of this. Surely you've got something better to write about. Hmmm?" He turns, looks away, then turns back. "Okay. What do you know?"

"Off the record?" Mom asks.

"Between you and me," says the trooper.

"The Baby Jesus is worth about twenty thousand," Mom tells him. "Italian fine art. Your non-crime is grand larceny."

"You're not serious!"

"You don't know this," she says and begins to walk away.

He grabs her arm, "What do you mean, I don't know this?"

She put her finger to her lips. "Merry Christmas, Bill."

"How do you know it's worth twenty grand?" I ask.

"I don't," she says.

Dad is shaking his head. "You lied to the police!"

My sister starts bawling.

"No. I didn't. It's worth something. Maybe not twenty thousand, but it's worth something. What the town selectmen put up every year on the village green is the Doris Loring Memorial Crèche. The Lorings, that wealthy family, used to summer in the area. Doris had willed the crèche to, quote, 'the dear people of Hush River.' So I did a little digging and called James Loring, her son. Turns out the Loring Crèche is a scaled-down copy of the Pittsburgh Crèche. And in case you don't know, the Pittsburgh Crèche is modeled after *the* one in the Vatican. The figurines are the work of Pietro Simonelli, constructed on wooden frames with clay hands, feet, and faces. They're covered in waterproofed papier mâché. The Pittsburgh and Loring figures are constructed the same way, but only the Pittsburgh crèche has the Vatican's stamp of authenticity. Something a bit too Catholic for the aging Congregational crowd in Hush River. James Loring tells me this and then says, 'We never told anyone about the crèche's provenance, and look, please, we'd rather not see our name in print.'"

"So, where'd you get the idea of twenty thousand?" dad asks.

She offers a smug smile and says, "I just took a small fraction of priceless."

Like I said, that's not what Haggarty gets, because she's got to respect the Lorings.

"So what have you got?" Haggarty asks when she comes back.

"Nothing you don't already know," she says, and Haggarty's face turns red like it's about to burst a blood vessel.

He leans on her desk. "Which is what, may I ask?"

She flips open her steno pad. "The Baby Jesus went missing sometime between nine p.m. on Sunday when it was last seen by Wilber Toggs and six-thirty a.m. on Monday when Alice Groober noticed it gone."

Whatever the truth of the matter, the next day Haggarty's head-line reads, "Jesus Held Hostage" in 72 points and immediately everyone in the tri-state area starts wagging their tongues, half of them picking up their pens to write Letters to the Editor.

Mom doesn't like it. She's worried the Associated Press will get hold of it and the next thing you know all of America will be laughing at us. She asks Haggarty, "Do you want to publish a story that makes us the butt of a national joke, like Hush River is the local one?"

"I have no choice," he says. "I've got a mandate for readership and profits, and this story sells. Maybe the biggest story of the year for us."

"Damn. Did you ask Santa to bring you a Pulitzer?"

He chortled.

The Weigold boys are the first suspects. After all, they have a history. Not that they're hardened criminals, but they had messed with the crèches before. Note that I said crèches. Plural. According to Paul Bassett, the first selectman, "Half the town used to put up nativity scenes on their lawns. Most of us don't do that now. Four years ago there was a twelve-foot statue of the Blessed Virgin taken from the Congregational Church and set up as the guardian of the gate to the town dump. We left it like that until after New Year's. And on Christmas morning the Satini family had a lawn decorated with six Josephs and the Johnson kids found Lisa Parvan's Baby Jesus up in the tree house in their back yard. Another Baby Jesus was put on the Synagogue steps down in Torrington. Wrapped up with a note that said, 'Take me in. Please.' We never tried to figure out who did it, but most of us suspected the Weigold boys."

"Is it Jesuses or Jesi?" Ned asks.

"Check the *Associated Press Stylebook*," Roy says. "Everything's in there."

"It isn't," Ned says a few minutes later.

The Hush River stringer had interviewed the boys' mother, Mrs. Arthur Weigold, back then and had written:

With the Weigold boys, Daryll was the one you had to worry about. "I know I should have never have named him Daryll," his mother said. "Guaranteed trouble. Some names you just have to stay away from. Stupid me. But I loved the sound of it. Like Beryl. You know, the jewel. Sure, I could have done worse, could have named him Judas."

More news that Mom brought home. I remember that paragraph because it fed the part of my imagination that likes dark things.

But Haggarty trimmed it and another twenty cents off the stringer's pay. Turned out that Bassett had it wrong. They didn't have to do much to figure it out because the boys had confessed. No one pressed charges so nothing much was made of it but a bunch of talk.

Haggarty sends Mom back to Hush River the next morning. "Be a Sherlock," he says as she's putting on her coat.

Ned quips, "He means, be a Shylock."

Mom does her best. She conducts interview after interview. She speaks with the town manager. "Ask anyone in the village," he says. "Nobody thought anything was going to happen for the holiday. Not here."

"Why is that?"

"Well, 'cause Daryll is out in Colorado and his brother's in the hospital. And even if Daryll were here, he would never act alone.

"Doesn't sound like much of a holiday for Mrs. Weigold."

"Believe me. She's less stressed this way. Daryll can drive his new truck home in the spring."

The people in Hush River are heated, and Haggarty is rubbing his hands together, gloating over a spike in circulation as the story brings the heat home and begs *The Citizen*'s readership to take sides. Haggarty takes a few of the calls himself. One woman berates him as though the theft was his fault. "Haggarty, this story better have a happy ending. It's the season, don't you know."

"Yeah, sure, Bernice. Whatever you say," he says and hangs up. "Happy endings don't sell. What does she know."

On my way out I hear an argument down at the classifieds counter. One man in overalls and flannel jacket is saying, "It's only a piece of cheap plastic. Poorly painted at that. Big whoop. That's what I say. Big whoop."

Another man in a suit and tie and overcoat replies, "But it's our tradition. The Loring crèche has been there for more than twelve years. It's not Christmas if that crèche isn't on the green." I figure the man must be from Hush River.

"Why don't you people go out and get a new Jesus? Get a new Jesus and carry on," Mr. Overalls says.

"You don't understand, it was a gift."

"And you used it well. Appreciate it for what it was. Maybe it's time for a change."

"You can't let a bunch of hardened criminals get the upper hand," says the man from Hush River.

"Hardened criminals? Vandals. Teenagers most likely," replies the Overalls.

"Vandals don't terrorize an entire village."

"Bullshit," says Overalls.

"Bullshit yourself," says the suit and tie. "They're holding us ransom."

"He, not they, is holding a piece of plastic for ransom. Get it straight. You'd be okay if you just let him have it. Screw the ransom."

"And what would we let him take next time? Sure as hell there will be a next time."

Overalls shrugs his shoulders. "Have it your way."

When Mom speaks with Reverend Milner, the minister of the Congregational Church in Hush River, he's a bit more philosophical.

"When a town begins to die, the living get out. What's left are the near dead… people who have lives like picture puzzles with the pieces all scrambled up, many of them missing. I mean really scrambled. This is what I mean… our lives seem to be messed up by pranksters. Each and every one of us, the ones who are left, we're the town's jokes." He watches my mother write that all down in shorthand. Then he says, "Don't quote me. They'd crucify me if they read that in your paper."

"What do you know about the connection between the Loring and the Pittsburgh crèches?" she asks.

"The what?" Milner asks.

"The Pittsburgh crèche."

"Nothing," Milner says. "It was given to the village, not to the church. You'd have to ask the town manager or the board of selectmen about it."

That evening the television networks pick up the story. NBC's Brad Chronan leads his six p.m. newscast with, "Will there be a second coming in Hush River? That's what the people in western Massachusetts are asking after their nativity crèche was stolen, or more precisely, kidnapped, and the village of Hush River was left with a ransom note. Reverend Milner of the Hush River Congregational Church said, 'Christ died as a ransom for us. Now, the question is, will the dear people of Hush River pay the ransom for Him?' Let's pick up the story live on location with reporter Sarah Baskin. Sarah."

Haggarty is fuming on Wednesday morning. "How are we going

41

to keep the lead?" he asks no one in particular. You see, he had gambled on the Hush River Hostage story. The downstate papers such as the *Hartford Courant* and the *Waterbury Republican* poured their front page ink into the Mad Dog Jaworsky Murders down in New Britain and the international story about Palestinian gunmen storming an airport in Rome, killing thirty and taking fourteen hostages. Haggarty had pushed those stories off the front page; he had gambled and won. And now, *The Courant* and *Republican* had also turned their eyes on Hush River and sent journalists up there to keep company with those from the TV networks.

Mom looks up from her typewriter. "What do you call the people of Hush River?" she asks. I guess "Hushites" didn't occur to her.

"Dickheads," says Roy.

"No, the people from Torrington are called Torringtonians, and the Winsted people are Winsteders, so the people of Hush River are what?"

"What about Hushdicks?" Roy offers. "And the folks from Norfolk are Norfuckers. Don't believe me? Check it out. It's all in the *Associated Press Stylebook*."

Haggarty looks at her. "Call them whatever you like, Reeney. If somebody doesn't like it, we'll get a call or a letter."

Mom avoids the uncertainty and settles for "residents."

Haggarty goes back to his office and stands looking out the window down to the life passing by on Main Street. Haggarty's office has a glass door, and the folks in the newsroom are watching him.

Ned nods towards Haggarty's door and says, "We'd better prepare ourselves."

Roy cranes his head. "What's he doing?"

Mom looks up, "He's just standing there, chomping on his stogie."

"He's doing more than looking out the window. The bastard is thinking," says Roy.

"Not a good sign," adds Ned. "You remember the last time he had a brain fart, Roy? You ended up sleeping in your car for three days."

A few minutes later Haggarty puts on his coat, and walks out of his office, slamming the door.

Roy gets up and comes over to Mom's desk. "Look, I got to go get a tree. Cover for me, will you?"

Mom shrugs.

Haggarty is gone for about three hours. He storms into the newsroom well after lunch. "Where's Roy?"

No one answers.

"Ned."

"Yes, boss."

"New development in the hostage case. Check the stores on Main Street and come back with a decent photo of one of the boxes."

"Boxes?"

"Half-dozen pics and fifteen inches in an hour. Get out."

"Fifteen inches!"

"He's got to have that much to cut down to five," says Ned.

Ned starts with the Desi's drugstore, then moves on to the dry cleaners, Winsted Cigar, the 5 'n' 10, the Strand movie theatre, Bridge Street Barber Shop. Each one has a collection box on the counter. "Jesus Saves. Now it's our turn."

Roy comes back with a decent shot of a box. He also comes back with eighteen photos—portraits of shop-owners holding or standing next to the boxes. He's also captured quotables. The front page story: "Citizens Take a Stand to Save Our Savior" features large photos, more photos than text. Haggarty cut the fact that he distributed the boxes himself and that *The Citizen* is the central collection agency.

Letters to the Editor pour in. Haggarty isn't without his detractors. "Poor taste," reads one that mentions the photo of Lemuel Scheib putting a dollar bill into the collection box and a caption that reads, "I don't mind giving a buck for the Babe." Another derides *The Citizen* as being a "tool of the evil-doers." "Render unto Caesar," the writer urges. But, for the most part, the letters are full of praise and support. Haggarty runs every one of them after he pencils in "expletive deleted" a few dozen times.

The next day more than eight thousand dollars are collected. That includes a few substantial cheques that are hand-delivered to the girls at the circulation desk. Others are a bit more media-hungry. Once Janet Dickson, secretary of the Rebekah Lodge, gets her mug on page two handing over five hundred dollars, a whole whack of media-hungry philanthropist wannabes demand greet-and-grin pictures taken of them handing cheques to Haggarty. And Haggarty can't refuse.

The Hartford Courant, Waterbury Republican, The Lakeville Journal, and *Millerton Independent* have collection boxes spread throughout the region and are calling each other regularly for updates. Paul Bassett drives down from Hush River to thank Haggarty and to have his photo taken giving *The Citizen* the $423.16 the dear people of the village had contributed. Haggarty runs a blow-up of that photo on page one of the Thursday edition.

Christmas is closing in. An unsigned letter is dropped off at the circulation desk and taken up to Haggarty, who shares it with Roy, Ned, and Mom. "What do you think we should do about this?"

"What about the crime?" the letter begins. "Why don't you report on what the police are doing? All this collection hoopla is a distraction, and the criminals are probably loving it. If there really are criminals. If there really was a 'kidnapping.' Is this a hoax? A put-on by the press? Tell us, what's going to happen with the money. And for God's sake, show us the note."

"Has anyone seen the note?" Haggarty asks.

"Nothing about dropping off the money. Whoever wrote that note is one stupid arsehole," says Roy.

"Or brilliant," says Haggarty. They look at him as though they're stunned by a more profound profanity. "It's open-ended," he says. "Ecumenical, so to speak. It gets more people to respond. Mention a drop-off and you're narrowing your possibilities."

Roy shrugs. "Maybe. You going to run the letter?"

Haggarty raises his eyebrows. "You know the policy."

The policy is that he'd run a paragraph saying that the paper had received an unsigned letter, and if the author identifies himself or herself and gives a telephone number for verification, *The Citizen* will run it.

Haggarty turns to Ned. "Go talk to the troopers. Get a look at the note. Take a camera, get a good shot of it if you can."

Ned comes back and a print is made. Passed around.

The note is a scrawl. "It doesn't read '50K for Jesus or no Xmas,'" Ned says.

"Sure it does," Haggarty says.

"Not to my eyes."

"Yeah, well, we'll see," Haggarty says, and runs it as the lead that evening along with a statement that the police are following up on more than a dozen tips they have received—another way of saying that there's no news from the boys in blue.

The debate flourishes on Saturday. Mrs. Ronald Burke writes in, "It's not a ransom note. Take a good look. It says 'Look for Jesus or No Xmas.'" Most of the other letter-writers agree with her. One offers the following, however: "We can't take chances in interpreting the note. Raise the $50 thousand to be on the safe side. It's nothing compared to the price He paid." It's signed Mr. Ronald Burke. A few rant on the "true meaning of Christmas," noting that if we do not look toward Christ, we will indeed have missed the spirit of Christmas.

Monday morning Haggarty comes out of his office looking like he wants to conduct a military inspection. Only, it's assignment time. He looks at his team of reporters. "Any of you hacks go to church yesterday?"

Roy, Ned, and Mom look up at him. No response. Haggarty shakes his head.

"Well, did you?" Ned asks.

Haggarty glowers. "Okay, Ned. Dig it out."

Ned walks out and is gone for most of the morning. He's written a two-column feature by noon about how attendance at the churches is up throughout the region. It normally rises this time of year, but the real spike comes on Christmas Sunday. Perhaps people went to get an inside sacred scoop on the story, because almost every minister, pastor, and priest gave sermons that made more than a passing reference to the Babe missing from the Hush River manger. They had the secular story from the newspapers, and the metaphorical version with a healthy dose of Christian virtue from the pulpits. According to Ned's story, Reverend Milner said that he saw people he's never seen before. "Were collections up?" Ned asked. "Not what you'd expect," said Milner. Staff at other churches confirmed this. Pastor Darby told him that he found a note in one of the collection baskets reading, "I gave at the cleaners." Bernice calls again. "Merry Christmas, Bernice," Haggarty says. "Don't worry. You'll get your happy ending." And he hangs up.

On the 24th *The Citizen* usually puts out a shortened version of the paper early in the afternoon, shuts down the offices, and sends everyone home. On the morning of the 24th Haggarty is the first to arrive. So Mom thinks. Roy, though, swears that Haggarty's home address is bogus and that he sleeps in his office. Ned is the second to arrive and Haggarty is waiting. "Call the police," Haggarty tells him. "Ask them to come to the back door by the loading dock. Bring a camera. When they arrive, you'd better get a front pager."

Ned gets a front pager, but nothing candid. He has to ask the police to pose. He gets one shot of Trooper Bill smiling while bending over the Loring Baby Jesus lying on the doorstep. He gets another shot of Haggarty and Trooper Bill standing on each side of the crèche figure, holding the found note between them. From the poses you'd think they'd just shot a rhinoceros. When they finish, another trooper moves in to dust the Baby Jesus for fingerprints. Haggarty yells at Ned, "For Chrissakes, get a shot of that, too."

Roy and Mom arrive a few minutes later. Mom's assignment is to call around to the other papers and to update the collection figures. She tells them about the note and says that *The Citizen* will be making a presentation at noon. They're welcome to cover the event. The note that Haggarty found scotch-taped to the Baby Jesus reads in the same scrawl as the first note: "Give it all to the United Way." This time there is no doubt; the message is unmistakable.

When she finishes her calls, the tally is $114,031.26. Haggarty has a dummy three-by-four-foot cheque printed for the presentation.

Christmas Day. Christmas dinner, then a round of visits. At the end of the day Mom and Dad are groaning with exhaustion.

"I'm sorry it's over," Mom says.

"Yeah, well," Dad says. "There's nothing left but the clean-up."

"No, it's not that. I'm sorry the Hush River case is over. It generated a special extraordinary community spirit. Every year people get caught up in the flush of the holiday. But this year was different."

"Too good to last," Dad says.

"Did they ever figure it out?" I ask.

"Figure what out?"

"Who took the Baby Jesus and left the notes."

She shrugs. "That day, Christmas Eve, I swear I saw copies of the note in Haggarty's waste basket. Like practice attempts."

"Does that prove anything?"

"No, but his wink did. He caught me looking. He put his finger to his lips and winked. In my mind's eye, you could have given him a beard and red suit, and with that wink, he could have been a colour advertisement for Coca-Cola on the back cover of *Life* magazine."

I wonder if she talked to Haggarty about her suspicion—he wasn't the type to entertain sentimentality or to suffer hearts on any sleeve. I wonder because the following Saturday Haggarty prints his weekly editorial. He recaps the Hush River Hostage case, lavishes praise on editors of the other papers and TV news producers. He comments on the post-Christmas letdown and then he writes, "Hush River gave us something special this year, an opportunity to truly share in a campaign of common purpose that seemingly transcended politics, class, race, and religion. If the outpouring of our generosity and the mounting evidence of our collective Christmas spirit were inspired by a crime, the *Winsted Evening Citizen* goes on record as saying, let the crime be committed again next year."

And so the tradition begins. For the next fifteen years the Loring Christ-child finds its place with the other figures installed on the village green in Hush River on or about December 10th. And it disappears on the third Monday of the month. Every year. The same day the collection boxes appear in the stores. The campaigns have been successful; every year the amount raised for the United Way increases. But the spirit is nothing like it was the year Lemuel Scheib gave a buck for the Babe.

Kindness Matters

❄ Liza Oliver ❄

I was fifteen, and times were not so good for my family. I was shopping for Christmas groceries at an IGA in Truro, Nova Scotia. My little sister, who was seven, was with me, her eyes big and round as she took in all the surroundings and smells at the store's bakery department, her shopaholic urges just developing. Everything was so pretty, so colourful, all sparkly green and red with bows, sprinkles, and captivating packaging.

Christmas tunes were coming from the overhead speakers, and a slushy mess sullied the supermarket's white floors as people hurried by with shopping carts full of special Christmas groceries. Impatient people with children wearing big bulky snow suits and wet mittens in tow hurried down the aisles, carts loaded to overflowing with endless supplies for the holidays, as if they might never eat again. My only concern was getting all the things on my list for forty dollars. That was the amount of money I had in my pocket. Mom had given me two crisp twenty-dollar bills. I opted to get a ham instead of a turkey because hams were on sale and seemed a better deal. Besides, I had reasoned, who needs a turkey anyway?

I continued shopping as my sister kept bugging me to purchase a Yuletide log. A tubular chunk of cake, blanketed with thick sugary white icing, accented with shiny sprinkles that glimmered blue and white in a certain light. The icing was scored with perfectly formed parallel lines. I, too, may have been mesmerized by it, but I knew it was not an option. At $9.99, it cost far too much for our budget. I can still hear her pleading voice as she tried to convince me it would be a good surprise for Mom. I did not disagree. It *was* beautiful, and it *would* look lovely on the table. I decided ignoring her would be best way to cope. She cried and pouted and stomped her feet and begged me to buy the cake. Then I became annoyed and spoke firmly to her, trying to explain that it was too much money and that we still had to pay for everything we had in our cart. I confess, though, I was tempted to steal the damn thing to make her stop crying.

After all, I had stealing experience. One time I robbed a chunk of Kraft cheddar. I stuck the stick of cheese up my coat sleeve when I thought nobody was looking and casually walked right out the door. But you couldn't do that with a Yuletide log and I did not want to go to Hell or jail. Instead, I convinced my sweet, chubby little sister, red-faced from her tears, how beautiful the six white cupcakes were with the mounds of icing on top and the edible Christmas sprinkles, and how we could each have our own mini-cake. After a while she seemed to forget about the Yuletide log and was happy. The cupcakes were on sale for a much more reasonable $1.99.

We continued to glide through the aisles gathering the items we needed. *There was no way I was getting gravy browning,* I thought, as I scratched that from the list. Instead, I plotted, I would stop at the snack bar and get several packets of soy sauce, which would work equally well and be free. By now I just wanted to go home. We arrived at the checkout where it seemed we waited a very long time for the girl to ring in everyone's overloaded carts. The packing boys were moving busily, the red-numbered parcel-pickup bins crashing into each other as they were pushed along the metal rollers. I felt a breeze from outside as the bins rolled through the hanging fringed rubber door to the outside, waiting to be gathered by weary shoppers. Finally it was our turn.

"Parcel pickup?" asked the girl without looking up.

"No thanks," I said. "We will carry them."

We headed to the direct line phones to call a taxi.

"Paradise Taxi," said the woman on the other end of the line.

"Can you send Ralph to the IGA please?"

Ralph was the driver Mom trusted. He would charge us less. I had saved three dollars and fifty cents for the cab ride home.

"Well, a request call will take a while today, Love."

"That's okay."

It did take longer, but pretty soon the big green car with the exuberant bald man arrived. Ralph was the kind of man whose face lit up a room, nothing visible beyond his brown skin but his kind eyes and his white teeth. He got out and helped us with the bags.

"After you, ladies," he said, opening the door and gesturing with his hands for us to get in the car, which he called our limo.

Before he closed our door, though, a woman handed me a bag and said, "Merry Christmas, girls," and walked away before I had a chance to say anything or thank her. Inside the bag was the Yuletide log that my sister and I had admired. My sister believed the woman was a Christmas angel. Now her little eyes grew big and round with anticipation. Maybe she was right. Maybe the tall round lady with the fancy blonde hair and perfect makeup, who handed me the IGA bag that day, *was* an angel of sorts. I let my sister believe it was a Christmas miracle.

"Now that's what Christmas is about girls," Ralph explained as we pulled out of the busy parking lot.

He didn't charge us for the ride home and he helped us with our bags again, suggesting, "Now get a gift for your mother with that money." He always tried to teach us something on our short cab rides.

When I entered the house I saw that we had a visitor, a woman I didn't know. She had brought a decorated cardboard box, which contained a turkey and all the fixings plus a small gift, one with each of our names on it. *Another angel perhaps?* This meant we could save our ham for New Year's Day.

Retrospect is a wonderful thing. I am forty-five years old now. I realize how much thought, energy, and concern people had taken to make sure we had a turkey that year and many other years, how much coordination, effort, and dedication were involved on so many levels. Every year as I listen to the CBC Radio turkey drive I know this is one place where Christmas angels start. I listen with great interest as the morning show hosts report the number of turkeys donated to date, and I remember how the gift of that turkey so many years ago helped ease the pressure and keep disappointment somewhat at bay. I think of how kindness really does matter. So, I will buy a turkey or two every year and I will drop them off at the CBC station to help the angels do their work. And if my little sister lived nearby I would buy her all the Yuletide logs she wanted.

Carolling

❄ Malcolm Murray ❄

She said the Carvers invited us for drinks. I didn't want to go. Once I'm inside my own place, however small and dirty and bare, I don't want to leave. I don't want to listen to people, or have them look at me, or have them judge me. She insisted.

We stepped inside their home and the Carvers greeted us effusively, as if we were relatives. They were already drunk, but they didn't offer us anything for the longest time. Without being offered a drink, I didn't know how to behave. I didn't know where to stand. If they offer me a drink right away, I can have something to do, though I don't like it when the glass is empty, and I don't like it when they count.

"Would you like a scotch?" Alan Carver asked me, finally. "It's Christmas Eve, after all."

I had forgotten it was Christmas. Although everyone tacks up Christmas lights to their trees and roofs, they go up earlier and earlier. There's nothing in particular to tell you when it's Christmas.

We sat in their living room by a fire. I swirled the brassy liquid in my glass. Everything was nice. The Carvers kept a clean house and they decorated it with good taste. Even the faucets in the washroom were polished chrome. It makes your own place cramped and cheap. Alan said something, and then she said something, and then Lydia, and then Alan, again, etc. Periodically I would think of something to say, but I never found an opening to say it. Lydia brought out a plate with cheese, crackers, and grapes, and since the knife reminded me of a dream I had, I said, "That reminds me of a dream I had," and they began to speak of dreams they had and I never got to say anything about my dream, which, in any event, wasn't really anything other than my looking at a knife.

I stared at my empty glass. Lydia Carver stood up and turned toward the fireplace to get warm. Her dress fit tightly against her buttocks. I was not sure what to think about that. Then she turned, catching me look at her, and said, "You know what we should do? We should go carolling."

Alan said, "Carolling? We need more scotch for that." He rose from the couch, took my glass, and entered the kitchen. I was glad he was thinking of me. My wife followed him.

Lydia Carver sat back down on the chair. She crossed one leg over another, leaned forward, and looked at me. She stared at me as if trying to figure something out, as if she believed she had the power to see into my soul if she stared deep enough. Her dark mascara had smudged. I saw the wrinkles around her mouth and didn't know what to say to her. Usually Lydia Carver speaks about how busy she is, how important she is at whatever it is she does. She makes you feel that you owe her something merely for her deigning to put aside her important work to listen to what you have to say. Lydia asked me, "So, what do you think of that?"

"Of what?"

"Of carolling."

When I was in grade school, Mr. Davis said that I could not sing. He asked me to run the projector, instead, and then he got mad at me for missing some kind of cue. Fearing that Alan would forget my scotch, I rose. In the kitchen, Alan was pressing himself against the backside of my wife, his arms around her. I returned to the living room.

"So, are we going carolling?" Lydia asked me.

"Yes," I said and stood there stupidly.

It was after eleven o'clock at night when we finally got around to going carolling. While we put on our boots and hats and scarves and whatnot, Lydia said, "Be sure to carol in front of the Wilsons. Remember when they called the police on us?"

"They called the police on you?" my wife asked. She thought that was funny.

"And the Wyatts," Alan Carver said.

"What did the Wyatts do to you?" my wife asked. She fell over trying to put on her boot and Alan righted her.

"The Wyatts? Well, they're just pains in the neck. You say 'Hi' to them and they look the other way."

"Why do they look the other way?" my wife asked. She reached out for Alan to hold her upright. I wanted to say, "They just do," but I kept my mouth shut. I didn't want to go carolling. To be honest, I didn't think they would carol. I figured we'd go for a walk, return, and have more scotch.

"And the Castlemans," Lydia said. "We have to carol at them, too. Their dogs always shit in our yard."

Alan put two bottles of beer in his jacket pockets, and he held a third one in his gloved hand, open, ready to drink. He saw me watching, and said, "Help yourself to some beers, if you want. They're in the fridge."

I took off my boots and returned to the kitchen to stock up on beer for the trip. I drank one right there, thinking I didn't have enough pockets. An orange fell out of the fridge and landed on the ceramic floor with a dull thud. When you are drunk, things like that happen and there's nothing you can do about it.

By the time I got outside, the carollers were already up the road. You could hear them bellowing the first stanza of "We Three Kings." They sang off-key, out of kilter, and no one knew the words. None of that seemed to matter to them. They thought they were funny. You could hear them laughing. I imagined children lying in bed wondering what had infiltrated their fairy tales. Lydia Carver walked up to a house and knocked on the door. Though lights were on, and cars were in the driveway, no one answered. She hollered "Merry Christmas" at the people inside the house the way one would curse.

It was a beautiful night. Black sky with its jagged stars and snow that squeaked when you walked, and the vapour of your breath. I opened another beer and let the assault carollers get farther ahead of me. I could hear them shouting the first lines of "Silent Night" in booming voices, punctuated by their laughter.

A Question of Colour

❄ Sean Wiebe ❄

Every time I recount this story it is taxing. Though it is probably more accurate to say that it taxes me only when I begin to think about how it might have turned out differently. I've told it to my latest girlfriend, and without much deliberation she said if I were to change a detail earlier in the story, then, by simple deduction, there would be no need for the ending to be different.

Her advice has been quite helpful. Of course I am still burdened, but it is true that when I think about what happened my regret is less. Deciding to accept the ending as it is has focussed my imagination on what might have been different earlier in the story.

The story itself is quite simple: There is this woman who is bumped sideways into a pool. She is mildly tipsy but abstaining enough to discuss what colour to paint the baby's room with Joseph, the one who bumps her.

But he swears their bumping was an accident, it being only a result of him trying to avoid contact with three men he didn't know, who must have been guests of one of his colleagues, and weren't paying attention to where they were standing, as sometimes can happen when there is a crowd of people and the talking is animated, like it often is later at night after a few drinks and the party takes on a life of its own.

I asked my girlfriend if this is an instance where a woman would be embarrassed, or if, from her experience, this is something that is nothing. She thinks there is something I'm missing; perhaps my unconscious, she says, is avoiding the central issue by keeping my imagination from discovering what else should be part of the story.

Engrossed in their conversation, the three men continue on inside, and as Marni climbs out of the pool, Joseph is not sure where the towels are kept and wondering whether he should search for one, or whether he should go introduce himself to three men, which might be easier if she had not been bumped. But now that she has been, how can he act normally?

If only he could slow things down and be the one who is quickest at thinking what to do. If he knew who they were, or they knew Marni, then he could replay what happened step by step and she would know it wasn't his fault. Polite conversation might still possible, but he is feeling guilty and supposes they would guess how he is really feeling, or think that he is the kind of person who avoids things, like being bumped in order to prevent a little beer from spilling.

In the story, it might be coincidence that Joseph bumps her at the exact moment she says the word "baby," though the timing is not entirely clear, even if it is entirely believable that Joseph is the kind of person to avoid contact wherever possible. Most distressing to him is why she denies being angry, laughing it off, as if these kinds of things can happen without any underlying reason.

It is hard to explain to my girlfriend why Marni keeps the anger inside her. Even though it is clear to me, the clarity always becomes less clear when I try to explain it, or rather, in the story, it feels unnecessary for Marni to explain her anger as if somehow Joseph should know there is always another explanation for something accidental.

Now I see how something in me has been avoiding the issue. Rather than explain her anger, maybe it would be better for me to try to imagine it. Perhaps while she is looking for a place to dry off, she thinks he is enjoying another drink, smiling and talking, even insisting to others that it was an accident, getting sympathy and using his humour as if it were a funny incident a few months ago and can be laughed at with friends who are having a drink together, reminiscing about the kinds of things that can go wrong when two people are walking together beside a pool. And while it is true that the bumping is in the past, for her, it is not enough in the past to be an event that one can talk about with a smile.

Or maybe she wonders why he was furthest from the pool? She might be thinking about how awkward it felt to be on his right side, walking along the pool's edge, for frequently she had been on his left when they walked downtown for drinks, though he is quite sure they don't have set sides when they walk. They always returned by cab so never walked in the other direction where she might have been on his right. Maybe she blames herself for not having tested this before, and now it is too late to know if he is the kind of man to shield her from traffic, or to keep her from being bumped into a pool.

Painting the baby's room is something they had talked about recently, even having taped swatches to the wall, but a firm decision is still to be made. Maybe having a decision to make feels like something she can hold on to, something she can look forward to in the evenings. Even if the swatches are tiny cards, perhaps she is happy about them. After all, she can look at them the entire day while he is at work. The decision is something they are going to make together, and she might be counting on there being more decisions of importance that lie ahead.

At the party, maybe when she is in the guest room upstairs, wrapped in one of the hostess's towels after drying off, she sees the perfect colour for the baby's room. That might explain her urgent text to meet her in the bedroom, but seeing her in a towel, Joseph isn't thinking about the colour of the room.

As I imagine what details I might change earlier in the story, what is becoming more clear is how his remark about the towel sets her into a rage, and why when she slaps him it is not with enough force to equal the amount of anger that she feels. My girlfriend agrees that this is something she can imagine doing in this circumstance, but not so close to Christmas.

It's true that Christmas and anger are incompatible. Although Marni would know intuitively that more painful than the anger in her is the loneliness of an empty house, this being why she continues to text him to return home, after a few days an awkward apology, then a suggestion that she cook a nice dinner, then a photo of her in a Christmas sweater, then one with her stockings rolled down, then nothing at all. He thinks the nothingness is similar to her loneliness. The absence of fabric pressing on her skin is like the absence of his skin.

I can see now, as is often the case in fiction, how I might not need to change anything that happened, only how the characters understand what is happening. My girlfriend is a stickler for endings refusing the sudden sentimental turn, and this was part of our initial attraction, a mutual distrust of authors who lack the courage to let endings unfold logically from their causes.

Maybe it would be better for the baby not to be born, even though, technically, it is not yet born. But that would overshadow the important question of what colour to paint the baby's room.

Peppered Hearts

❋ Ruth Mischler ❋

It was four in the afternoon, the end of November, early dusk lurking behind a curtain of snowflakes as I pulled up in the parking lot at Sobeys. Just a few little items left on my list. With my head turned away from the wind, I almost ran into him. A Japanese guy with a backpack and a city map, toque pulled low, hands shaking slightly, a lone straggler frozen in the wrong season.

Could I show him on his map where he was, he asked in broken English. Everything was written in Japanese, our little old town transformed into an exotic locale I hardly recognized, the streets snaking through and around brushstroke characters with a flourish. No matter which way I turned the map, I was getting as lost as he was. The tourist information, that's what he wanted. He kept nodding his head, smiling with a frown. I handed him back the map, and told him I would give him a ride if he was still there when I came out of the store. I caught myself nodding and smiling as I rushed in and back out again. Of course he was still there.

The tourist information office was closed. The second X on his map was a B&B a brushstroke away, the OPEN sign blinking blue under a snowy hat. Although I had known him for only a few minutes, I felt a touch of responsibility when he gathered his belongings to leave and walk up the steps of the B&B. A student, Yusuke had travelled across Canada from Vancouver by train and bus, he said, and was here to look for a homestay to finish off his year's working holiday. I gave him my phone number in case he had problems. Five days later he called. The few homestays offered on PEI in the winter were off-limits for his tight budget. We met for coffee, my eldest daughter tagging along. Not that she would have known any better than me what a Japanese axe murderer looked like, but if I was going to offer our home to a stranger, she would have to approve.

Yusuke lived with us for almost four months, paying half of what a homestay would usually cost. Being slight and short he blended right into our family; only his facial features framed by black hair, coarse and straight, set him apart. After he asked me to bleach it, his hair not only had the texture of straw, but it turned flaxen with an orange tint. The coincidental connection was lost on him. Yusuke hadn't come to the Island for Anne. Instead, he went sledding with my kids and our dog, who had a habit of snatching hats off people's heads when they were down in the snow. Yusuke was shy, so shy he had problems calling our dog by his name. Sensei, meaning "teacher" in Japanese, was completely wrong for a dog, in his opinion.

Yusuke crafted big charts of the two Japanese alphabets for us. He designed and painted coasters at Fired Up. Wrapped them for Christmas. He studied, practiced, and questioned English lessons from a book each day. He learnt to cook chili, taught us to make sushi. While the snow piled up in everybody's yards, and lights appeared on houses and trees, we got busy in the kitchen baking ten kinds of cookies, my sacred Christmas tradition.

With a black sweatband keeping his hair at bay, an apron protecting his clothes, Yusuke was ready for the job. For days he helped me knead and roll dough, cut out shapes, brush them with sugar water, egg yolk, egg white, or lemon icing, and arrange them on cookie sheets. I kept control of the right temperature in the oven. The ginger Christmas trees, hazelnut fingers, chocolate balls and hearts, almond moons, cinnamon stars, nut squares, butter hearts, and coconut drops all reached their respective tins in the traditional way, but the jam hearts were caught on a snag. Getting comfortable with cookie baking, Yusuke lost all shyness and started throwing his own ideas into the mix.

Is it a Japanese tradition to trick people and have a good laugh afterwards? I doubt it. Was it the seeds in the raspberry jam which tempted him and led him astray? I noticed him taking pepper and milling it with the jam. Pepper to enhance the flavour of fresh strawberries, yes, but raspberry jam? When he asked for hot sauce, I balked. I had baked the bottom hearts and the top hearts with smaller hearts cut out so the jam would be visible. He had started spreading the peppery raspberry jam on the bottom hearts with a knife. It became clear that he was kidnapping my jam hearts, messing with my long-standing Christmas favourite.

What's wrong with a little fun? Yusuke argued and argued till I softened my stance. We came to a compromise. He was allowed to pepper a few. The recipients either didn't notice or were too polite to say anything. I let him mix the raspberry jam with hot sauce for half a dozen more. Those who bit into a hot-sauce cookie froze and never thought about being polite once they caught up with their breath.

That day my jam hearts lost their innocence, while Yusuke hid behind a hand, silently doubling over with mirth, his orange hair catching an angelic glow in the candlelight.

thanksgiving 2011

❄   Lee Ellen Pottie   ❄

An American friend made a Canadian
Thanksgiving dinner last night: gluten-free, quinoa
veggie loaf, buckwheat gravy, and cumin-red
pepper mashed potatoes. Her husband's from the 'Chi:

the Miramichi, famous for salmon runs, bear and moose
hunting, beer-drinking out at the cabin, famous
celebrities doing catch and release, some local girls
living down in New York because the handsome

baseball players' hooks and pockets were deeper. I wonder
what that Chatham boy thinks about tofurkey, land flatter
than a becalmed ocean, drawling accents and nasally vowels.
Does he wish for the smell of a roasted or deep-fried bird,

mustard and honey ham, baked sweet or red potatoes, peas
and carrots boiled till they're a pile of mush? That gravy
from giblets and pan juices, white flour and onions.
The row of pies—apple, pumpkin, sugar—and squares

with all that sweet icing and sparkles,
ice cream on the side. The family fighting over
who gets to sit next to Grandpa, Maman.
Ice fishing or quail hunting next morning. The kitchen now

full of neighbours dropping by for fiddles, guitars,
old tunes handed down from Irish, Scottish,
Acadian ancestors. People knowing that your
family voted red or blue, never orange and green,

and always attended the same sturdy church,
were buried in the same churchyard for ten generations.
That love takes you in unfamiliar directions.

The Christmas Cake

❄ Dorothy Perkyns ❄

I swung around the kitchen door, that raw December afternoon, my gas mask bumping on my hip as I entered. My mother looked up from her recipe book to smile her usual after-school welcome, though today I sensed her preoccupation with the baking. Her bright blue eyes shone radiantly in her round, rosy face. This was a moment she had been waiting for, and she was taking time to savour it.

"I've got everything I need at last," she declared, triumphantly. "They finally had a delivery of currants at the Co-op this morning, and we were allowed half a pound per family. The manager weighed mine out. He said we were lucky to get any food at all from overseas, with German warships and U-boats out in the Atlantic. Canadian sailors are risking their lives every time they set sail for England. You'd hardly expect…" Her voice trailed off and for a brief moment she was lost in thought before seizing her dog-eared cookbook to check the recipe.

Ingredients for the cake lay marshalled in precise military formation. Two green enamel containers, one labelled FLOUR, the other SUGAR, each protectively guarded an end of the line of smaller items: a jar of syrup, pats of butter and margarine, a cup containing dried egg powder, tiny boxes and bottles of spices and flavourings, all systematically and secretly hoarded for this combined operation.

To the right of the formation rose a neat barricade of mixed dried fruit. Hiding behind it crouched three precious government-stamped shell eggs, tensely awaiting their signal to be broken, like grenades ready to be tossed. It was the mouthwatering display of currants, raisins, sultanas, and dates, studded with scarlet glace cherries, which captured my attention. To my war-conditioned eyes it epitomized former days of peace and plenty. Now it was 1940. After long months of strict food rationing, I knew better than to help myself to even the smallest pinch.

I quickly went to dump my coat and gas mask in the hall cupboard.

"Just make sure the fire's all right," Mum called after me.

As I hurried back, intending to perch on the tall kitchen stool, I poked my head round the door of the dining room, where our bake-oven was part of a large range heated by an open coal fire. The little room was as warm as on prewar days. Flames from a meticulously selected heap of coals were drawing keenly, causing the tiles in the hearth to wink and flicker. When I returned to the kitchen, Mum was carefully cutting a liner for the cake pan from margarine wrappers. After months of stretching meagre rations to keep us fed, she was going to make a real cake, and she was determined to enjoy this special experience to the full.

"I waited this late to make the cake so that we could all enjoy the fire," she explained. "Dad will be home, too. It's not a Home Guard night, and it's not his turn as air-raid warden."

The Home Guard was a volunteer army of able older men who drilled and practised military manoeuvres in the surrounding countryside. Dad considered he was "doing his bit" as part of a force ready to support the regular troops in the event of a German invasion. Air-raid wardens were neighbours who undertook to be on overnight watch in pairs.

As Mum talked she plied her wooden spoon. With an expertise I'd almost forgotten, she vigorously beat fats and sugar, added eggs and syrup and finally the flour and fruit. She scraped the thick, golden mixture into the pan, levelled the surface, and carefully, almost reverently, carried the cake to the oven. I was left to find what "licking" I could from the sides of a well-scraped bowl.

Dad came home from work, his normally florid complexion drained of colour, for he was chilled to the marrow from waiting for a bus in the damp cold of the darkening afternoon. He took off his overcoat and unwound the long khaki scarf I had laboured many hours to knit as part of his Home Guard uniform. His tired brown eyes brightened at the sight of the fire and the smell wafting from the pot simmering on a trivet. For the first time I noticed that his straight brown hair, from which I inherited my own straggly locks, was turning grey above his ears.

Before sitting down to eat, he drew the long, heavy blackout curtains, for it was illegal to let any light show to the outdoors after dark. I knew that lentil and vegetable soup was one of his least favourite meals, but he stolidly spooned up his bowlful, offering no complaint. It would have been unthinkable to ask for anything different. Either we ate what my mother struggled to provide or we went hungry.

While I helped with the dishes, Dad switched on the six o'clock radio news. I usually tuned out at the sound of the cut-glass BBC voice, but he listened with avid concentration, sometimes reacting with a deep sigh and a sad shake of his head. Mum and I returned to the living room as the bulletin ended, and we all settled down to make the most of the unusual luxury of a really good fire.

"The cake smells good," Dad remarked, as he filled his pipe with tobacco and opened the newspaper. "You managed to buy currants at last?"

"Yes, just today. I'd begun to think I'd have to manage without them. I always used to make my fruit cake weeks ahead, so that it could mature, but now…" Her words faded to a sigh.

My father shook his head sadly and half-closed his eyes as if thinking about something he did not really want to believe. He was usually reluctant to share his thoughts at moments like these. I now know he felt it his protective duty not to worry Mum and me more than necessary. Tonight, I was surprised that he actually murmured an observation. "I reckon somebody cares a lot about us if they make sure we have currants for Christmas."

I dragged out my Geography textbook, from which I was to read over topics already explained in class by Miss Shuttleworth. She was a skinny, poker-straight woman of indeterminate but older age, who always wore shapeless tweeds and flat-heeled, laced shoes and wore her greying auburn hair twisted into earphones. With patriotic enthusiasm she had decided that grateful awareness of our vast British Empire should be instilled into our unreceptive brains. Today she had concentrated on Canada.

The source of her knowledge of this country is still a mystery to me, but as in all her teaching, she was quite dogmatic in what she told us, illustrating her information by vigorously tapping a sketch map hung over the blackboard. Canada was divided horizontally into three sections. The section just above the United States was coloured dark green to represent coniferous forests. Most Canadians, she said, lived in this area. They were tall, fearless lumberjacks who felled many trees, stripped them of their branches, and flung the trunks into rushing rivers. The rivers knew, as if by magic, where to take the logs.

The stripe above the green area was mauve and represented tundra. Here, ice melted only long enough in summer for small flowers and bushes to flourish briefly. At the top of the map was an incredibly jagged white area depicting permanent ice and snow. This was where Eskimos lived in dome-shaped houses made of blocks of frozen snow. They survived by eating seals, fish, and whales.

"The port of Halifax remains ice-free all year round," the assigned section in the book began. My eyes drifted from the words to my mother's precious fire. Among the glowing coals a forest sprang to life. Through this a man was anxiously hurrying. He was tall, fair, and fearless, and carried an axe. Breathless, he rushed to where a ship rode at anchor on the dark waters of Halifax Harbour.

My reverie was shattered by the all-too-familiar, strident, repeating wail of the air-raid siren.

"Oh, no!" exclaimed Mum. "Not just now. Do we have to take cover?"

Automatically, I slipped into my siren suit, a sort of poor man's snowsuit fabricated from one of her old coats. With resigned sighs my parents bundled themselves up, too.

"We've never had a raid as early as this," muttered Mum, thoroughly disgruntled as she fixed the wire fireguard to prevent sparks flying onto the hearthrug.

"Let's hope it won't be much," Dad answered sympathetically, picking up a flashlight and the small bag of family papers that lay ready on the dresser.

We trooped through the kitchen, making sure to switch off all lights before opening the back door. The flashlight bulb was covered with green tissue paper to dim its brightness. Already, as we picked our way over the frosty stones on the little path, we could hear the distant rumble of guns and the drone of approaching aircraft.

Usually, I did not mind a night in the air-raid shelter, the body of which was made from corrugated iron sheets arched and bolted overhead. Flat sheets of the same material formed the end walls. About six feet long and just over four feet wide, our uninviting refuge was barely high enough for an average man to stand upright in. The bottom half was sunk in the earth, fixed into the rectangular hole that Dad and friends had dug. All the displaced earth and sand bags were now piled on top of the shelter. At one end a small rectangular hole covered with a movable screen provided the only access, through which we crawled in and out.

There was something adventurous about sleeping outdoors on a camp bed, and normally nothing disturbed me. Tonight, however, was different. Scarcely had we settled down before I found myself flung about a foot above the mattress to the noise of falling bricks and broken glass.

"That's close," I heard Dad say under his breath. "They'll be aiming for the power station."

Our home was in a small development of modern houses at the edge of a straggling village about six miles north of the industrial city of Manchester. Although the surrounding countryside was besmirched by the presence of coal mines and cotton mills, there were still plenty of woods and fields to enjoy. In a gentle valley about a mile away meandered the River Irwell. From any point on its riverside trail the giant cooling towers of the power generating station disrupted a comparatively unspoilt rural view.

Mum ignored Dad's remark and kept silent, listening to the drone of the planes. "What about my cake?" was her eventual tremulous reply.

"I'll hop out and see to it later," Dad promised. "There's sure to be a break before long."

But there was no break. Hour after shattering hour the bombardment continued, the crashing, thudding, deafening roar of bombs and responding ack-ack guns. At one point the duty wardens, on their rounds to see how neighbours were faring, tugged open the shelter screen. I saw their tin-helmeted silhouettes against a sky that flashed incessantly as in a bad thunderstorm.

"You're missing all the fireworks," one of them called with forced cheerfulness.

The next moment an extra loud crash sent the two men falling flat, face down on the garden. It was some time before they dared stand up again and go on their way.

After that I must have dozed fitfully. The ship that had lain at anchor in Halifax Harbour was now gliding over the blue-black ocean. My brave lumberjack slept, too, lurching and rolling with the waves in a high bunk, while an icy torrent erupted onto the deck above, and I awoke to the high-pitched whine of the all-clear siren assuring us that it was safe to creep from our hiding place.

Mum leapt out and dashed along the garden path before Dad and

I even emerged. When we reached the dining room, she was kneeling by the cold hearth, a tired but relieved smile on her face. The cake, clasped protectively in her mittened hands, looked perfect.

With dogged resignation, my father got ready for work. I ate a slice of toast and then went out to view the most recent damage. Windows were missing from a few houses, but walls and doors were almost totally intact. Some kids were hunting in the street for bits of shrapnel to add to their collections. As I came back to pick up my books and gas-mask, Mum was talking to our next-door neighbour over the garden fence.

"Mrs. Peters at the end of the avenue had a little boy at three o'clock this morning," I heard our neighbour say. She dropped her voice at my approach, for this was clearly a conversation I was not supposed to hear. "The doctor couldn't get his car out. His garage door was blown in. The midwife rode all the way here on her bike and looked after everything, cool as a cucumber."

I sauntered away, pretending to scour the ground for shrapnel. As I turned the corner of the house, I just caught my mother's sympathetic enquiry: "Is everything all right? Poor woman. What a world to bring a baby into."

On the way to school I briefly compared the night's experiences with my friend Sally. Our conversation then switched to the more important topic of the last few rehearsals for the pantomime *Cinderella*, in which we were to appear with other members of our Sunday School just after Christmas.

Because of my loud speaking voice and regular attendance on Sunday afternoons, I was always cast in a major role. This year I was to be an ugly sister, dressed in a "fashions for rations" creation Mum was concocting from an old evening dress and a nightgown. Sally, whose attendance was sporadic, was merely a courtier. She was afraid she might lose even that part if, by next rehearsal, she did not know the words of "There'll Always be an England," which the whole cast was to sing in the grand finale.

During the last two days of term, pre-Christmas excitement was unquenchable. With all the men teachers away on active service, the middle-aged women left to run our school entered into our eager anticipation. They schemed and devised ways for us to make decorations for the classrooms from all sorts of unlikely scraps of coloured paper, old ribbon, and even twigs from our gardens. Friends and relatives were cajoled into donating last year's greeting cards for us to recycle and send to each other. On one occasion we were herded into the school shelter for an hour because of a daytime raid, but we sang carols lustily, glad of an excuse to think of Christmas instead of long multiplication.

At home I had an artificial tree laid away from prewar days. I cautiously unwrapped it for decoration with a few lovingly preserved glass balls and dulling lengths of tinsel. By some miracle the ancient chain of fairy lights still worked.

My mother fussed over house-cleaning, and the cake reappeared to be decorated. I stared in fascination as Mum pounded soya bean flour and almond essence into mock marzipan.

"I don't know what I'm going to do about the royal icing," she murmured, wrinkling her forehead and biting her lip.

I arrived home on the final afternoon of school to find her vigorously shaking powdered milk and granulated sugar in a jelly bag, which she then flattened by forcing it through the heavy wooden laundry wringer. She dampened this unpromising substitute for icing sugar with boiling water and spread it over the marzipan. By morning it had achieved the texture of granite.

Christmas Day dawned bright and crisp after a two-inch fall of overnight snow. Although I had secretly abandoned my belief in Santa, I never doubted that there would be gifts, and I was not disappointed. There was a large, shiny box of paints, two books, a board game, and even small packets of candy and an orange weighting down the toe of my overstretched stocking.

Soon after breakfast, the tantalizing smell of roasting chicken permeated the little house, for we always ate Christmas dinner at midday. While our feast sizzled we walked the short distance to church, where a congregation, bereft of its younger men, prayed for their safe return.

Nothing that Christmas, however, made quite such an impression on me as the wonderful tea. My mother had invited my grandparents, several aunts and uncles, and my three young cousins. We squeezed round the dining table, where she had laid a mouthwatering spread of canned meats, pickles, salad, trifle, and scones. In the middle towered the cake, an invincible marble fortress, its walls now crenelated with a week's candy ration of sugar bonbons.

"I don't know how you manage to do all this," remarked one of my aunts, whose corporal husband had left for an undisclosed destination "somewhere in England" two weeks earlier.

"I save up for months," answered Mum, "an ounce of this, an ounce of that, from the rations. When we're allowed a tin of anything, I try to keep it by."

Towards the end of the meal she stood up and carefully pulled the cake towards her. There was a lull in conversation as she gripped the bread knife and firmly cut the first slice. I sensed the apprehension under her tight-lipped concentration as she cautiously laid it on a plate. It was perfect. No cake ever held fruit so evenly dispersed through such a firm golden texture. Though the hard mock icing began to crack as she served it, the cake was the personal victory she had dreamed of, a triumph that thumbed its nose at anyone trying to destroy Christmas and all it stood for.

The womenfolk made short work of the dishwashing. As soon as they returned from the kitchen, my mother announced firmly, "It's time we played a few games to amuse these children."

The well-tried routine of Hunt the Thimble, Hide and Seek, I Spy, and Forfeits followed. I had previously enjoyed this immensely and joined in today with apparent enthusiasm. Secretly, however, I was beginning to find some of the activities childish and could not share the intensity with which my cousins, all younger than me, hunted for a thimble planted in full view among ornaments on the dresser. My grandmother, an indefatigable knitter for the armed forces, took out her needles and wool to work on a khaki sock and enjoy the games as a spectator.

I still loved the carol singing with which our evenings always ended. Three of my uncles and one boy cousin were church choir members, so the sound we raised was fairly tuneful. It did not last long, for by ten o'clock the visitors were swathing themselves in coats and scarves. From our darkened hallway we watched their grey shadows shuffling across the snow, like a column of the fleeing European refugees shown on every newsreel at the cinema.

As we cleared away scraps left over from the meal, Mum mused over the compliments to her cooking. "Who would've thought it could possibly turn out so well?" she asked, as she packed the remaining wedge of cake into a tin. "It's the best Christmas cake I ever made."

"It should be," replied my father in a strangled tone I did not recognize. "It cost the most."

Sighing deeply, my mother shook her head and bit her lip. I thought she was going to weep.

Embarrassed, I slipped away to bed. As I undressed, I decided to try out my new box of watercolours the following day. In my dreams I painted all night long at a vast, action-packed mural. My smiling Canadian lumberjack, now resplendent in naval uniform, was balanced high on a ship's bulwark. He brandished his fearsome axe above the roiling waves, in which the shadowy outline of a skulking U-boat was slowly sinking out of sight.

Only One Wish

❄ Diana Lariviere ❄

The gears of the school bus ground ominously as it trudged its way up the long, steep hill. There had been two snowstorms in less than three days and the one tiny track on the road sparkled with ice, swaying the bus in zigzags as it boldly forced its way to the top. I sat praying that I wouldn't have to walk the two miles to our house, with my brothers and little sister in tow, as often happened over the winter.

I breathed a sigh of relief when the bus edged its way over the last knoll.

It wasn't that we lived so far from town. In autumn and spring it was quite a nice walk—barring black-fly season, of course. But, in winter, it was just too cold a trek through the snow and blowing wind. The school bus would head away from school in the opposite direction from us and then circle back. We were first on in the morning and last off at night, as were most of the kids who lived on the "other side" of the tracks.

As we drove through the familiar route, many of our neighbours' houses shone brightly with the blue, red, and green of flickering Christmas lights. Some of the children were still playing outside, building snowmen and snow castles. I so wanted to be out there with them; but there were just too many things to do at home to allow for playtime.

I knew envy was wrong in so many ways, but I could feel it oozing from every pore in my body, like water passing through a sieve. I wanted my old life back—life before the iron lung.

When we lived in India, Daddy was a mining engineer working for one of the large petroleum companies. It was sometimes unbearably hot, but still a wondrous place.

We had a huge house, with a cook and a housemaid. My sister, Molly, and I had our own bedrooms, while the twins, Alfred and Matthew, shared another. We even had a nanny to take care of our clothes and baths and all the other little details that take so much time with children, so there was little for us to do except go to school and enjoy ourselves—and enjoy ourselves we certainly did.

We were busy with all sorts of activities—from riding lessons to swimming, art, tennis, badminton and, of course, the ever dreaded school. One of my best birthday parties was when my parents arranged for a whole array of Indian animals for entertainment, including a monkey that played a little music box and an elephant that we were allowed to ride.

Thinking back, I know for sure that it was my mother who had the huge task of making sure everything ran smoothly.

When I was ten, everything changed. Daddy got really sick and went into hospital. My mother cried a lot, and, although she tried to smile when we were with her, we would huddle together at night listening to her sobs and wondering what we had done to make her so unhappy.

One day, a large truck arrived. Everything in our house went into boxes and the boxes went into a truck.

My mother huddled us together, explaining that Daddy had to go to a hospital in Canada to help him get better. Daddy had polio… and, because he had been so athletic, the disease had had particularly severe consequences.

A few hours later, we were on a flight to England, en route to Canada. Molly cried herself to sleep on the plane. It didn't help that her precious doll, Anna, had been packed along with all of our other belongings and wouldn't be seen for weeks.

At first we lived in the city, not far from Daddy's hospital and our school. My mother spent hours at the hospital with Daddy but she was always home in time to make supper, help us with our homework and our baths, and tuck us into bed at night with a story.

I begged my mother incessantly to let me see Daddy; I missed him so, but she said I would have to be patient because Daddy wasn't well enough yet to see anyone. That scared me. I was so afraid that my handsome, energetic father was going to die and I would never see him again.

My persistence eventually paid off and my mother relented. My mother cautioned me that I shouldn't be shocked and that I shouldn't tell the younger ones how Daddy looked. I had no idea what she meant and I didn't care. I wanted to see him so badly.

When I walked into Daddy's hospital room, there was no bed and I couldn't see Daddy at first. The room was dwarfed by a huge metal container—an iron casket of sorts. A bedside table lay littered with syringes and other medical instruments.

"Charlotte," came a low, rasping voice. "Charlotte, are… you… okay?"

My mother's hands gently steered me to the head of the iron casket, where only my father's head peeped through. He smiled.

"Daddy?"

The iron-embodied face that stared back at me bore no resemblance to the happy, laughing father I knew; but I knew it was him. I knew that voice. I loved that voice.

"Daddy," I choked, "you're… looking well." Oh, how foolish could I be to say such a thing.

I tried to smile. I tried to be brave. My eyes welled with tears that I dared not shed.

"I love you, Daddy."

"I… love… you… too… poppet," Daddy said in laboured breath. Oh, how I had missed those words.

I visited Daddy every Sunday after that and I never again questioned my mother's long absences. I willingly assumed more responsibility for Alfred and Matthew and Molly. I promised myself from that moment on my mother would never have any extra worries about her children; she had worries aplenty with Daddy.

When I was twelve, Daddy was able to breathe sufficiently well to leave the iron lung behind, but not well enough to come home. My mother explained that Daddy still had lots of therapy and rehabilitation to endure. But my heart surged at what I knew to be progress and I couldn't wait until he would be well enough to run and swim and play with us again.

I didn't always understand the anguish on my mother's face when the mail came in. I was oblivious to all the bills that were piling up; but I was grateful for my mother's honesty. Mother explained that our family savings had run out because of Daddy's hospital bills. We would have to move to the outskirts of a nearby town so that we could keep costs down and Daddy could undergo his therapy at one of the smaller, less expensive hospitals.

The house we rented was a huge old farmhouse, but would more easily be described as a barn with doors and windows. There were holes in the roof that my mother tried hard to fill with old tar she got from one of the local farmers, but it still leaked when it rained. The cracked floorboards were an open invitation to every rodent, but we became adept at trapping and very skilled with a broom. We each worked at stuffing the sides and bottoms of the windows with old straw to stop the drafts.

My mother took in sewing. Since she had been raised on a tea plantation in Ceylon (now Sri Lanka) and otherwise been a wife and mother, sewing was one of the few marketable skills she had. Late into the night, I could hear the sewing machine whirring its way into a repair or evolving a new pattern for the meager dollars that it would bring in.

My mother was a proud woman who would not accept handouts, despite our dire situation. She did, however, manage to salvage mountains of used clothing or bits of cloth and turn it all into wearable items for the four of us. Boots and shoes were harder to come by. Somehow the other kids knew that our "new" clothes were reconfigured hand-me-downs. I'll never forget when one of the boys called out to Alfred on the school bus, "Hey, Alfie... ain't the seat o' your pants the sleeve from my old man's barn jacket?" All the children laughed. Alfred's embarrassment shone through in the red flush on his face, but he only stared coldly at his verbal attacker. Alfred swore he would never wear those pants again—not that he had a choice. He cried himself to sleep in my arms that night. None of us would have said a word to my mother. Despite our own disappointments, we knew she worked so hard for all of us.

The absolute worst was at Christmastime. We had spent three Christmases without Daddy and were heading into a fourth. The first two weren't too bad. We decorated a tree and my mother had one gift for each of us. Although there was nothing for her under the tree, my mother said that she felt blessed—with four caring and well-behaved children, a husband who was on the mend, and food on the table.

But as money got tighter, my mother sold off the elaborate Christmas ornaments that she had collected over the years from the many different countries to which she and Daddy had travelled. Much of our furniture, cutlery, and china went the same route. Then, there wasn't anything left to sell.

Our meals also slowly diminished. My mother managed to exchange some sewing for two chickens... so we had eggs, and eventually we had more chickens, thanks to the rooster across the way. We learned to collect seeds and to let a few potatoes grow "eyes" so that we could plant a garden. We learned to can and preserve and conserve, and my mother and I became adept at vegetarian cooking.

When it came to meat, there was little to be had. We talked about getting a pig or lamb or cow, but we had no way to keep it fed and definitely no money or means to have it butchered. There was also the worry that it would be hard to eat one of our pets, so it seemed a futile option.

Christmas number four without Daddy was fast approaching. On our school bus, children were sharing their letters to Santa, with long lists of the toys and clothes and other things they were wishing for. I had only one wish and I doubted that Santa would bring it.

On Christmas Eve, my mother drew us all together by the fireplace.

"My sweethearts, I love you more than life itself. I can only imagine how much you would like to have a Christmas like the ones we had in India and like most of our neighbours are enjoying. But I can only promise you the simplest of Christmases this year. We must be thankful that the fates have seen fit to keep us together, to keep us healthy and to watch over Daddy as he gets well enough to come back to us."

We did manage to have a tiny tree that Alfred and Matthew had cut from the forest near our house. Molly and I gathered pine cones and filled a bucket with straw and dirt to keep the tree straight.

My mother plopped her sewing basket filled with fragments of material and wool and thread and buttons into the middle of the living room. Molly and I tied bits of old cord and sewing thread onto the pine cones and hung them on the tree like Christmas bells. Molly took pieces of thread and hung them over the pine cones like tinsel. We strung the bits and pieces of cloth, thread, and buttons together, passing the ever-lengthening cord from one to the other. Then, Alfred and Matthew wrapped the Christmas cord up and around and through our little tree with the same enthusiasm as if they were decorating with ornaments from Sears or the Bay... or even Harrods of London.

To our child eyes, the tree glistened in the flickering light of the fireplace. My mother surprised us with hot cocoa... and marshmallows. We laughed and sang and shared stories of days gone by as we sat in front of the fireplace. But, as we grew tired, we also grew somber. We missed Daddy terribly.

At midnight, we hugged each other and recited a yuletide blessing and a wish for Daddy to come back to us soon.

On Christmas morning, we were awakened by a scream from

Matthew that brought us all flying into the living room in our pajamas. There, under the tree, all wrapped in the comic pages from a newspaper, were brightly decorated packages. What could be better than presents under the tree on Christmas morning!

Alfred's gift was a turnip that he peeled, rinsed, and threw into a pot. Molly's surprise was a large tin of peas that I helped her open. Matthew's package had six potatoes that he promptly washed, peeled, and sliced. And I was the proud recipient of a large ham. My mother pulled five hefty carrots out of a nearby pot.

In the remaining packages we found flour, sugar, and a container of baking powder. My mother smiled and said, "I think we might have the makings for a cake, except for eggs." Alfred and Matthew quickly threw on their coats and boots and headed off to get that last ingredient from the chicken shed.

As the pots of glorious food lay bubbling on the stove, we read and played checkers, trying desperately not to focus on the wonderful smells emanating from our soon-to-be Christmas feast.

Around noon, we heard the siren of the big red fire truck that was the pride and joy of the local volunteer fire department. It stopped—right in front of our house. My mother peered out the window and said, "Children, I think another Christmas present is here."

My mother opened the front door and there, in a wheelchair, sat our father, with a smile so broad and bright that it would have lit an entire room. We stared, stunned, and then all of us rushed toward him, nearly knocking him over. Mr. Brady, the fire chief, had brought my dad home, wheelchair and all.

But our Christmas surprise didn't end there. All sorts of cars and trucks and even tractors were pulling up. Almost every one of our neighbours was heading toward our house. There were even some of the nurses and doctors and other staff from the hospital. We were awestruck. My mother had known about Daddy coming home, but it was pretty obvious that even she didn't have a clue about the rest.

Mrs. McFadden, the mayor's wife, was the first through the door. Sugar pie in hand, she hugged my mother firmly with her free arm and said, "Dear, you must simply accept that we are neighbours and neighbours help each other, no strings attached."

Everyone brought food to share and gifts for each other. Mr. Killigan brought a big tree that he placed out of the way, near the bathroom door. It was beautiful, even if it didn't have any decorations on it. Mr. McCurdy, the janitor from our school, was decked out as Santa; he played the part exceedingly well with his blustering "Ho ho ho!"

Our house was filled to the rafters that Christmas with people and, most of all, with joy and good will. I hadn't seen my mother that happy since before we left India.

When everyone left that Christmas day, we gathered around my father's wheelchair, overwhelmed by the wonder of having him home at long last. But there was yet one more surprise to come.

"Look," Daddy said, and there in the corner by the washroom door was the tree that Mr. Killigan had brought, no longer abashedly naked, but covered in almost every Christmas decoration that our family had originally owned.

With my fourteenth birthday just around the corner, this was by far the most special, superb Christmas ever. Daddy was home and we had become an accepted part of our community.

Over time, Daddy learned to walk again and even to drive an adapted vehicle—very much a wonder for that time. Daddy was never again mobile enough to take part in any of the sports that he had loved, or to run and play with us. But, somehow, he never seemed handicapped to us. I don't think Daddy missed a play or game or other event that any one of us took part in.

My parents are both gone now, having lived a long and happy life together… and I miss them terribly. But nothing will take away the wonder and magic of that Christmas when we were united again as a family.

The Dress

❄ Louise Lalonde ❄

1962—the year that Marilyn Monroe died of an overdose of barbiturates, Gregory Peck won an Oscar for his role in *To Kill a Mockingbird*, and the Cuban Missile Crisis began and ended as abruptly as it started. It was also the year that Polaroid introduced colour prints that developed in sixty seconds, the first Medicare plan was launched in Saskatchewan to great protest by doctors, and Canada's last two executions took place, on December 11th. If that weren't enough, it was the winter that I began to shed my tomboy image.

I have very few vivid memories of my childhood, so I have to assume that my life was pretty much uneventful and that I'm not suppressing some traumatic existence that is better left buried in the bowels of my mind. My oldest brother has an incredible memory. He recounts stories where I was one of the main players and I remember nothing. One of those few vibrant memories is the first time that I fell head over heels for a piece of clothing: a dress, and I wanted it.

I was the first girl in a brood of four whose birthdays spanned five years. We had good Catholic parents. Apparently, my mother had been praying for a girl that she could dress up since she had gone into procreation mode, but had had to settle for three boys in a row. I would hate to think that I was a disappointment since, up until that winter, I just wanted to be one of the boys, and ruffles did not fare well when I was building a tree house, riding a bike, or wrestling.

Early that December on my way to school, I passed by the only mercantile store in our small town and there in the window, on a headless mannequin, was the most beautiful dress I had ever laid eyes upon. I stopped to take in the sight: the dress was made of lilac organza with cap sleeves and a huge crinoline skirt. On each side of the square neckline sat a small cluster of crystals that shone like diamonds. I pried myself away from the big plate glass window and went on to school, but I couldn't get the damn dress off my mind. What the hell was going on? Just two weeks prior, my mother had been ranting about how I could have at least combed my hair before having my school photo taken. I still have the pictures that prove she was fully justified.

When I got home that afternoon, I mentioned the dress to my mother, who very nonchalantly dismissed me, nodding and suggesting we discuss it later. Minutes after, she was freshening up her lipstick and out the door, asking my dad to look after us while she ran an errand.

You see, in those years, my father ran a grocery store and we lived upstairs, so business and family responsibilities often overlapped. As an intercom system, he had a buzzer behind the counter that he used to get our attention upstairs. He would buzz once if he needed help, three short buzzes if he wanted us to quiet down, and the dreaded "leaning on the buzzer" when he was on the verge of losing it. At that point, we usually had enough sense to stop whatever we were doing that was annoying him, and if we weren't doing anything annoying, we knew it meant that he urgently needed assistance in the store.

Sadly the dress fell off the radar that night, but the next day on my way to school, I stopped by the store window to admire it and, much to my chagrin, it was gone. With the resilience of an eleven-year-old, I swallowed my disappointment and went about my life. After all, it was almost Christmas and there was a lot going on. That year we had so much snow we could slide off my friend's porch roof. She was an only child and pretty much did what she wanted. We would take our boots off at the door and go traipsing up to her bedroom, boots and card boxes in tow, climb out a window onto the roof and down an icy path on the snowbank to the church parking lot next door.

Finally, Christmas Eve came and our apartment above the store was fully decorated and filled with the smell of donuts frying and cinnamon and cloves from the freshly baked *tourtières*. Growing up, we traditionally celebrated on Christmas Eve after Midnight Mass, which we, French Canadians, call a *réveillon*. After Mass, even kids were allowed to stay up to feast and open one present, play with it for a while, and then get out of the way of the card players. Our parties were always dry since neither of my parents imbibed. The story goes that my father had given it up a year into their marriage mostly because he would become belligerent after one beer. My mother didn't drink because she didn't feel like it. She had a terrific sense of fun and didn't need the crutch.

That Christmas Eve, I remember listening to the theme song for "Davy Crocket, King of the Wild Frontier" over and over again, singing along with one of my brothers who wore his coonskin hat. We were big fans of Disney's Frontierland, and one of my uncles had brought the record over from his collection. Another of the adults eventually got fed up and pulled the plug, switching it over to Christmas music. We were soon distracted and moved on to the feasting part of the festivities.

Finally it was time to choose a gift to open. As we scanned the pile of gifts under the tree, trying to decide which direction we would go, my mother came out of her bedroom with a large box wrapped with shiny silver paper and a huge red bow. The gift looked like something straight out of a movie. She suggested I should open it first and I willingly obliged. I carefully removed the bow and, while everyone watched, I managed to unwrap it without totally destroying the paper to expose a pristine white box. I lifted the cover and, much to my surprise, inside, enveloped in sparkly multicoloured tissue, was the lilac organza dress in all its glory. I vaguely remember hearing angels sing when I saw it, but it was Christmas, so there may very well have been angelic voices resonating somewhere in the background. I wore it proudly the next day to our grandparents' house for Christmas dinner and my mother was ecstatic.

While visiting some of my cousins recently, one of them pulled out some old photos of us as kids, and in one of the pictures, the youngest cousin of the bunch was wearing my lilac dress. She excitedly told me the story of how our aunt had made it especially for her and how much she loved that dress. I let her keep her memories.

Skates for Christmas

❄ Jeanette Scott ❄

In 1948, Barbara Ann Scott became the Olympic Female Figure-Skating Champion. Among other honours she achieved were a World Championship and two European, two North American, and four Canadian Championships. She became known as "Canada's Sweetheart." When I was seven, I received a book of cut-out dolls featuring Barbara Ann Scott, and like many other Canadians, I was soon captivated. I longed to become a figure skater just like her.

At nine years old, I got my first pair of skates. They were well-worn hand-me-downs that offered little support to wobbly ankles, but they were skates, and I envisioned gliding over the ice just like my idol. Adjoining our property was a farmer's field that featured a large low spot, which in winter made an ideal rink where neighbourhood kids skated and played hockey. This was to be the stage upon which I would become a champion. Much to my chagrin, I did not glide gracefully. My parents assured me that I could not expect to learn to skate the very first time.

Over that winter and the next few winters, I went back again and again, each time coming home with painful blisters on my ankles. As I grew, I had other hand-me-down skates, and each time I was hopeful that maybe this pair would make me skate like "Canada's Sweetheart." Time after time I was to be disappointed, but I stubbornly held onto my dream.

During my first year of high school, my class went on several occasions to the town rink for a skate. The first time, I watched from the sidelines since I had grown out of my last hand-me-downs. The girls from my class glided effortlessly across the ice on figure skates just like those worn by Barbara Ann Scott. "Oh," I thought with excitement, "that's the answer. If I had figure skates like those, I, too, could do that."

Christmas was coming up in a few weeks time and I asked for skates: new skates—figure skates. I was filled with eager anticipation as I spied the box that had to contain the answer to my dream. When I opened the box, my heart sank. They were brand-new skates, it is true, but they were not figure skates and they were trimmed with a lamb's wool collar at the top. I expect they looked warm and attractive to an adult, but they were nothing like the sleek, stylish ones I had seen my friends wearing. I tried to swallow my disappointment and put on a smile of delight because I knew they had probably cost money my parents could ill afford.

I did wear them a few times that winter, but like the old hand-me-downs, they did not transform me into a star. That was the year I realized I would never skate like Barbara Ann Scott. In fact, I decided that I was not meant to be a skater at all. And thus it was that I abandoned my dream, hung up my skates, and never put them on again.

Decades later, I look back on a lifetime of dreams. I feel satisfaction with those that have been realized and acceptance of those that have not. Yet even as I thrill at the graceful artistry of a Patrick Chan or a Mao Asada, I hear faint whispers of disappointment and regret from the child that lies deep within me.

Christmas Eve Debutante

❄ Margôt Maddison-MacFadyen ❄

St. Christopher's Church is overflowing when we arrive, so Mom and I are pressed in beside the altar, looking back into the main part of the congregation that is squeezed into pews. There's no debutante's ball, like Mom would've attended in ritzy Shaughnessy when she was sixteen. Midnight Mass on Christmas Eve has to do.

Mom specially made the plaid Jane Austen-style dress I am wearing. "You'll wear this to a few events," she'd said, pinning up the hem, me standing still and erect on a chair. "Other families will greet you, and maybe there'll be an interested son who's going to be a doctor. We're looking for doctor material."

My younger sister Kate had run away the summer before and had lived on Ambleside Beach with the guy who makes leather belts and sells them at the market. When she finally returned home, she'd had a tattoo of a bluebird on her wrist.

"Oh!" Mom had said when she saw it. "Oh, my!"

So I smile at Mom's hope for doctor material and keep the peace.

The dress sweeps to the floor, and a bright red sash cinches me in just below my breasts. My hair, long and honey-coloured, is tied back, but strands pulled out at the sides dance along my shoulders.

St. Christopher's features a gargantuan pipe organ that climbs the wall and fills the space behind the altar like a Virginia Creeper. Diminutive Miss Rochester, the organist, wears a burgundy tam with a small hawk feather held in place by a glittering silver pin. She sits on a large bench pulled up to her keyboard at the far side of the pews.

She has been playing Christmas hymns softly, but suddenly she amplifies the sound and breaks into "All My Heart Rejoices" when a procession of black-and-white robed figures, one carrying a huge, brightly polished brass cross enters at the back of the church and makes its way up the centre aisle. Frankincense puffs out of the thurible swung side to side by the altar boy who brings up the rear.

Chatter stops and some children who'd been sleeping like lap dogs, small collapsed lumps in the pews, wake up. The minister, carrying a gold-embossed bible, smiles at me when he reaches the altar. I am sure he wonders why I have suddenly reappeared in his church after a three-year absence, and why I'm dolled up in a Jane Austen dress like I'm at a late-eighteenth-century genteel English ball.

When I found out in confirmation classes that the Anglican Church was formed because Henry XIII couldn't get a divorce from Anne Boleyn, and that he had lopped off her head, I'd decided it was a pretty sketchy beginning. So after the big day in my white dress, white wrist-length gloves, and white shoes, with the Bishop of New Westminster, the purple-and-gold pointed mitre upon his head reaching halfway to heaven, I had distanced myself.

The altar, covered with a white floor-length cloth richly embroidered with a pattern of seasonal birds, is decorated with shiny-leafed, dark green holly festooned with bright red berries. Two enormous white candles, one on each side of the short tabletop lectern upon which the bible has been placed, burn with long yellow flames, and a silver snuffer lies between them. Fir boughs lavished with gold-sprayed cones and red velvet ribbons adorn each of the twelve pillars that line the nave.

Turning and facing the congregation, his black cassock swirling, the minister says loudly, his voice deep and resonant, "Let us pray."

It sounds like a crew of carpenters banging hammers furiously on wood as the congregation flip out their kneelers and lower themselves solemnly, some with their foreheads resting on the backs of the pews in front of them.

"Before beginning the main part of the service," continues the minister, "let us remember in our prayers Tom MacIntyre, who fights for his life in the Lions Gate Hospital."

I haven't seen Tom for five years. The news that he is in hospital shocks me, and I feel guilty for forgetting him, for letting so much time go by.

Just beneath the floor I'm standing on is the large Sunday school room, where Tom and I, our mothers both Sunday school teachers, had earned perfect attendances. The stories we'd learned still animate my mind—*The Garden of Eden, Noah's Ark, The Coat of Many Colours, Elijah and the Prophets of Baal.*

I see us sitting at a low table cutting out paper elephants and giraffes to paste on a mural of an ark.

I see his bony knees, paper-thin skin showing blue veins beneath the surface, pinched face, and thick shock of dark hair. I see his kind chocolate-brown eyes the size of walnut shells. And his two tow-headed sisters dashing about at the back of the room—free to run, to jump, to fall, to scratch and bruise a knee, while his movement is restricted to a wheelchair.

"Thomas! Stay in your chair!" instructs his mother, when we are doing stretching exercises. "Margôt, do not encourage him."

A year later, when I am eight, I ride my new bike to his house one brilliant spring day when the daffodils have opened their faces to the sun, and it is warm enough for outside play. His sisters have a playhouse set up on their front lawn. There is a toy stove and appliances, including a tiny pink toaster with a push-down lever, just like a real one.

My bike, a CCM, is red with whitewall tires and a loud bell. I ring it all the way down the hill and up the other side to Tom's house. He is waiting in his wheelchair at the end of the driveway when I pull in.

"That's a wonderful bike," he says. "Let me have a try?"

"I got it for Christmas," I say. "You know I'm not allowed to let you ride it. I really want to, and would, but I'm not allowed."

He is out of his chair and standing, for he can walk very well, and is only made to sit in it for safety. If he falls down and gets cut, or bruised, he is raced to the Lions Gate for serum injections and transfusions, and he is gone from school for days.

I daren't let him try my bike.

"Please, Margôt, let me," he says desperately.

The kitchen window slides open. "Margôt, do not let Tom on that bike!" yells Tom's mother. Then the window bangs shut. She watches us for a few minutes, and then she is gone.

The bike sparkles red in the sun.

"Please, Margôt. I'll only just sit on it. I won't actually ride it."

His imploring eyes convince me. I recognize his adventurous spirit. He is not meant to be a bookish person hanging about in a wheelchair having no fun. His is the spirit of a mountain climber, an astronaut, or a racecar driver. Maybe even an Olympian track biker sprinting around an oval at forty-five kilometres per hour, his wheels just centimetres from the wheels of the other riders.

At first, he does just sit on it, but lured by the promise of movement and wind on his face, he pushes off. The first ten seconds on the bike are worth the disaster that follows. I see brief elation in his smile, a gentle breeze sticks its fingers in his hair and rustles it up, but then he wobbles, heads for the ditch, and crashes.

We hear the wail of the ambulance long before it sails into Tom's driveway. When it is gone to the Lions Gate, I am banished.

"And don't bring that bike back here," says his mother.

A month later, Tom returns to school. His father has bought him a motorized wheelchair, but it is the 60s and wheelchairs are still teetering, skinny-wheeled contraptions. He has a speed control, and there are brakes, one to each side.

He zooms around the playground. Soars through the halls. Takes the concrete ramp that connects the two floors at full speed, pulling on the left brake at the halfway mark to spin him 180 degrees to continue down in the opposite direction.

All colour drained from his face, the school principal, Mr. Smith, yells, "Tom! Stop at once!" but Tom doesn't listen.

Hark the Herald Angels sing/Glory to the new born King, sings the choir, and I am back at Midnight Mass, fully embodied. Miss Rochester, whom I've known for as long as I can remember, has begun a new hymn with gusto. Her hawk-feathered tam, just visible over the tops of the congregation's heads, bobs up and down rhythmically. The low, low notes of the pipes resonate through my rib cage.

After the service, church ladies serve coffee, tea, and thin deviled-egg sandwiches downstairs. A faint smell of musty mothballs assaults my nose, and I sneeze. I half expect to see Tom's and my mural of Noah's Ark on the wall, where we had pinned it ten years before.

"Such a fine young lady," says Colonel Hawkings, who, retired from the British Army, has settled in West Vancouver. "And con-firmed in the church, too." He has a huge handlebar moustache and eyebrows like wire brushes.

His son, a renowned pothead who chronically skips school, is not doctor material, and his daughter is anorexic. She is so skinny and weak she slipped on slush in their front yard and tore all the soft tissues in her knees, but there is no sense in mentioning this to my beaming mother.

"Lovely to see you again, my dear," says Mrs. Taylor coolly. She lives in a ridiculously large and posh house in the British Properties. Its driveway is lined with sculpted, potted shrubs as if it was a Tuscany villa. "Georgia, your daughter has grown to such a fine young woman."

Her son, who got a gold-coloured Corvette for his eighteenth birthday, was up on speeding, drinking and driving, and resisting arrest charges when my Law 11 class was on a field trip to the West Vancouver Courts. The judge was sympathetic because of his age and had reduced the punishment to three months without a driver's license and a three-hundred-dollar fine. But did her son say, "Thank you, Sir, for your kind consideration of my case"? No. He said, "Whatever. My mother will pay the fine."

"Georgia, this can't be your eldest?" says Miss Rochester. "The little girl who used to come to church dressed in blue velvet the colour of the sky, and who always sat in the pew next to the organ?" Her eyes catch the light and twinkle like topaz gems.

If she'd married and had a son, and if he'd married and had a son, that boy might have been the doctor material Mom is after, but she didn't. There is the whole Anne Boleyn incident to consider, so I understand perfectly well that she may not have married for self-preservation.

It is raining, and we slosh through puddles as we dash for the car.

Mom, disappointed that there was no one suitable at Midnight Mass, says, "The Anderson wedding is coming up in April. Maybe there."

I remember the tattooed bluebird and the look of astonished dismay on Mom's face, her lips a perfect "O" as she said, "Oh! Oh, my!" so I ease myself silently into the car, pulling the bottom of my dress up to my knees to keep the floor from dirtying the fabric.

The windshield wipers flop heavily from side to side as we drive home.

The true doctor material—if there really is any such thing—frail in body but strong in spirit, is fighting for his life at the Lions Gate.

Mass Confusion

❄ Shaun Patterson ❄

One minute Patrick was thinking about going to bed and falling asleep as soon as possible so that he would wake up early on Christmas morning, and the next minute, it seemed, he was sitting in church trying to picture himself as a baby held by his parents and the priest over the baptism bowl.

Even though people talked about it as though he was there, he could never remember being baptized; he was a baby at the time, of course. His friend Chucky told him that they dip you in the holy water and that means you are friends with Jesus now. Chucky always got things only half right, so Patrick wasn't so sure he believed him. Besides, the little basin of holy water would barely hold a baby. The whole thing sounded very embarrassing. Now, sitting in the pew, Patrick looked over at the holy water basin with people constantly putting their hands in it and then on their forehead. He had been dunked into that? Yuck.

Sunday school was a weekly ritual and, although it could not compete with the fun found in comic books or watching cartoons, it was a passable way for a seven-year-old like Patrick to spend a couple hours on a Sunday morning. His mother would drop him off in the church basement before going upstairs with the other dressed-up adults. He wasn't sure what they all did in the big church room together. He imagined that they must be giving God some sort of weekly report on how good they were being and, of course, apologizing for their children's bad behaviour. When Patrick asked his mother if God said anything about how bad he was this week, she just turned a bright shade of red and glanced embarrassedly at the other parents. Patrick was puzzled, as he thought that this was a legitimate question.

What did it mean to be Catholic? What did it look like and what did it feel like? These were the kinds of ideas that the Sunday school teacher liked to talk about. Whenever one of these questions would be directed at Patrick, he would look around the room thoughtfully before answering.

"Being Catholic means wearing sandals and not getting along with Romans, I guess," Patrick said with an earnest look on his face. The other kids laughed but Patrick knew that they wouldn't know the real answer either.

Summer turned to fall and fall turned to winter. Their small town was now awash with holiday cheer. Christmas lights on everyone's home and a sense of cheer and charity that seemed to be elevated beyond the norm. Patrick and his brothers were incredibly excited about it being almost Christmas. This year they had started writing their Christmas lists in August. They wanted to make sure that they all asked for different things, or the same thing if it was an important item. Patrick was still haunted by the last Christmas, when his two older brothers both asked for skateboards and, because he didn't specify that he wanted one as well, his parents got him one of those silly scooters. He tried to pass it off as okay, but he lived with that disappointment for months. Patrick was six at the time and on the verge of manhood, so how was he supposed to be able to get a girlfriend or a wife eventually if he didn't even know how to ride a skateboard.

The outlook this year, however, was good. The tree was packed with presents for tomorrow morning and with Santa on his way in a couple of hours, this would surely be a Christmas to remember. All Patrick needed to do was get into his jammies and cruise through this evening and go to bed early. After dinner, though, a curious thing happened. Patrick's mother started laying out clothes for him and his brothers. They weren't just regular clothes either; they were dress clothes. What terrible twist of fate was this? thought Patrick. Where could we possibly be going in clothes like this on Christmas Eve?

Normally, Patrick would have put up a fuss about the situation, but in his astonishment, he complied with his mother's request to get dressed. As he marched out to the minivan with his brothers, there were looks of shell shock on their faces as the cold weather nipped at their cheeks. They buckled in and drove down the street to a destination unknown.

The family vehicle slowly turned into the packed church parking lot, and all Patrick could think was that this was surely turning into the worst Christmas Eve ever. Sundays were for church. Christmas Eve had always been a time to go to bed not long after supper, to will oneself to sleep so that one would wake up early.

"Stop fidgeting with your pants," Patrick's mother said. The wool was uncomfortable and the pants were on the verge of being too small for him anyways. As he looked down at his patent leather shoes, he thought that there surely must be a law against making kids dress up in this torturous manner. At least he wasn't in it alone. His family rushed into the church and tried to find the choicest pew that was close to the door, yet not too obviously close. Taking a look around he saw his brothers and sisters in arms, other children, with blank expressions on their faces, some trying desperately to stay awake. The little kids were lucky; they could always throw a fit and, based on their acting skills, they might be lucky enough to be taken outside. One cranky two-year-old in the row in front of Patrick's family started fussing as soon as the family was seated. Her father had to keep telling her to sit quietly. Patrick was all too familiar with this technique. She was acting up just enough to be noticed, but not too much that her restlessness would elicit a harsher response or punishment. Patrick appreciated this "slow burn" technique and wished that he was still young enough to pull it off himself.

The priest at their church was an old Polish man. He spoke in a friendly, deliberate manner, which Patrick found soothing, even though he could rarely understand a word that he was saying. Sometimes he would be able to pick out the name of an apostle, and repentance was always something that jumped out to let Patrick know the general nature of the sermon.

The Mass seemed to last for hours and Patrick's brothers were getting anxious. As they pushed past him to take communion, they both gave him a punch on the shoulder for good measure. Last year, one of Patrick's brothers had pocketed a couple of communion wafers so that Patrick could try one. After tasting the odd and quickly dissolving wafer, Patrick was confused about why this was something that people lined up for every week. When Patrick asked his father about this he said, "People will line up for anything that's free." Patrick's mother was clearly not impressed by this and shot him a look that Patrick recognized from when he had learned some new curse words at school last year and decided to share them with his family around the dinner table.

Now that communion was over, Patrick knew they were on the home stretch. The priest would talk for a few minutes more and then they would be done. Patrick could feel the crowd's anticipation as women slipped on their jackets and put their purses in their laps. He could see some parents zipping up their children's coats and a few of the men jockeying for position to be the first out the door. For some reason at this time of year, moms needed to be dropped off and picked up at the curb instead of walking across the snowy parking lots. Patrick assumed that they didn't want their expensive perfume smell to blow away before all the other people in the church could enjoy it. But that didn't explain why they needed to be picked up after Mass, too.

The night was finally over and by the time the van pulled into the family's garage, it was bedtime. The kids all looked like they had gone through a battle. Shirts were untucked and jackets were buttoned in the wrong holes. Even Patrick's dad's tie was hanging loose on his neck, like it did when he got home from a long day's work. The gang trudged into the house and everyone seemed quieter than usual as they got ready for bed. As he brushed his teeth and then was tucked into bed, the house took on a gentle quiet tone at this late hour.

After thinking about it for a bit, Patrick surely understood why his family had taken him to church tonight. It was all a test. All the chores, good grades, and minding his manners had led up to this ultimate gauntlet of naughty or nice. He felt bad for the kids who had managed to hold it together all year, only to be broken by this final ordeal. They surely wouldn't be seeing a new train set or Barbie doll under their Christmas trees tomorrow. But Patrick had succeeded and now looked forward to a day filled with presents and his parents' blessing. A day spent in his jammies, with junk food, no baths, and no brushing his teeth. He couldn't imagine that life could get any better, and was certain that Christmas would always be his favourite day.

A Charlottetown Hanukkah with Kafka

❋   J. J. Steinfeld   ❋

Nightfall, first day of Hanukkah
serene, safe, embraced by memory
I stand in front of my old menorah
brought from Europe by my parents—
an indestructible artifact Hitler missed
my father would say, a little sarcasm
with forceful historical allusion
an objet d'art a century old
my mother would say, a little nostalgia
with much ongoing warmth—
the *shamus* candle in my adult hand
sensing my little boy's long-ago grip
I ready to light the first night's candle.
As I stumble with the Hebrew words
of a candle-lighting blessing
I wonder if Kafka as a boy
ever lit a Hanukkah candle
connecting to the past
celebrating the miracle
of one day's menorah oil
lasting eight days in the Temple
liberated by Judah and the Maccabees.
I remember myself as a boy
year after hopeful year
gathering in a little Hanukkah *gelt*
spinning the playful *dreidel*
with its four Hebrew letters
lighting the candles
eight days of observance
thin colourful candles
their box proclaiming dripless
dripping to my childhood delight
in random dreamlike designs

nurturing imagination
even then pursuing other worlds
and fanciful creatures
as if Hanukkah were a holiday
to be celebrated every day.

Kennebecasis

❄ Richard Snow ❄

Christmas Day 1973, my fourteenth. The river had frozen as we slept, and, in the distance, snow glistened atop the pines of Long Island. Awake before anyone else, I lay in my bed listening to the wind whistle outside. Across the room, my brother Brian slept, his lanky thirteen-year-old frame already starting to overfill his bed.

When our family moved into this bright, new, two-storied home overlooking the Kennebecasis River, Brian and I graduated from bunk beds to matching twin beds in a large room facing the street. Our sister, Shari, a year younger than Brian, got her own bedroom next to ours. Two years after we moved in, our family grew by one, when our baby sister Betsy was born. Brian and I moved downstairs to make room for the new addition.

Our home was in a newly minted subdivision, just outside of Saint John, New Brunswick. On a peninsula jutting into the river, Kennebecasis Park drew its name and the quality of its existence from the water that mostly surrounded it. Our childhood was filled with summer days at the beach, swimming, canoeing, and sailing. In the winter we skated on the ice and snowmobiled across its expanse.

On that Christmas morning, tiny stingers of snow danced across the windowpanes of our room, and I was grateful for the warmth of the glowing red wood stove across the hall. This time of the year, its familiar smell was cut with the fragrance of the huge pine that filled the family room. Dad always insisted on cutting our own tree, and though it often seemed a little too tall, the result was somehow fitting.

From upstairs I could smell the lingering aroma of coffee cakes, which Dad and I had delivered to relatives and neighbours the night before. Mom made a dozen or more every year, including the one on the cutting board, waiting for our Christmas breakfast, sending the scents of nutmeg and cinnamon throughout the house.

A faint whisper filtered through the silence.

"Rich."

I hopped out of bed, wriggled into my slippers, and climbed up to where Betsy was leaning down the stairs.

"He came!" she said.

"Ha," I said, "You were right."

"I knew he would. You should always listen to me, especially when it comes to Santa."

"Come on. Let's get our stockings."

"Yay!"

"Shsssh," I said, as we tiptoed into the living room. "No one else is up yet. We can go back to your room and open them."

It was a rule Mom and Dad had. We could open our stockings if we were up early, but we needed to wait for the rest before we went to the tree.

We settled on her bed, and sorted through our treasures.

"Casey!" Betsy said, pulling a puppet from her stocking. "How did Santa know I love Casey and Finnegan?"

"Oh. He just knows. I'll bet even Santa Claus watches Mr. Dressup."

"He does?"

"Yeah," I said as she leaned back on her pillow and danced the puppet across the bed.

"What else do you think Santa brought me?" She shook her empty stocking and looked around.

"I think we'll have to wait and see. Shouldn't be too much longer now."

"Awww…"

"You know what?" I said, "I know a story about another Casey."

It was a game we played on family drives. She'd point at signs along the way, and I would make up stories about the origins of the places we passed, with names like Grand Bay, Belleisle, and Kennebecasis.

"A long time ago," I said, "a little boy, about your age, was playing along the shorefront where our house is now. Despite the wishes of his mother, he had come along with the men on the day's fishing trip.

"'Casey will be fine,' his father had said to his mother. 'It's time for him to start on his path, to see some of the world around him.'

"His mother sighed, and nodded. When they were ready to leave, she met them at the shore with a small packet wrapped in a bright kerchief.

"Partway across the river, a brisk northerly wind came up and the boats rocked with the motion of the waves. Casey was green when the party arrived at the other side.

"Casey's father looked at the boy gently, and said, 'That may be enough adventure for now, eh?'

"The boy nodded and clutched the red kerchief his mother had given him.

"'You can rest here on the beach,' his father said. 'And watch us.'

"Casey stepped off the boat carefully and tucked his knees under him, scattering pebbles aside as he settled in the lee of a speckled rock.

"'You can play in the sand,' his father said, as he pushed off. 'But do not go into the water.'

"After a few minutes, Casey's stomach had calmed again, and he sat watching the men from his village in their sleek birchbark canoes fishing the water of the cove in front of him. Eventually he lost sight of them, as the narrow craft rounded the nearby point and headed downriver, following the current and the fish.

"He amused himself throughout the morning, building a village from the sand, peopling it with bits of wood and clam shells he found. When the sun was high above him, he settled at the water's edge, unwrapped the bright red kerchief, and ate the lunch his mother had prepared for him.

"His belly full, he wandered along the edge of the shore, stopping occasionally to toss pebbles in the water. After a while, the sun kissing the back of his neck made him drowsy and he fell asleep on the shore, his toes dangling in the warm water.

"When his father returned, Casey was nowhere to be found. The men searched up and down the beach, but found no trace of him.

"Then one of them spotted a splash of colour in the woods behind them.

"'Can it be Casey?' he said as they rushed to the trees. But when they arrived, it was only a wild flower peeking through the bushes.

"Casey's father saw something from the corner of his eye. They hurried to the opposite end of the cove, but again it was just a flower.

"Each time they looked, it was a false sign, the red wild flowers growing along the shore fooling them again and again.

"As the sun began to go down, and they were starting to lose hope, Casey's father called frantically, looking at the river, 'Can-it-be-Casey, Can-it-be-?'

"But wait, that's not right," Betsy said, stirring on her bed beside me. "He can't have drowned. And, it's s'posed to be ca-sis, not Ca-sey," she said, emphatically.

"Ha! You're right. But I wasn't quite finished my story."

"When the men were ready to give up, one of them spotted a splash of red on a boulder around the point.

"'Can it be Casey?' his father said, not daring to hope.

"When they reached the boulder it was just another of the confounding flowers. Casey's father looked around in sorrow.

"And there was a figure huddled fast asleep in a small stretch of sand nestled between two rocks.

"'Casey!'

"The men gathered around him, and his father clutched him close. 'I thought we had lost you,' he said. 'But where is your kerchief?'

"'There,' said one of the other hunters, pointing to a dab of red out on the water.

"When they had gathered in their canoes and headed back across the river, the bit of red was missing. Gone to the bottom or floated off, it had disappeared.

"One of the men looked around, pointing, and shaking his head. The others chuckled, 'Can-it-be-Casey's?'

"Casey's father sighed with relief, aware of the fine line between the laughter about a lost kerchief and the sorrow over a lost boy.

"As they crossed the river, the men would occasionally look again and laugh heartily at a spot real or imagined. 'Can-it be Casey's?' Casey, who was revived from his nap, joined in the fun. 'Can-it-be-Casey's?'"

"Ha-ha," said Betsy, "I knew he couldn't drown."

Outside the room, I could hear the rest of our family starting to stir.

From across the hall, our sister Shari appeared.

"Hey, Bets…"

"Shari! Santa brought me Casey."

"So I heard," said Shari, smiling.

Shari was wearing bright new Santa-red PJs. Betsy put her hand on Shari's shoulder and giggled as she followed her down the hall toward our parents' bedroom.

"Can it be Casey's? Can it be Casey's?" Betsy sang as she skipped along, pointing at various spots on Shari's pajama top.

After Mom and Dad had thrown on their housecoats and slippers, we headed downstairs where the sparkling tree nestled over a burgeoning pile of presents. Sprawled on the couch, Brian grinned sleepily. "Took you long enough."

Shari took up her customary spot under the tree and handed out the gifts. Despite Mom's best wishes in the matter, the distribution of the loot hovered on the edge of organized chaos. When the dust had settled, nestled at the back of the tree was a large square present with a huge pink bow.

"New skates!" Betsy said, proudly displaying the open box. "I want to try them out."

"After breakfast," said Mom. "But stay in the cove."

"I know, Mom."

Given the capriciousness of our maritime weather, it was not unusual for the river to be still open on Christmas Day. The ice in our little cove, which we shared with a few neighbours on either side, had been frozen for a week and was pretty secure. The main part of the river had iced over just the night before.

After we ate, Shari went off to a friend's house. Brian, Betsy, and I laced up our skates and headed out onto the gleaming surface of the river. A friend of Betsy's, Ellie, came down to join us. She and Betsy skated in circles, as Brian and I passed a puck around. Time scooted on past, and then I noticed a sleek Cadillac pull into our yard.

Rene and Bob. My mom's parents had always preferred the familiarity of first names.

"I'm too young to be a Grammy or a Nanny, dear," Rene would say when anyone asked. They had been on a once-in-a-lifetime world trip and were not supposed to be home for another week.

Brian and I pulled off our skates and headed up to see them.

Betsy and Ellie were still doing laps.

"Your mother just got a little homesick, I guess," Bob was saying to Mom as we came into the house.

We went into the living room, which had a magnificent view of the Kennebecasis. In the summer we would stand at the floor-to-ceiling picture window and watch lightning over the water, illuminating the hills of Long Island two miles away.

After a few minutes, Bob looked out the window and said, "Those kids are quite a way out."

"Huh?" said Mom.

"The ice hasn't been frozen that long, has it? Do you think it's safe?"

"It's fine in close," said Dad, as he came around Bob.

"Where's Betsy?" Mom said, joining them at the window. She looked down to the little cove below us. Empty.

"Oh, god."

Mom ran to the sliding glass door that led to the deck off the kitchen and pried it open.

"Betsy!"

Dad appeared behind her. "It's no use," he said, "they're too far away."

I looked out on the ice, where two tiny figures were skating along, maybe halfway to Long Island. On ice that only yesterday had been open in spots.

"I'm going after them," Dad said.

"No," said Mom, "you're too heavy."

"The boys," he said, looking at Brian and me. "Get your skates on. Quickly."

"Dick, no," said Mom.

"They're light enough. They can take their hockey sticks for support, in case they break through."

The idea, once floated, had a mind of its own.

As the sun got higher in the sky, the ice would only get weaker. We needed to be away.

"Watch for open spots. Changes in colour," Dad said as we skated off.

The ice was a shade of polished mirror. My reflection flickered back up at me as I skated along. The river groaned, and I tried to think of something, anything else. I looked up, concentrating on Betsy and Ellie in the distance. Brian was a little ahead of me already, the better skater. I dug in and focused on the rhythm of my skates cutting into the fragile surface below, wary of each change in the hue.

As I glided along, I looked at the hockey stick in my hands, and heard Dad's voice as we laced up our skates. "It'll give you something to hang onto if you go through."

My father knew a little something about the fickleness of river ice.

He had put his snowmobile through the ice into open water on three occasions. The first two times he managed to get free with very little trouble. The third time was another matter entirely.

It happened the winter we were building our new home on the Kennebecasis. Brian and I, five and six years old, were riding in a little trailer attached to the back of Dad's skidoo. We had stopped at the construction site when an old family friend, who was to be our new neighbour, came over to say hi. Brian and I spied some other kids tobogganing nearby and went off to join them. When Dad was ready to go, we were happily ensconced on the hill. He called for us, but we refused to budge. He started across the yard toward us, but then, laughing, he stopped, and turned toward our family friend. "I give up."

"Not to worry," he said. "You go ahead. I'll run them home when they've played themselves out."

Dad sighed, unhitched the trailer, and headed off on his own. I think he was a little put out, but to this day he credits our little desertion for saving all of our lives.

When Dad returned from his visit, it was just after dark. He was going hard to get home for supper. Mom insisted on the family sitting down for a meal together every Sunday, the one night we could count on being together. He blasted across an inlet that had been iced over that afternoon.

Suddenly he found himself in the air, the machine slipping beneath him into the deep water.

He started to pull himself up onto the ice. It broke under his weight. He fought through the slush, kicking his legs until he could get another grip on the fragile slip of ice, but again it cracked.

As he fought for his life, he looked up and saw lights in a house just up from the shore.

His voice breaking with the cold, he called out, "Help!"

Again he tried to heave himself up, the ice crumbling, his body sliding back into the frigid water.

His strength failing, he called with a weaker voice, "Help."

Then, as he was about to sink into the icy slurry, he saw a silhouette on the shoreline.

"Hang on," he heard. "I've got a rope."

His sodden snowsuit pulling him down, he struggled to keep himself afloat.

And watched as the rope sailed by, too far away to reach.

He floundered toward it, but his strength was almost gone, and he started to slip beneath the surface.

Then the rope came again and landed in front of him. With a feeble kick he brought himself forward and wrapped it around his frozen hands.

The ice breaking around him, he felt himself being hauled toward shore.

"Betsy!"

It was Brian, still a little ahead of me, his voice cutting through my thoughts.

The two girls were approaching the overhang of Minister's Face, an aptly named protuberance at the northern tip of Long Island. *Crap*. The waters there hardly ever froze solid, the current constant and dangerous at any time of the year.

Something in Brian's voice must have caught their attention, though.

Betsy turned, and waved.

I dug in and caught up to Brian.

Betsy waved again, and started to jump and dance happily.

"No, Betsy!" I called.

"Huh?"

"Stop jumping!"

"Why?" she said, in mid-leap.

The brittle ice moaned as she came down.

Ellie backed away toward Long Island.

"It's too thin," I shouted.

"Aaaw," Betsy said.

"Girls!" Brian yelled. "Stop."

For a moment we were all still, like a tableau.

Then, finally, Ellie turned and skated back to where Betsy was waiting.

"Now," said Brian. "Carefully, you both need to come here."

Brian and I retreated as they approached, drawing them away from the thinner ice.

"Hey," Betsy said. "What are you guys doing here?"

"Betsy," Brian, said, serious, "we need to get home."

"You're out too far," I said.

"We were just skating, and having fun," Betsy said.

Ellie was silent, defiant or chastened, I couldn't tell.

"Well, we need to get back," Brian said. "It's not safe."

"Huh," Betsy said, pouting.

"Rene and Bob are here," I said.

"They are?"

"Yeah," I said. "Come on. You can show them your new skates."

"Okay," she said.

The groaning ice seemed to thin with each careful stride we took on the way back.

We separated to spread the weight; Brian took Ellie, and I skated with Betsy. Her face was red as she skated beside me, little legs digging in to keep up.

Suddenly, her toe caught a burr on the ice, and she started to go down.

Reaching back, I grabbed for a hand and pulled her up.

"Easy," I said, seeing the panic in her eyes. "Don't worry. We'll make it."

Betsy and I were pretty close. The nine years between us had brought out the paternal instincts in me, I guess. I had saved her once before, on a family trip to Florida. Wading into Lake Kissimmee, she slipped on a rock, and fell under the water. Without thinking, I rushed to where she had gone down and fished her out before she could swallow more than a mouthful.

I tried not to think of the water now below us, as we gingerly glided toward home. Like skating on eggshells.

The sun was higher in the sky, and little puddles were forming on the surface. I looked down at my soaked legs, the weight of the day suddenly pulling at me.

Finally, we neared the shelter of our cove. Mom and Dad were watching anxiously from the edge of the shore.

With a last effort, we practically dashed across the firmer ice.

"Betsy," Mom said, "what were you…"

Then breathless, "Come here." She gathered Betsy into her arms.

Later, the eight of us gathered around the dining room table, my father poised to carve the first slice of turkey. As always, Mom was the last to settle, closest to the kitchen, looking across her family to the view of the Kennebecasis.

Her hand on the back of her chair, she froze suddenly, and inhaled sharply.

"Mom?"

She was looking out on the river.

Turning in my seat, I followed her eyes.

The sun was low in the sky, casting long shadows onto the treed hills of Long Island. Minister's Face, like a silent sentinel, gazed out on the ice. Then I saw it, not far from where we had been skating, exactly on the spot where Betsy had done her little happy dance. Open water.

And as I gazed over the surface of the river, I realized that wasn't the only open area. Across the breadth of the ice, dark spots had appeared. Like spring thaw come early, the Kennebecasis was a mishmash of ice and water.

For a minute, we were all looking, and silence filled the room.

Then Mom pulled her chair the rest of the way out, and sat down.

"Well," she said. "someone was watching over us today. Thank goodness we're all here, safe and sound."

It hadn't hit me while we were making that mad dash across the river. The balance of our future had rested on narrow strips of steel cutting through the ice. Was it chance or some unseen hand that guided our fate? No matter. Somehow we had all made it through, unscathed. Across the table Betsy sat, Casey in her lap, the day's adventure forgotten.

As I swiveled back in my chair, I thought I spied a bit of red floating on the open water. But when I looked again, it was gone. Probably a trick of the light, the sun setting on the Kennebecasis. I turned back to the table where our Christmas dinner awaited, thankful for the meal and so much more.

My Incredible Performance

❄ Helena Sullivan ❄

Money was not plentiful when I was growing up. There were no lists of requested toys and games made up for Santa Claus to bring and put under our tree. We received two Christmas catalogues, one from Eaton's and one from Sears. These catalogues were not to extract lists from but were just "wish books" for us. My two brothers and I would take turns looking through them and would turn down the corners on pages of dream items that we wanted to show our parents or each other.

I always loved the Eaton's catalogue the best as it had pages of mouthwatering candies that I would drool over as I envisioned picking them off the page and putting them in my mouth. My favourite hovered between the pink, white, and chocolate coconut-filled bonbons and the thin butterscotch wafers that came in a brightly decorated Christmas tin. I haven't been able to find these delights in years, which is probably a good thing for my weight maintenance since I would buy more than my wise share.

When I was seven years old I showed my mother a picture of a figure skater in the Eaton's catalogue. The girl had long blonde hair and looked like an angel as she glided along the ice. She wore a royal blue velvet outfit with white fur trim along the sleeves, neckline, and skirt. Her navy leotards sparkled like diamonds. Mom said that, indeed, it was a beautiful outfit. She laughed when I replied, "No, not the dress. The skates. Look at her skates." I was mesmerized by the brilliantly white figure skates and would have traded a box of bonbons for them.

Up until this point, I had worn my older brother's brown skates or my "training" skates, which had two side blades and leather ties to strap them onto my boots. Mom patted my hand and told me that when I got older, and when my feet stopped growing so quickly, she and Dad would see about getting me a pair. I sighed and tried to be content with the fact that, someday, I would have real figure skates, not boy's skates, not baby's skates, but true figure skates.

Christmas morning finally came and my brothers and I woke Mom and Dad up around five a.m. to see if it was time to check out what Santa brought and to open his gifts. Although they groaned at the early hour, they swung themselves out of bed to join us in the living room by the Christmas tree. Santa's presents were always under our Christmas stockings and in front of our gifts from our parents, great grandmother, aunt and uncle, and godparents. In our stockings, we usually found a Christmas apple (we called them the delicious bumpy apples, later to discover that they actually are called Delicious apples), a big orange, a handful of purple grapes, yellow and red barley candy (one would be on a sucker stick and one we would wrap in wax paper while we sucked on it), and a small bag of hard Christmas candies with a few gumdrops and soft white and pink cream sugar candies thrown in the mix. Santa had left me a paper doll with three outfits, which had to be carefully popped out along the perforated lines.

I tried not to show my disappointment when I opened my gift from Mom and Dad, only to find a pair of hand-knit socks. I murmured a halfhearted thanks to them. When Mom slid a box out from under the couch towards me, I looked up at her and she motioned for me to open it.

I screeched with delight when I saw the box contained white figure skates. Not only real figure skates, but a red pair of plastic skate guards to boot.

"They're not brand new but they still have lots of wear on the picks left to get you stopped," Mom said, "and your father polished and buffed them three times for you."

"They're the most beautiful skates in the world," I gasped as I held them as reverently as Midas would gold.

"They might be a little big on you but we thought the socks would fill up the added space, plus keep you from getting blisters," Mom added.

I looked at my parents with tears threatening to spill from my eyes, my heart bursting with love for them. Dad winked at me and suggested that as soon as it was daylight, I should try them out across the street at our neighbour's homemade rink. He cautioned me that the picks in figure skates would take some getting used to as they made quite a bit of difference in skating. He said I would have the space and privacy I needed to get used to them if I went over before everyone else landed there. I gazed at him, thinking that he was the smartest person in the whole wide world. I would have hated to try out my new skates in front of the neighbour kids only to fall flat on my face. I quickly looked outside and whirled around to announce that it was almost light enough out.

"Dear Lord, child!" Mom laughed. "It's only six a.m. Come have some porridge and wait until at least eight o'clock. That will give you an hour before we have to get ready for church."

A rooster wouldn't have announced daylight any quicker than I did that Christmas morning. Since I was already dressed, as soon as I got the nod from Mom I laced up my new skates, put on the skate guards, threw on my hat, coat, and mittens and walked across the street to McInnis' front yard rink.

Mr. McInnis had laid down a wooden two-by-four plank along the side so that we would have a place to sit and rest or put on our skates. I sat down and lovingly took off my skate guards and slowly went on the ice. I wobbled and felt as if I was going to fall head first, but holy smokes, all of sudden, I took off skating like a seasoned professional. I thought I would try a figure eight like I had seen a skater do on the television. Holy Hannah, I could do it first try. I decided to try to throw in a jump and a twirl. I was like a fish taking to water. Lord Dinah, it was as if I was born to be a figure skater. I was twirling and jumping and spinning as if there was no tomorrow. By this time, people driving by had noticed me and stopped their cars to witness my incredible performance. They were clapping and whistling and cheering me on. It was as if I was flying! All I could hear was the chanting of "Helena! Helena! C'mon Helena!" Then the loud cheering faded, although I could still hear a faint "Come on, Helena." Something wasn't right. "Helena, wake up. Come on honey, open your eyes. Everything is okay."

What was going on here? I slowly opened my eyes. I was lying flat on my back and looking directly up into Mrs. McInnis's face as she bent over me.

"Oh, thank goodness," she said. "I was looking out the front window and saw you go out on the ice and fall. You knocked yourself out cold."

Mrs. McInnis's face kept fading in and out, alternating with the crowd's chanting. I felt confused, and gently lifted my head to look around. There were no crowds of awed people. There was no cheering. I wasn't doing all those magnificent jumps and twirls. I wanted to cry. But wait. It wasn't all bad. If no one was there cheering me on, then no one was there to see me fall and knock myself out. It would have been harder to live that down than to try to live with all the fame.

"I'm great, Mrs. McInnis." I tried to smile as I eased myself upright. "We don't have to tell anyone about this, do we? I only fell because I'm not used to my new skates yet. Look. Dad and Mom gave them to me for Christmas!" I proudly lifted my legs to show her my beautiful figure skates.

"Oh, child, I should really come home with you and tell your mom. You gave yourself an awful crack and were unconscious. However," she chuckled as she saw the look of pure anguish on my face, "promise me that you'll take it easy for the rest of the day and tell your mom if your head aches or you get sick to your stomach. Also, you have to promise me that you won't skate here alone until you're used to those gorgeous new skates."

"I promise, Brownies honour," I declared, knowing that, as a Brownie leader, Mrs. McInnis would know how much this meant to me.

"Okay then," she laughed and added with a wink. "I 'Brownie honour' promise I won't tell anyone. It will be our secret."

I gave her a big hug and tenderly put my skate guards back on for the trip home across the street. As much as I loved my new skates, I was more than ready to hang them up for the day and would try again tomorrow. My head was starting to ache so I thought I would take Mrs. McInnis' advice to take it easy, especially since it was Christmas Day. There were still candies and special fruit to eat, as well as popping out my new paper doll and her outfits.

Within a week, though, I had mastered the picks on the figure skates and was able to remain upright. I never did master the leaps and twirling jumps that I dreamt while unconscious, but I never knocked myself out again either. Life has a way of balancing some things out.

The Silver Wren

❄ Sam Jensen ❄

(Transcription of an audio interview
with Mr. Connor Allen, age 87)

"Well now, it's been a long while since anyone's asked me about that night. I bet I'd be the last person who remembers it, too. You see, I was just a little kid when it happened. Five years old, I was. Far as I know, no one else from back in those days is still around.

(Mr. Allen pauses.)

"Well, all right, let me see what I can tell you. Now, don't you go thinking my memory's gone, 'cause it ain't. I know I'm getting old, but I'm still sharp. I pride myself on that. And that night, well, I remember it plain as day. I just need to get my thoughts in order. All right, first you need to remember that I was living in Fountainstown, which wasn't more than a little village out in the country back then. Far from the cities, we were, but we had one hell of a view of the ocean. It was a quiet little town, a great place to grow up. There was a forest nearby, too, lots of pine trees and some, what do call them, the ones with the leaves. Deciduous, that's the word. Mostly fir trees, though, and full of all sorts of birds and creatures. Now, that Christmas Eve you want to hear about. As I said, I was five years old at the time, a few months shy of six, in fact. I loved Christmas, ever since I could understand it was special. Least, that's what my mum told me. I don't really remember any of the Christmases before this one, see. I mean, how could I remember anything clearly from before I was five? So this Christmas Eve you're asking about, well, it's my oldest and clearest memory from my childhood.

(He pauses again, and audibly sighs.)

"Now let's see, it was a beautiful sunny day, a little below freezing so there was snow on the ground, but not too cold to play outside.

I was beside myself with excitement, I was so anxious to see what Father Christmas would bring me. I was looking forward to the food, too. And my cousins were coming over later that evening. So I spent the afternoon running around in the snow, making snowmen. Standard kid stuff. Around four or five o'clock, the sun started going down, so I turned around and headed home. The streets were full of carollers and people heading for friends' or relatives' houses for dinner. I got past the crowd of happy people and continued toward my home.

"Around the church, I stopped for a minute. It had clouded over, and big snowflakes were starting to fall from the sky. It was so quiet and peaceful, and the town looked so beautiful, all those little windows and street lamps shining through the snow. So I just sat there and watched for a while. It was well dark by now, and I was alone. Then, I became aware of some kind of noise behind me. It sounded like singing, and I heard instruments as well. Some kind of horn, and some stringed thing, maybe a harp. Now, like I said, there were carollers around the town square, but I was on the hill by the church, and behind me was the forest. That's where the music was coming from. I thought it was pretty strange, but I wasn't afraid, mind you. Kids are braver than we give them credit for. I just turned around and watched the woods. The music got louder, and soon enough I could see a flickering light coming through the trees. A group of people emerged—some of them had torches and the rest had baskets and sacks of some kind. They looked heavy, but the people were dancing as they walked. Not like any dance I'd seen before, but they were swaying their arms and their hips as they walked. All of them were singing.

"Just then, the bells started ringing in the church bell tower. A minute later, Father Patrick came out and stood beside me. He had heard the song, too.

"'Who are they,' he asked me. As if I had any idea. I just shrugged. Father Patrick was a kind man, probably in his forties then. He was quiet, and he wore small glasses so low on his nose that he ended up looking over rather than through them. Gave his whole life to the church, he did. Anyway, I shouldn't get off track. The priest and I just stood there as this strange group came out of the forest, and they were strange, let me tell you. They were all wearing long dark cloaks or robes, with hoods that made it hard to see their faces. In fact I couldn't see a single face clearly, but we were still far away. I thought maybe we'd recognize them when they were closer. There were men and women together, far as I could tell, but the robes made it hard to be sure. Most of them were fairly tall, but not unusually so.

"They walked from the forest to the little road that led into town, which ran straight past the church, so we stood there and watched them walking towards us. The way that they moved, it was odd and rhythmic, and I couldn't look away. I couldn't make out the words of their song, either. It wasn't English, maybe it was some kind of Gaelic, but I didn't recognize it. Whatever it was, they sure could sing. It was beautiful. Father Patrick was very quiet, and I couldn't tell what he was thinking. He had one of those faces that was hard to read. He mostly looked like he was lost in thought. Anyway, as they got close to the church, a few other people from the village came up to where we were standing. Guess they heard the music, too. They asked the Father who the strangers were, but he didn't say anything.

"In a minute the crowd of people was walking right past us. They never stopped singing and they never stopped walking, they just waved their arms at us, like we was supposed to follow. Now that they were close, I could see that their robes were dark green and blue, or burgundy, like a good red wine. They had big wide hoods and scarves over their faces, so we couldn't see more than their eyes. They all had these big bags and baskets, like I told you. There were, oh, I'd say maybe thirty of them altogether. As they went by, they kept waving their free arms, the ones they weren't carrying stuff with. So we did what they wanted and we followed them.

"They were walking straight into the middle of town, and we trailed a little behind them. Most of the people from the town who were walking with us were asking questions under their breath. Who were these folks? Where were they from? What were they singing? But no one talked too loud, I guess 'cause they didn't want to drown out that beautiful music. As we marched along, more townsfolk joined us. They heard the commotion and came outside to see what was going on. Others watched our little parade through their windows, and I could see them through the glass asking each other what was happening. So these dancing strangers kept a steady, slow pace through town, and our group of spectators grew.

"We got to the town square, and suddenly the cloaked figures all started spinning and hurrying about. They were putting down their baskets and taking out all kinds of things. They pulled out some tables, I don't know where from, and started laying out food. All kinds of food—there were turkeys, and vegetables, and baked goods stacked a foot high on big bronze plates. They set out a pile of lumber in front of the statue in the town square, and in no time at all they had a big warm fire going. They were heating the food over it. They still hadn't stopped singing. In fact, once their bags were unpacked, some of them pulled flutes out of their pockets and started to play.

(Mr. Allen pauses to take a drink.)

"Now we were all dumbfounded, we didn't know what to think. Here were all these folks we couldn't recognize, setting up a feast outside in our town. We didn't know who they were or where they were from, or even what their language was. But they were beckoning us over again, inviting us to eat, by the looks of it. The whole crowd was murmuring. What should we do? Who are they? A lot of people were asking Father Patrick, but he was still silent.

"Then Albert, a fellow who lived a few houses away from my family, turned to the rest of us and said, 'I don't much care who they are, I ain't never said no to a meal.' Father Patrick nodded, and Albert headed off towards the feast. Everyone else stood frozen to the spot for a minute, but then slowly a few more people followed him, and soon enough we were all together by the fire.

"About then, my mother found me. She scolded me for being so late to dinner, said she'd been sick with worry. Then she asked me what on earth was happening and who the people in robes were. I told her I didn't know. She grabbed my arm and led me away, but I didn't want to go. We found my father, a little ways from the crowd, and my parents stood there discussing the bizarre scene in the square. Soon enough Father Patrick joined us and told them how he and I had been the first to see them come into town, and what had happened as we followed them. I wanted so badly to go and join the people in the square. The food smelled incredible, and the music was so joyous. I just had to be there.

"'Probably folks from the other village down the road,' my father reasoned, 'come to give us a surprise and play a bit of a trick.' My mother still looked a bit uneasy, like she thought something wasn't right. But Patrick said he saw no harm in joining everyone else in the square, and my parents agreed. They were still a bit wary, though. They had always been careful people, the both of them. Great people, don't get me wrong. They were just a bit too cautious is all.

(Mr. Allen coughs and blows his nose.)

"So we were all down there together, the whole town. Well, maybe not all of... no, you know what? Even the old folks were there, I think we really all were. Who could stay inside on a night like that? It was a party like no other, I'll tell you. These strangers in their cloaks were still playing music and singing, but they joined us in the feast. They were eating and drinking... lifting their scarves a bit to get to their mouths but never enough to give us a clear look at their faces. Right, I forgot to mention the wine and the cider. They had brought small barrels of each. I only had the cider, 'course. Mom wouldn't have liked to catch me with wine, let me tell you. Everyone's questions had long since died away. It didn't matter anymore who these people were or where they came from. They were here, they were kind, they had brought us all food and song the likes of which we'd never experienced, and it was Christmas Eve. On a night like that, we're all supposed to trust each other and act like family, right?

"After everyone had eaten their fill of turkey and veggies, they passed around biscuits and pudding and cakes, and all manner of delicious treats. I could scarcely believe my luck, and I ate 'til I was nearly sick. The strangers never really talked to any of us, not as such. I suppose that might have given away who they were. They gestured, though, like in charades, and we all got along splendidly. They laughed a lot, those guests of ours. At one point, old Albert had had one cup too many of the wine, and he said to one of his friends, 'I've got to know who these guys are,' and he leaped up and tried to pull down the hood of one of the strangers. But the guy spun out of his reach, and poor Albert nearly fell face first in the snow, but someone caught him and propped him in his seat. Bit of a drinker, he was, but harmless, and people mostly liked him.

(Mr. Allen's voice begins to crack.)

"Dear me, I beg your pardon. My voice isn't as strong as it once was. To finish my story... we ate and drank well into the night. Even my parents both loosened up and enjoyed themselves. Thank the Lord it was a mild night. I guess the fire kept us warm too, 'cause no one complained of the cold all evening. After everyone was too full to eat another bite, the strangers started up another song. Now, this moment I'll remember if I live another eighty years.

(Mr. Allen laughs.)

"They all started to twirl around, faster and faster, and their long clothes fanned out and spun around them. It was… mesmerising. The patterns on their cloaks, around the borders of the cloth, the way they moved in circles with their arms outstretched. The shadows they cast in firelight on the houses. I've never seen anything like it, before nor since. They carried on like that for what seemed like hours, 'til the fire was starting to die. Oh, I wish you could have seen it. How I'd love to see it again. I don't think I'd ever been more excited, but I was still a little kid, and it was well past my bedtime. Eventually I started to nod off.

"I do remember—and this is a bit hazy now, 'cause I was pretty much asleep in my mother's arms—but I remember one of the strange men leaned down in front of me and handed me something small. The next thing I remember, I woke up in my own bed on Christmas morning. I felt something clutched in my little hand. I looked down, and saw it was a small silver bird. A wren, it looked like. I was a bit confused until I remembered the man handing me something.

"I went into the kitchen, and asked my parents about the previous night. I was glad to hear that they knew exactly what I was talking about, because even with the tiny silver bird in my hand, I had been worried that it had somehow all been a dream. Well, in fact, I soon found that everyone in town remembered the feast and the singing and dancing as well as I did, though we never did figure out who the strangers had been. They left in the night without a trace, and we never saw them again. My father still thought that it must have been folks from one of the neighbouring towns having some fun with us, but no one from the area ever admitted to being behind it. Some said that we had let a band of ancient pagans who had been living hidden in the forest right into our town, but few took that idea seriously. One old lady insisted that they had been angels, and that we had all been blessed. She wanted Father Patrick to back her up, but he just told her that while we may have been blessed, some miracles have earthly explanations, too. Ever the diplomat, that man. He had faith, but he was practical, too, and didn't talk as much about angels as some priests I've heard since. The truth is, no one knew exactly what had happened that night. Whether it was an anonymous good deed from some neighbours, or a hidden tribe from the woods, or angels straight from heaven, it was still a miracle in my mind.

"A lot of people don't believe me when I tell this story. Heck, my own son thought I was crazy once he got older and starting doubting everything. You know that phase kids go through. And, to be honest, I've sometimes doubted it myself. But whenever I start to think I dreamed the whole thing up, I remind myself...

(There is the sound of clothing rustling, and Mr. Allen removes something from a pocket.)

"... that I have the proof right here in my hand."

Christmas Unwrapped

❄   Michael Conway   ❄

"Christmas waves a magic wand over this world,
and behold, everything is softer and more beautiful."

—Norman Vincent Peale

Excited as I was to see if Santa had arrived, I didn't want to get out from under the coziness of my blankets. Waking, I just knew that today was going to be a good day. Most days I woke feeling nauseated and lethargic. On Christmas Day, 1956, I was a small, sickly girl with poor eyesight. School was difficult and learning a challenge. It would be another six years before doctors would discover a growth on one of my kidneys and remove it along with the upper half of the offending organ. Then, like a butterfly emerging from its cocoon to flit from blossom to flower, I came alive with joy and exuberance. Everything became easier; school was exciting, outside play, fun. Until that time came, however, I usually felt ill, remained small for my age, was painfully shy, and never strayed far from home. This day, while I felt well, I was too timid to venture downstairs to the Christmas tree by myself. For the time being, I was content to lie in comfort, admire the magic of Jack Frost's intricate window art, and rethink the events of the past two days.

Mom had worked hard finalizing preparations for a perfect Christmas. It was a family joke that nearly as much of the preparations went out the back door as those that came in the front. Mom not only believed the Christmas lesson, she lived it. Generous to a fault, she was the anonymous purveyor of many Christmas hampers; her efforts guaranteed the less fortunate would have more during the holiday season. This was her attitude throughout the year, but it was more apparent at Christmas.

I had been a big help ensuring Mom's Christmas cakes were perfect. It was my job to count the eggs and I took the job seriously. Baking was secondary to the kitchen camaraderie we shared because working alongside Mom at this important time increased my sense of well-being. Self-satisfaction washed over me as I thought of Mom's praise for a job well done. I would share in the success of the feast.

My thoughts turned to the Christmas wonderland that would greet me downstairs. I closed my eyes and imagined creeping downstairs, followed closely by my twin brother, Darrell. We went through the kitchen with the smell of the twenty-five-pound turkey roasting in the oven. Mom would have put the huge bird in earlier so that it would be ready by noon. Leaving the kitchen, we would be overwhelmed by the sweet fragrance of the fir tree. Is there anything that speaks of Christmas more than the wafting scent of a Christmas tree? By now we would be dizzy with the anticipation of entering the front room where the tree and gifts were. And, oh, what a tree. It was covered from top to bottom in angel hair. Twinkling lights peeked from behind the fibrous wisps, causing the whole tree to glow while enhancing every decoration. The beauty of Mom's Christmas tree is still talked about during family gatherings.

I knew that when we entered the room, apprehension would subside and pent-up excitement about Santa's visit would be rewarded with reality. Each knew where his gifts would be and the type of toys in the vicinity proved it. There would be a doll and doll clothes for me, trucks and a hockey stick for Darrell. Other family members would be relegated to various areas of the room. Dad's gifts were always stacked neatly under the tree.

Finally, I thought about how lucky Darrell was to be here for the Christmas celebration. Yesterday, he had been stumping ice cakes at the wharf while I watched from shore. I was too diffident to be involved with anything of that nature. As I watched, I was horrified to see him miss a jump and land in the water. The weight of his winter clothes quickly pulled him under. I became hysterical and started to cry. Darrell calmly swam five or ten yards, then walked the rest of the way to shore. His stocking hat had managed to stay in place. Ice had already started to form on his clothes. He looked as if he was encased in a sheath of ice and quickly suggested we go to Gramma's. He knew that we were forbidden to be on the waterfront and that stumping ice cakes would be hailed with a lengthy grounding followed by a mandatory short leash restriction requiring us to be within earshot of the front door. I was still crying, but followed him up the wharf to our grandmother's house.

Gramma was surprised at Darrell's condition. She got a hot bath ready and sent Aunt Gail to Johnny's Fish and Chips to get him an order of French fries. While Darrell got bathed, warmed, and dried, Gramma scolded me for allowing him to go ice cake stumping. I started to cry again so she sent me home.

My thoughts were interrupted by Darrell standing in the doorway of my bedroom.

"Get up, Darlene. Let's go downstairs to see what we got." I just looked at him. I was still smarting from yesterday, but threw back the covers and crawled out of bed.

We crept downstairs. We were four steps from the bottom, when sixteen-year-old brother Reg Jr. bounded down the staircase. He ran through us like he was playing Red Rover and someone from Hillsborough Square had just "called him over."

"Sorry, kids! I wanted to see the excitement on your faces when you see what Santa Claus brought you. You're okay? Don't tell Dad, you little gerbils."

We entered the kitchen almost as one and the blending of delicious smells wafted around us. There was the October smell of mustard pickles, the plum pudding of early December, and the fruit cakes— both dark and light—from a few weeks previous, savoury meat pies of five days ago, and the tantalizing aroma of the roasting Tom Turkey. I could almost taste Mom's melt-in-your-mouth shortbread cookies. The secret was in the butter. Or so she told me. I felt so mature when Mom had trusted me with the secret. I wondered if my older sister Beverly knew.

Everything was a glorious banquet for the senses, but this time we barely noticed the fragrance of the fir tree as we dashed through the TV room and into the living room. We stopped and surveyed the wonderland that Mom and Dad had created. Junior plugged in the lights to complete the ambiance. Standing there amidst the splendour, though, I sensed something was not quite right. Santa had indeed found us. In my designated corner, I could see a doll and doll clothes, and, in Darrell's corner, a brightly painted truck, and a book, *Treasure Island*. Junior, meanwhile, stood there looking sheepish.

"I guess I got carried away," Junior said.

"What do you mean?" Darrell asked.

"I went to Midnight Mass and when I got home, I thought I would open one gift. Well, one gift led to two, then two to three.

I was so excited I opened all the gifts. I hope Dad won't be too mad. I didn't open any of his."

A quick glance confirmed that Dad's gifts were under the tree and intact.

"Who cares, anyway?" said Darrell. "You never touched any of the good stuff. All you opened was junk, like socks and underwear."

Junior could see I was close to tears and quickly passed a gift to me. It was a small wicker basket full of the green, grasslike material used in Easter baskets. Lying on top were small twin dolls, a boy and girl. I loved them immediately.

Junior explained that he had won the dolls at the Notre Dame Academy bazaar especially for me. He'd gone to the bazaar with a friend, who had suggested that he give the dolls to one of the girls who had accompanied them to the bazaar. Although the girls thought themselves too mature to admit they still liked dolls, both had hopeful expressions that Junior would make the dolls a gift to them. Not likely. Junior told them that he had a seven-year-old sister who would make a great mother to these dolls. Furthermore, the sole reason he played the game was to win that gift for me.

Junior reminded us that we should get dressed if we were to be on time for the eight o'clock children's Mass at the Basilica.

Darrell and I met at the front door. We were bundled up against the bitter cold, and started our walk up Dorchester Street. I wanted to go past Notre Dame to see if the nuns had put the Baby Jesus in the manger. The large nativity scene was in place a week before Christmas, but without the Infant. The Christ Child wasn't placed in the manger until early morning on the 25th of December. To my satisfaction, Baby Jesus was there. He was wrapped in traditional swaddling clothes and laid in the manger on a fragrant bed of straw. The ceramic figure reminded me of my new dolls and I remember thinking, "Unto you a Saviour is born!"

We arrived at Mass on time and were pleased to see that the priest who would say Mass was not old, crotchety Father Pat. Christmas blessings continued to come our way. I tried to be holy and concentrate on the prayers but I couldn't wait for Mass to be over so we could go home.

One long hour later, Mass was complete and we started home. We were excited, but our return was not without trepidation. The eagerness grew all the way down Dorchester Street as we witnessed other households in the midst of their celebrations. The apprehension was the result of what may be in store for Junior when Dad realized that he had opened others' gifts.

When we entered the house I got a heavy, sinking feeling. Seated on the couch side by side were Alfred, Junior, and Beverly. The three resembled the stone carvings on Mount Rushmore—not quite so noble, but just as immobile as they stared glumly at the wall opposite. Mom and Dad were just coming through the TV room to greet us.

"Merry Christmas," Darrell and I chirped, almost in unison, as much to provide some levity to the room as to offer the traditional greeting.

"Merry Christmas," they replied, also almost in unison.

Dad stood in the doorway of the living room as Mom squeezed by and took her seat in the corner diagonally across from the couch and Mount Rushmore.

Dad stared at Junior. "I've got a little crow to pick with you."

Junior was quick to pipe up. "Dad, I got wrapped up in the moment. I came from Midnight Mass and thought I'd open one gift. As I told the twins, one became two and two became three. I just got caught up in youthful ex... youthful ex..."

"Exuberance," offered Darrell.

"Yeah that's it," said Junior.

"That's funny," said Dad. "I was just going to show you some old man exuberance."

Just then a knock came on the door. Mrs. Doyle, our neighbour, came to give Darrell a dozen sugar cookies. After exchanging holiday pleasantries, she said, "I baked some cookies for Darrell, but with raisins in the centre because Frank likes them that way." She turned to look at Darrell. "Just pick them out, dear."

"The heck with Frank," Darrell mumbled under his breath, low enough so that only I could hear him. Then with an angelic smile he thanked Mrs. Doyle. Darrell leaned over to my ear and said, "And the heck with the raisins, too!" Mrs. Doyle took her leave with everyone's wishes for the happiest of holidays following her out the door.

This was the perfect opportunity to exact retribution for yesterday's ice cake escapade. Mom and Dad would be furious that Darrell would make such a rude comment to an adult. But no, I thought, let bygones be bygones. I wouldn't want anyone to tell on me if I had said something wrong. I wrote it off to jealousy because Darrell had been treated to fries and gravy. I knew my silence was the right decision, but the hurt remained.

"Dad," I said. "I know you think Junior ruined our Christmas, but like Darrell said, he only opened socks and underwear. Look at our gifts! How could our Christmas be ruined? This is the best Christmas ever and we never ate yet and that's your favourite part. At least you say that's your favourite part."

Mom smiled and Dad's demeanour changed. He stepped into the room and looked at me and said, "Pass me my gift in the green wrapping paper, please."

I think of this scene from time to time throughout the year but, at Christmas, it is front and centre in my bank of yuletide memories. When Junior gave me the gift of the dolls, he had no way of fully knowing the value and meaning I would attach to them. The dolls are long gone now, but as I look back, I realize that it was never the dolls in the first place, but the *receiving* of them that was the gift. They had arrived at a time in my life when I was most vulnerable, seven years old, small for my age and timid, and still smarting from the day before. Why had Gramma blamed me for Darrell's misbehaviour on the ice cakes? I knew I had done no serious wrong. Yes, we were at the wharf without permission. Darrell, however, was the one courting disaster. It could have turned out differently, with deadly results. Yet Darrell's inappropriate behaviour of the day before was rewarded with an order of French fries from Johnny's Fish and Chips and, as a result, I was getting mixed signals from an adult and, at that stage of my life, I was incapable of dealing with it in a logical manner.

On the other hand, Junior had resisted his friend's suggestion to give the dolls to the girls. At an age when he should have been cultivating a gallant image amongst his peers and female friends, he chose instead to surprise me. As with countless children, I was raised to believe that it's better to give than to receive. But for that to be true, recipients are equally necessary. Grateful recipients, like me, that Christmas day in 1956.

Little Miracles

❄   P Susan Buchanan   ❄

I've hardly said a word since the night of the fire and things are deadly quiet in Nanny and Pop's house as it is. The only sounds at the dinner table are Baby Johnny's happy babblings and the low words of the CBC Radio news announcer. Nanny and Pop are worried about me. I can tell by their tight frowns and the way their wrinkles crease around their eyes. I don't blame them. I've done a lot of stupid things since I moved in, starting with piercing my nose and my belly button on my own, chopping my hair off so I look like some kind of freak, and getting into trouble just about every day at school. And then there's the issue of my not eating. I've always had baby fat that hangs off my belly and hips and I've always hated it. Now I've found the solution. Fuss with the food on my plate and eat a few mouthfuls of each thing. Already I think I look better and that's the only good thing that's happened since the fire.

I'm worried, though. What if they can't cope anymore with all the idiotic things I've done? What if they send me packing? I'd have to go live with Great Aunt Margret and that would be the most horrible thing imaginable. She has whiskers on her chin. And whenever she does see me, all she does is stare. So I better get my act together soon.

Conversations around Nanny's table go something like this.

"How's school today, Katherine?" asks Pop. They call me Katherine, never Kate.

"Good," I say.

"Baby Johnny sat up and rolled over, then started crawling like a son-of-a-gun," says Nanny, smiling proudly. That amount of talking is almost a speech for her.

"Cool," I say and put my head down.

"Gurgle, gurgle, blub, blub," says Baby Johnny, in agreement. By the way, Baby Johnny is named after my dad, Big John. Poor baby might always be known as Baby Johnny.

Then back to deadly silence. Just like all the non-talk about the fire that brought us together at this dinner table in the first place, the silence keeps us hanging in limbo waiting for something, anything, to happen. At this point, I want something to happen. I can't keep hanging in space like this. I might start screaming and never stop. I have images inside my head that make me want to scream, but, like my grandparents, I'm the silent type.

I'm also thinking they're missing my mom, Mary Ann. She was their only child and even though she gave them lots of trouble as a teenager, I know they loved her. I know they love me and Baby Johnny, too. That's why I need to make sure things work out here. I need to stop doing stupid things.

The fire. It's been two long months since everything good about my life went up in flames and burned down to a smoldering mass. It feels like that smoldering mass lives in my gut. Like a huge hole has opened up and swallowed me. I feel nothing else. Just plain numbness. I can still smell the smoke. Still hear myself screaming for my parents to wake up. Feel Baby Johnny's arms wrapped tightly around my neck as I run from the flames. The roaring heat as our trailer seemed to melt around me. But that's where all the feeling stops.

I've stopped caring about anything except Baby Johnny. I think I hate him but I know that can't be right so I try to fill my head with his cuteness. He makes me smile the way he crawls across the floor and puts absolutely everything in his mouth. Even the cat's food. He's starting to toddle when held up by Nanny's strong fingers. I can tell that already he really loves her. Inside his little baby head, he's probably forgotten Mom and Dad. Not that they were ever much when it came to being parents. Except loving. They were both good at that. And that's why my feelings about them, the drinking, and the fire get all mixed up. If they hadn't been partying and drinking, they'd still be here. And since all that is a secret that no one knows about, especially not Nanny and Pop, I can't say a thing. That knowledge would kill them and I need them both alive right now.

Mom and Dad drank. All the time. That's why they never woke up the night of the fire. They were passed out cold, drunker than drunk. And that's why I hate them now and my feelings are all tangled up. They've left me alone with Baby Johnny, a kid I've never really liked no matter how cute he can be. See, right from the start he has mostly been my responsibility. That's a bit much for a twelve-year-old kid who likes to disappear into her own life and shut the world out. Call me selfish. Call me mean. I don't care. Especially now. Despite all the drinking and all the responsibility, things used to be pretty good at home even with Baby Johnny seriously putting a crimp in my style. Lots of love and lots of laughter crammed into a rusty old trailer that saw better days long before I was born.

Our trailer was really small with only two tiny bedrooms, one for my parents and one for me until Baby Johnny came along and they rammed a crib into my already cramped room. A squalling, wrinkled baby became my responsibility. When he fussed in the middle of the night, I'd drag my groggy self out of bed, warm a bottle at the kitchen stove, and walk up and down our narrow hall, feeding Baby Johnny until he was all milk dopey. I'd change his diaper, put him in a dry onesie, and snuggle him back into his crib. Then I'd repeat the whole process in the morning, pack his diaper bag, and drop him off at the sitter before school.

I hated everything about this. And Baby Johnny. But I didn't hate my parents then. They drank because their lives were miserable. They were always struggling to get better jobs but it never seemed to work out. Mom was always saying things like how she wanted a better life for me and my brother, that it made her sad we didn't have iPads and fancy clothes and sneakers. But during the sober moments, life was good.

When Baby Johnny was born, Dad did some work on my bike as a surprise. New paint job. New seat and handle bars. It was pretty cool until he added the baby seat. That way I could take Baby Johnny with me when I went riding with my friends. It's as though they couldn't see how embarrassing that was. There were times Dad would take us to the beach for the whole day and I'd spend hours jumping off his shoulders into the sparkling water. Or Mom would make me money cake for my birthday, wrapping coins in wax paper so my friends and I would gobble up all the cake.

Birthdays and Christmases were always a big deal in our little trailer. We'd decorate like crazy and always have an amazing pancake breakfast and then a delicious dinner with all the trimmings—stuffing, cranberry sauce, a big fat turkey, gravy, and potatoes.

On the day Baby Johnny was born, my dad took me out for dinner and told me how cool it was to be a big sister and how much I should love my baby brother. I felt very special that day.

I feel bad about hating my little brother now because he's all I have left. It's time to get over my hate but I have no idea how to do this. Nanny and Pop show us all kinds of love just like my parents did. They took us in even though I know they can't afford us. We had nothing left after the fire but they took care of that. Pop started bringing me home books abandoned at the bus depot where he works as a janitor. I think he knows how painful it is for me to have lost all my precious books. Nanny took me to Value Village and we filled a cart with cute baby clothes and good, plain school things for me. Nothing shiny or sparkly. Nanny isn't that kind of woman.

Maybe that's why my mom rebelled so much when she was young. She wore tons of makeup, all kinds of cheap jewellery, and the shiniest, tightest clothing possible. I was so embarrassed by the way she dressed and looked that I'd never tell her about parent/teacher nights or school concerts. And of course there was the drinking. Mom drank all day long, sipping Long Island Iced Tea like it was Kool-Aid. She'd be looped by the time I got home from school dragging Baby Johnny on my hip.

School became a nightmare after the fire. My teachers treated me oddly, letting me get away without doing my homework, ignoring the fights I got into. The only teacher who treated me halfway normal was Ms. McKay, my English teacher. I loved her. She gave us the coolest assignments and I always did them. For example, we made collages out of magazine clippings and we took the meaning from the pictures and wrote a poem about ourselves. So much fun. After my parents died, Ms. McKay took me aside and told me that if I ever needed to talk, she'd listen. So many times I was tempted to take her up on her offer but I always shied away. I was worried I'd start to cry and never stop. I haven't cried a drop yet.

"Kate?"

I was just leaving third-period English one day. Ms. McKay put a gentle hand on my shoulder. I almost burst into tears right then.

"I was thinking you might like to do a special assignment for me, to make up for the difficulty you're having with your other grades. Maybe you'd like to write me a short story about anything you like. Just turn it in a few weeks before Christmas. How does that sound?"

"That... that sounds good, Ms. McKay. Thank you."

I knew that if I didn't get away from her soon I'd be a blubbering mess. And with Sapphire glaring at me from in front of her locker, that was the last thing in the world I wanted to start doing. Sapphire would make sure I'd never live it down. I could tell by the way she was staring that she was jealous of the special attention I was getting from Ms. McKay.

Sapphire is my big problem at school. I mean, who calls a kid Sapphire except parents who believe they have the perfect little Disney princess? Sapphire is more like the evil stepmother. She has been my tormentor for years now. She's bullied me since grade four and I loathe her. She probably watches that movie *Mean Girls* just for practice. She's the one who started the white trash, trailer park crap and it's followed me ever since. All the kids chant it behind my back. It makes me sick to my stomach. What am I supposed to do about being a poor kid who lives, or rather lived, in a crappy little trailer park? It's not like I could move or something.

Sapphire thinks she's hot stuff. Keeps her long blond hair in a big messy ponytail. Also slaps on tons of makeup and wears big chandelier earrings. And she has boobs, the real deal. I still have pathetic, painful little chest bumps and haven't started my period yet. Sapphire makes this out to be a badge of freaking honour. She's the queen bee and the rest of us are nothing but little girls in her eyes.

I think I might have to do something about Sapphire before I can do anything else about my new crappy life.

"Sapphire, screw off," I say and give her a hard push. She gives me a shove back and pretty soon we're in a screaming, cussing, hair-pulling match.

Mr. Allen, our math teacher, and Ms. McKay separate us. Ms. McKay takes me into her room and hands me a Kleenex to wipe the snot off my face. I'm crying hard and I don't know why.

"Kate. Is there anything you want to talk to me about?" She has that gentle hand on my shoulder again. I'm blubbering like Baby Johnny when he loses his pacifier. I put my head down on a desk and sob. I may never stop.

"Kate? I could call your grandparents, if you like." She sits down beside me and waits, quietly.

"No," I gulp, and wipe my face on the back of my hoodie sleeve. "I'll be all right." I know this is a lie and so does Ms. McKay.

"Have you thought about seeing a counsellor?"

I look up in horror. Only dweebs see counsellors. "No, I can manage on my own."

"Have you thought anymore about that assignment I mentioned? It's getting close to Christmas."

"I have," I lie again. "I thought I'd start it this weekend." Truth is I'd forgotten all about the assignment.

When I get home from school, Baby Johnny is gurgling in his playpen and Nanny is surrounded by several boxes. I can see that it's all a bunch of Christmas stuff.

"Katherine, I thought you might like to start helping me decorate for Christmas. Mary Ann always loved to help and I've always loved to get things up early so we have lots of time to enjoy it all. Oh, and by the way, Baby Johnny said his first word today. I think I heard him say Nanny." Nanny has a big smile on her face. She looks pretty and reminds me of the way my mom looked when she smiled. Nanny has started to talk to me more and it makes me feel strange and special at the same time.

My stomach does a funny kind of twist. Baby Johnny should be saying, "Mama" or "Dada." Or even "Kate." Just goes to show you how far he's come and how far behind I am.

Christmas. It's crept up on me. Time is passing and I'm stuck back in a burning trailer.

"Nanny, I'm sorry. I can't help you. I've got a big assignment I need to get started."

And that is the truth. If I'm going to haul my butt out of the gutter at school, I need to start writing.

I go into my bedroom and close the door. It's a funny thing, having an entire room to myself. In a way, I miss Baby Johnny, especially at night. My room is too quiet without him. I pull out my English scribbler and stare at it. I think about the fire and how it's changed everything. I think about Sapphire and how I wish she'd cut me some slack right now. Then there's Nanny and Pop and Baby Johnny and how I need to get used to them being my new family. And I think about Christmas. But despite my head being a jumble of confused thoughts, or maybe because of it, nothing comes to me. I put the scribbler back on my desk and go down to set the table for Nanny.

That night Nanny pops a bunch of popcorn and shows me how to string it with cranberries to make garlands for the tree and mantel. It's actually kind of cool. Pop plays on the rug with Baby Johnny, who giggles and stands up using the couch to balance himself. He's cracking himself up as he "walks" from the couch to

Pop's chair and back again. Everyone is smiling, even me.

"That little lad will be walking soon, mark my words," Pop says, laughing with Baby Johnny. "Maybe even before Christmas."

Wow, that's quite a speech, coming from Pop. I go to bed, thinking about my assignment.

The next day in school I cringe when I see Sapphire coming toward me.

"Look, Kate. I'm sorry about yesterday. I'm sorry about everything." She smiles at me and walks away.

Huh? Shock city. I don't know what bolt of lightning struck her, or if I can trust what just happened. But I'll take it as a hopeful sign.

"Kate, if you need some help with that assignment, come see me after school," Ms. McKay says, passing me in the hall.

Huh, again. This is starting to be a crazy day.

By the time I get home from school, I'm humming "Away in a Manger" and looking forward to stringing more popcorn garlands. I'm also wondering if I'm maybe losing my mind. What's with all the warm and cozy feelings?

The dinner table is quiet, as usual, except for Baby Johnny. He's babbling away.

"Nan-nan. Nan-nan."

Nanny's eyes are glowing and glistening in the corners. Is she crying? Pop has a huge grin on his face.

"Katherine, I'm going to cut down a Christmas tree tomorrow. I thought you'd like to come with me after school. I could use an extra pair of hands and you might even have fun. We could stop and bring pizza home for dinner."

Now I know I'm losing my mind. I think Pop just strung more words together than he has in his whole life.

After dinner (a meal where I ate every bite), we all gather in the living room. I curl up on the couch and continue with my popcorn garland. Pop pulls out a bunch of old records, dusts off their ancient record player, and puts a stack of records on. Christmas carols fill the quiet, happy space. Nanny unwraps Christmas ornaments and starts showing me all the ones Mom made for her over the years. She has quite a pile by the time she's finished and some of them are really pretty. I'm impressed. I didn't know Mom was a crafty kind of person. Baby Johnny pulls himself up at the couch by my knee, reaches for one of the sparkly ornaments, and takes his first step,

126

right into Nanny's arms. Her smile lights up the room. We all start laughing and yelling at the same time.

That night, I pull out my scribbler and sit at my desk. I have a cup of steaming hot chocolate by my school books. Pop made it for me and he calls it hot cocoa. I love the old-fashioned things around Nanny and Pop's, like the popcorn garlands, the record player, hot cocoa. They make me feel warm and cared for. I decide I don't need to tell anybody about my parents' drinking. It's not that important right now. I pick up my pen and write the first lines of my special assignment.

Tonight, Baby Johnny took his first step. It's been a day of little miracles.

The Little Santa

❄ Catherine Edward ❄

The small girl wore a brown tweed coat with two pleats in the back. She skipped along so that her new coat swung. Her shoes were worn and her name was Ivy. Her mother carried her baby brother in a handmade sling. The day was grey and windy in the way of the last days of an Island November with dried leaves hugging the curb.

"I'm going to be an angel!" announced Ivy.

"Umm, lovely... Every day?" asked her mother Mary. "No, Mummy. You know. In the Christmas Pageant. My second year as an angel. Tinsel in my hair and a white gown. I love it. Miss Rose and Mr. Graham got the costume rack out at Sunday School to see who fits things. This Sunday we'll begin practicing. I'm so excited."

"That's great, Ivy. Did you know that Mr. Graham asked if Rafe could be the Baby Jesus?"

"Really? My baby brother? Can he, Mum?"

"Well, he's three months old now, so I think he would make a fine Baby Jesus."

"Will he cry? What if he doesn't like the manger?"

"He'll have his angel sister there to make him laugh."

"Goody. What will he wear?"

"Swaddling clothes."

"Oh yeah, like raggy things."

"Exactly," said Mary, pointing, "and there's Our Bookstore."

Our Bookstore was owned by a distinguished-looking gentleman who came from the Old Country.

"Hello, Mr. Miller," said Ivy's mother. His name had been translated into English from Malūnininkas when he first arrived from Lithuania and settled in Charlottetown.

"Hello, Mrs. MacDonald," said Mr. Miller. "Nice to see you and Ivy and baby Rafael." He took a peek at the sleeping baby in his sling.

Ivy was swinging back and forth so her coat swayed. "Mummy

made my new coat from hers. It's a town coat."

"It's a perfect coat for such a lady as you, Ivy. Turn around. Yes, yes, very stylish."

Ivy beamed and moved her head just so, with her chin up a little.

In the store were many books, from small picture books to thick, gold-edged volumes. Also greeting cards, wooden pencil boxes, ribbon bookmarks, small gifts, and carvings—many kinds of birds as well as small animals just in time for Christmas crèches. There was one Santa that caught Ivy's eye. Santa was kneeling, his fur-trimmed red hat on the ground beside him, his hands folded, head bent as he knelt, adoring the Baby Jesus. It was a handsomely painted sculpture. Ivy was fascinated and looked at it for quite some time. She touched the Baby Jesus's tiny hands.

Mr. Miller noticed and said, "It is beautiful, isn't it?"

"Yes," said Ivy, "very beautiful."

Mr. Miller, who knew these regular customers, said to Mary, "It was made by an artist from Lithuania who lives in Quebec now. His name is Naujakos. You can see he tooled it on the bottom edge of the piece, just there."

"I love that Santa," said Ivy, eyes looking up to her mother.

"Today we're here for Christmas cards. I'll choose those and you can choose a book."

"Okay." Ivy looked at the books as though she had something in mind.

"Can I help you? Anything particular you are looking for?" offered Mr. Miller.

"Flowers. I'm looking for winter flowers," said Ivy.

"Hmm. Flowers don't grow in the winter, Ivy, but here's a nice book of flowers."

"No. Those are summer flowers. I like winter flowers."

"I see. What sort of winter flowers were you thinking about?"

"Well, frost flowers that grow on the windows. All lacy but they melt when the sun comes out. And the ones that Mummy grows inside. They're small and white for Christmas and they smell like angels."

"And what do angels smell like?" asked the book man.

"They smell sweet like the white flowers. Or like babies, like Rafe, and he's even named after an angel," Ivy answered, thinking how slow grownups are.

"I see. You make a good case for such a book. Sadly, I don't have one. Maybe you could make one. Here's a box of pencil crayons and some construction paper I'd like you to have. The next time you come to my store, you can tell me how you're doing with your book. Such a book is needed, as we both can see." Mr. Miller winked at Mary.

Ivy bounced with excitement. "I will. I'll make a book. I'm a good drawer. Daddy always says that. He saves all the cards I make him and Mummy puts my pictures on the fridge. Thank you, Mr. Bookstore."

The little bell over the door tinkled as they left the store.

The wind was mostly at their backs on the way home, which was not so far, just a nice walk. Mary listened as her bright little daughter talked unceasingly about her book, her new pencil crayons, her new coat, how happy Rafe was in his sling, what a dear Baby Jesus he would be, and how she loved the little Santa. Time passes swiftly in the company of a skipping chatterbox and soon they were home.

Ivy sat at her small table to make a thank-you card for Mr. Bookstore. Making cards was one of her favourite things. At seven years old, she had lots of ideas and read way beyond her year in school.

She began by drawing a picture of the bookstore window. Among the things in the window was a big card that said, "Thank you, Mr. Bookstore."

The inside of her card showed the inside of the store with a smiley, big man. There were books all around, and a small, rounded, red-and-white shape, which, if you knew about it, would be recognized as the little Santa.

The card said, "I like my pencil crayons. I will make a book. Thank you, Ivy."

As her father tucked her in, Ivy fell asleep talking about the little Santa.

"Ivy loves the Santa at the Bookstore," Tim told his wife. "She's quite smitten with it. Is it expensive?"

"It's a wonderful Santa, but too expensive. Never mind, she was happy to show off her new coat." Mary lived with an unassuming knowledge of how having just enough was enough.

Mary had cause to visit the store several times before Christmas.

"That's one special little girl you have," said Mr. Miller.

"We know. Today's a school day or she'd be here with me. In fact, I came today with a mission. Ivy asked me to give this to you. She finished it at last." Mary handed him Ivy's little book. The blue pages were held together by blue yarn. Ivy had chosen blue paper so all her white drawings would show up.

While Mr. Miller read the book, Mary admired the little Santa. He opened the book carefully. The title page read,

My Winter Flowers
by Ivy Mae MacDonald
For Mr. Bookstore

There were eight pages of Ivy's beloved ice lace and narcissus, drawn alone or together. On the last page she wrote, "These are enough for me, because I love them."

Mr. Bookstore was deeply touched.

"I will write Ivy to thank her."

When his letter arrived, Ivy was beyond thrilled. Mr. Miller had drawn green ivy all along the border of the page. He thanked her for teaching him about winter flowers and said he would treasure her book forever and always.

Ivy was allowed to choose one gift to open on Christmas Eve. She chose a box wrapped in brown paper with green ribbon, which had arrived in the post. It was quite heavy. The card said, "For a particular family." Inside, under many layers of newspaper, was a note: "Merry Christmas, from Santa Claus."

If ever a gift had found its way home, this was it. Ivy could only say, "oh" and "oh" and finally, "the little Santa."

The little Santa took up a cherished place in the family's Christmases for years to come. Ivy grew and grew and eventually grew up. In the way that happens, she met a young man, fell in love, married, moved away to meet opportunity. Which is how Ivy and Robert ended up on the Oregon coast. In her silent heart, Mary asked, "But does it need to be so far?" Ivy intuited this and assured her mother, "You know we'll come home whenever we can."

Ivy and Robert settled into life on a shore where the waves arrived from the west, not the east. With the birth of their daughter, Mary Elizabeth, the young family yearned for an Island Christmas. But air travel was expensive. They saved up and, finally, the year had come to head home. There would be the little Santa again at last.

The thing with the little Santa is that its gift must come to one's heart in private. So Ivy quietly watched as two-and-a-half-year-old

Elizabeth stared at the sculpture, which had taken its usual place on a low table so children could see it well. Light from the stove fire shone gold around the little Santa. The magic seemed no less for Elizabeth, who rubbed the smooth red suit, kissed his bald head, touched his hat on the ground by the manger, and held the Baby Jesus's tiny hands. The little girl was so quiet.

The Christmas visit home was heaven to Ivy and Robert, and to Elizabeth, who delighted in the attention of her cousins. Two weeks had spread out before them like a long feast, but how quickly time seemed a mean measure. It was a new year. They returned to home on the Oregon coast.

The rhythm of the seasons completes its habit year in, year out, moving through spring, summer, and then autumn, which gives up everything. November. December. Another Advent arrived. Ivy was missing home, especially with Christmas on the way. She called her mother.

"Hi, Mum. It's hard to believe another year has gone by. I'm missing you."

"Me, too, you."

"Well, I have an 'Elizabeth story' for you. You'll love it. This morning Wee Girl and I were out doing a little Christmas shopping. We went to the mall, where there's a Santa. Some official with the mall asked me, 'Would my little girl would like to sit on Santa's lap?' The store needed a picture. You know me, having been scared of them when I was little, I'm not much for store Santas. I was going to say 'no' but the man looked so kindly at me and the Santa did look like 'a right jolly old elf' and your granddaughter is very outgoing and loves talking to people, so I said 'okay.' You'll never guess what happened. Elizabeth climbed up into Santa's lap. Santa asked, 'What's your name?'

"'My name is Elizabeth. Mary Elizabeth Reed. Age three-and-a-half. And you are Santa. Are you the real Santa?'

"Santa smiled at that. 'Would you like to pull my beard?'

"So she tweaked his beard, which luckily was real. Undeterred, she continued.

"'Is the top of your head bald?'

"Santa removed his hat, revealing his bald spot, to Elizabeth's delight. By this time she had decided he was the real Santa and snuggled into his lap.

"'And what would you like for Christmas, Mary Elizabeth Reed?'

"Elizabeth thought carefully and finally said, in her inimitable three-year-old philosophical way, 'A present would be nice.'

"'Can you think what sort of present would be nice?'

"'Um, I want,' she said, noticing his bushy silver brows and his soft brown eyes like milk chocolate, 'to know…' She touched a big brass button on his coat and, still looking right into his eyes and maybe his heart, asked, 'Santa, do you kneel before the Baby Jesus?'"

In the Temple of Jerusalem

❄ T. N. MacCallum ❄

Marina watches her mother pack the tan suitcase, its leather cracked at the edges from countless excursions. She is all too familiar with the woman having to leave somewhat abruptly for business, but Hanukkah is less than a week away and her mother has told her that she will be gone well into the New Year. Ramming all she can into the small carryon, her mother reveals the light but efficient packing skills acquired from working as an anchor in the news biz. Anything for a story.

Marina pets her cat, Blue, while her mind escapes the sight of the lady securing toenail clippers, wrapped in a bra, into a small side compartment of the suitcase. She knows that she will be shipped off to Olive's place, her mother's BFF. Olive's abode will furnish some ridiculous excuse for a Menorah—one the woman will have probably purchased at a box-store, or worse, one she'd found at some moldy garage sale when she'd been antique-hunting. Marina's mother will not let the beautiful Menorahs leave their house. And this will be Olive's service: rubbish to replace Marina's tattered hopes that Hanukkah will be somewhat normal in this woman's Christmas-filled home. She can see it now, the suffocating glitter of tinsel and Santas and an overdone tree. Olive will probably say some bullshit about how their religions are comparable while she stalks Marina's space, prodding her to ignite the nightlights of some junky candle-holder. She realizes she's inflicting her rage on Blue's tail when he bites her. Marina sucks at her finger as she sits, stewing on the stairs: Mother will hear about this when she gets back; but for now, the silent treatment will do just fine.

Ever since Marina lost her father to his duties last spring, their Jewish culture has become something she clings to; but now she feels as if she's losing grip, her fingernails digging deep into her faith—the talons of a hawk clutching to its food for survival. Her father had been stationed in Afghanistan for the past seven months, and they've asked him to stay another twelve. He'd always made

Hanukkah a special event in their household, as his mother did for him growing up. Marina strokes the Menorah on the table of the hallway across from her parents' room and remembers her father's dimples framing his face—his gentle laugh threading through her memories of past Hanukkahs. She is twirling an imaginary *dreidel* with him, really Blue's tail, again, when her mother enters the hallway, suitcase in hand. "Ready, Marnie?"

Marina is still spinning the toy in her head when she gets out of her mother's SUV in Olive's driveway, downtown. "Okay, Sweets. I'll see you when I get back," her mother says in the porch of the heritage-style home. The woman thanks Olive with a care package she'd made up before they'd left the house. Marina had seen the bottle of wine and Pandora bracelet that her mother had laid out on her bed before placing them in the shiny gift bag. Marina does the calculations: her mother has already bought Olive the bracelet for Christmas, so she must think the wine is fair trade for Olive's assistance of taking Marina in, that she is worth only a bottle of wine. Her mother left more for the neighbour boy to check on the cat.

When her mother goes to hug her daughter before leaving to catch the flight, Marina dodges the open arms and red lips, leaving the porch for the sitting parlour to the right. She can hear Olive saying goodbye to her mother, not to worry because she'll make sure that Marina has a *good* holiday. As if Hanukkah is a summer vacation or something. But she wouldn't expect Olive to understand. Nor her mother, being a phony and all—her mother had converted to Judaism to marry her father before Marina had been born. Unlike Marina, her mother hadn't been born into the religion; and now that she is abandoning Marina at Hanukkah, at a time that is so important to her father, she seems like even more of an imposter. A stranger; a sham.

In the SUV on the ride over, her mother had said, "I love you. But like your father, I have a duty to our country, too. To multiple countries. Someday, when you grow up, you will understand. When you're working a career, you see that it's not always about yourself. I love my job, Marnie. And I love you. But sometimes I have to make sacrifices." Remnants of the parent she once knew: gone with the commercials between newscasts. It's not like her family resides among the *Halacha* law of maternal lineage, anyway. Their reformed Jewish family starts with her father and his heritage; so, they don't really need her mother.

Now orphaned, Marina peeks over the sofa's huge swirling antique arm to catch a final glimpse of her mother in the porch, passing Olive an envelope, whispering something before leaving into the cold night. That's it. That's the one, the payoff for taking her in for good. Olive catches Marina staring at her and she stuffs the envelope in her cardigan before hurrying to the kitchen, saying she's going to make them a snack. Yeah. Right. She's just gone to count the dollars.

Marina is lying in bed, counting the days to when her father said he could Skype with her. But she figures it won't happen. Their computer dates rarely work out with his long days in the *sand trap,* as he likes to call it. She'll be lucky to get an email. Instead she goes over her memories of Hanukkah from the past few years. The songs they'd sing; the tradition of lighting a new candle on the Menorah every day; the special gifts he'd give her—one for every day of Hanukkah. Unlike the parents of her Jewish friends, he didn't just give her the gifts. He would make a treasure hunt out of the holiday, drawing a map with clues to lead her to find her presents. Along with the searches he had woven in lessons on the philosophy and traditions of their religion.

Her favourite memory is from Hanukkah of 2006: she'd been six and curious. It was the first year her father had planned a Hanukkah treasure hunt. On the first day, he'd given her a beautiful Menorah—the one with the gorgeous blue and white colours that sits upon the table upstairs in her old family home; she doubts she'll ever see it again. On the second day, as she lit the first two candles of the Menorah, he'd brought her a map he'd made. The map was a picture of their backyard's landscape, scaled into the shape of Israel; she'd recognized this shape from her Hebrew studies. Every day after she'd light another candle on the Menorah, he'd give her a fairly easy question about their religion. The answers were clues to use on the treasure hunt, guided by the map. Small presents would be hidden among the gardens mulched for winter and the naked trees. On the last day of the treasure hunt, the clues led Marina to the frosted tool shed, where her father came out dressed in a sheet, wearing a long wig and beard. He'd said, "Welcome, little one. I am Moses. You have made the long trek across your ancestors' past and their land of Israel. Welcome to the Temple of Jerusalem." He then asked her a final riddle: "What has six points, soars in the air of the land you just walked, and is found on the end of a pole, as well as in the night sky? It has protected David, and it shall protect us if we believe in our God."

There was a small chalkboard set up in the shed, to which Moses pointed. "Don't tell me child, show me." And he gave her a blue piece of chalk.

Marina knew the answer when he'd said *six points*; the mention of David confirmed this. She drew the Star of David on the board. He'd removed the Moses wig and hugged her, throwing his six-year-old daughter up high on his shoulder, and took her inside. There on the kitchen table sat her final Hanukkah present: a pair of binoculars. He knew how she loved to watch the birds when they went snowshoeing on the trails in the winter.

Marina longs for her perfect family, now. The one with the father who'd read to her and her mother on Sunday afternoons from famous novels: *Huckleberry Finn, Anne of Green Gables, Donkey Odie.* The same family whose mother's tender touch and kind words brought them strength. Like nothing could ever take away what was theirs. The smell of cookies baking, *dreidel* games, and bedtime stories. Their snowshoeing adventures in the winter, and their swimming at the beach in the summer. The perfect family: a memory that was growing more distant every day. Looking out the window of the guest room at Olive's, Marina daydreams her father had left her another map for this Hanukkah, and it leads her to the Temple of Jerusalem where her parents are dancing with the Star of David painted upon their faces. Just when she goes to hug them, they morph into actual stars and float way up into the sky where they settle in with the night's constellations. She reaches for them, but all that is left is stardust on the temple's floor.

The next day, when Marina is doing her final homework before Christmas break in the sitting parlour, Olive's antique rotary phone quakes its shaky ring—like a bomb warning from one of those 1940s movies that her father used to watch. Olive comes in, apron on and her hair swept in a bun, to answer the phone. Marina wonders why she doesn't have a touch tone. They don't even have a landline back in their house uptown. Cell phones are the new way, her father used to say before leaving for his deployment. She can tell by Olive's silly *oh-my-goodness-hello* and high-pitched tone that it's her mother on the other end. The two squawk like chickens every call. Marina pretends not to eavesdrop; and when she can see in the corner of her eye that Olive is about to the hand the phone over, she leaves so quickly for the bathroom that anyone would believe she may not have heard Olive calling to her.

The days come and go, and sure as the snow that has frosted the streets, a Menorah has been placed in the spare bedroom for her. It isn't so ugly either; rather pretty, in fact. But Marina never mentions it, and she dare not light it. She has to have Olive believe how her mother's abrupt parting for the reporting gig has woefully affected her, in case the imposter lady decides to return. This ensures she will hear all about Marina's heartbreak from Olive. *She never even lit a candle.*

Marina takes care never to be mean to Olive. The woman is, after all, kind to her. She has made Marina great lunches, ones with mini-chocolate bars for dessert; and she is always playing great music in the kitchen, or taking Marina for drives while she runs errands. She even took her shopping the other day.

But the bonding is bittersweet and Marina misses the days when her mother took her on errands, even to work when her mother interviewed people in town or talked on the radio. She'd shown Marina the big microphones and cameras, and one time she'd even bribed the network to let Marina make her own weather forecast on the local news for her birthday when she was five. Now that her mother has been replaced by the imposter who works for the big networks, she knows those days are long gone. She figures she'd better make do with Olive.

Later that night, when the phone sends out another bombing alarm, and Olive exchanges the bird-octave pitch, Marina decides to oblige when Olive motions for her to take the phone. She doesn't say much to the mother who'd abandoned her for the holidays, but the woman on the other end sounds so much like her old mother, she listens to every word.

"You'd love the snow-covered park here, Marnie. Its trails look super for snowshoeing. Wish I had you and your father here with me to try it out. We'll have to plan a hike when we're all together, again."

When Marina says goodbye and sets the rotary monster back in its place, she notices a small pair of binoculars sitting on a bookshelf across the room. They are dusty and cheap, nothing like the beauties her father had gotten for their bird-watching expeditions; but she takes them to her eyes, standing at the huge parlour window that looks out on the town, and steadies them to the night. She imagines their ocular range has the capacity to peek in on her father, who is working the sand trap. He is happy, his dimples showing as he waves to her. She then points to his left, encouraging him to look over his shoulder, and she steers her lenses there, too. Her mother waits on a snow-covered path with three sets of snowshoes, waving to them to come join her.

Christmas Eve, the last day of Hanukkah. Marina has received a short email from her father stating he's sorry but he will not be able to meet her online tonight. Though he'll try his best in January. She isn't angry, but she decides to light her Menorah. She wants him here with her; she wants her mother here with her; heck, even the imposter would do. She can smell Olive baking in the kitchen, and she lies on her bed listening to the visitors who are coming and going, dropping presents off to Olive, her giving them gift bags in exchange. The pile under the small Christmas tree in the sitting parlour is slowly growing larger, and Marina wonders what the presents are. She considers going down at one point, maybe shaking the wrapped boxes to guess what's inside, but she knows that is too much effort. Still, she's good at guessing; she'd always done it well with her Hanukkah gifts.

It is then she realizes that Christmas is indeed similar to her own religion, not just some of the religious stories or biblical representations, but the tradition of giving and people coming together over the holidays. She knows Olive wants to go to church later this evening, but she respects that Marina's religious beliefs do not quite permit the comfort to attend such a celebration of Jesus. And Marina knows that the sacrifice to stay in is Olive's gift to her. The presents under the tree with Marina's name on them, or the fact that the woman has taken her in, are all Olive's sacrifices; yet, Marina knows the woman wanted to do these things and she is coming to appreciate the welcoming gestures in the heritage home.

That night, when Marina is blowing out the candles on her Menorah, hushing the flames for yet another year, and wishing that her family would be with her the next time she lights one, Olive comes to her door.

"Hey, you. I have something for you. I want you to open it at six a.m., sharp." She sets an envelope on the dresser beside the Menorah, placing a wound alarm clock nearby. "I know you don't celebrate Christmas, but you might as well partake in some Christmas joy while you're here." *While* you're here. Olive says it as if her parents *are* coming back for her, and Marina hopes it is true. Olive says goodnight, and leaves her.

Marina, studying the envelope, thinks it's probably some silly letter from Santa Claus, telling her to get up and see all of the presents he'd brought her. She can't believe others believe in such crap.

As she falls asleep, she notices the white flakes falling outside her window, the sound of the wound clock ticking precisely—a perfect sound, like a tiny clap applauding her lids when they finally close.

Marina wakes to the alarm and she rubs her eyes before she takes a moment to figure out the silly clock, fiddling with the dials. Why Olive uses these old contraptions, she'll never understand. The lady seems to have money, otherwise. Can she not afford a decent phone or good clock? She remembers Olive telling her mother, it's all about the character. The antique character. Marina rolls her eyes at the shadows.

The envelope is staring at her, and she decides to open it after she brushes her teeth. Marina can hear her father as she rotates the toothbrush: a fine Jew is one with fine teeth—so he has said since she was just a tot. Upon her return to get dressed, she tears the envelope open: inside, *a map*.

She doesn't take a breath until she gasps. She can see it is a map of Olive's house, and she bursts out of her room, running down the hallway in her pyjamas. A note at the top of the stairs, *Where is Israel?* Marina remembers an antique map on Olive's wall in the sitting parlour: the Middle East. She descends downstairs and finds another question tacked on the map, a sticky-note: *What has two eyes, good for viewing birds?* Marina dashes to the binoculars on the bookshelf, but no note is attached to them. She fiddles with them until she decides to look through them instead. Written in one lens with a white marker: *outside.* She turns to the window, still looking through the lenses, and sees a Moses that only she would recognize waving at her from the front yard; a woman dressed in similar biblical attire beside him. Marina runs out the front porch and into their arms.

"Too much for a teenager? Guess you're outgrowing these gags," says her father, his bathrobe wet at the bottom with snow.

But Marina can't speak, no words will come, only tears into the arms of the woman who has removed her wig; for she is not an imposter, but the mother she's been yearning for.

"There, there, Marnie."

Her father's arms around them both. The family makes their way back into the house, Marina's slippers tracking snow into the kitchen where Olive has an exuberant breakfast waiting for them: the smell of sausage, eggs, and pancakes sift throughout the home as they tell stories and plan snowshoeing adventures.

Marina listens, and watches them: her mother and the old, familiar, uplifting smile that she has missed so much; her father, who looks as if he's been missing out on sleep, but seems so very happy to be home; and Olive, glowing in all her generosity. She watches how her father and mother joyfully interact, their eyes bright despite the fatigue she knows they have both been facing with their jobs. Marina realizes her mother has missed her father as much as she has, and now that he is here with them, the mother she has missed so much is home, too.

"I'm sorry," Marina says, quietly, to Olive.

"Oh, child, you have nothing to be sorry for," says Olive. "Your parents love you very much." And she puts another pancake on Marina's plate.

"We're sorry, Marnie," says her mother. And her father adds, "We know things have been rough on you."

Her father touches her cheek, "How about those birds?"

They head out into the yard where they see the chickadees, goldfinches, juncos, and blue jays foraging for seed at Olive's birdhouses, and on the freshly fallen snow. Marina's father is still wearing his Moses costume, robe dragging on the ground like a king's on a cloud. She notes her mother and Olive chatting on the sofa through the front window, their arms flailing as they squeal and laugh like school girls. What had annoyed Marina last week seems delightful now, and she giggles at the women. Her father takes a seat on the front steps and she sits on his lap, watching the birds flit on the snow and flutter around the branches. The trees are menorahs, the birds flickering.

Christmas Train

✳   Dianne Hicks Morrow   ✳

Christmas Eve, the midnight train to Montreal,
my first year of college, flirting
with a handsome young manager from Halifax.
He joins us for Christmas morning breakfast—
white linen, CN silverware, jam in silver jars.
Sits beside me in the observation car,
Mom and Dad across the aisle.

A skiff of crusted snow on the ground near Montreal.
Far ahead, Engine #1 does an odd jerk,
then straightens out. I stare, puzzled.
Engine #2 syncopates.
The next cars lurch—unlike the heavy engines,
too light to make the surprise switch to the parallel track.
Rail ties tossed like spilled toothpicks.
No sound reaches us.

Dad angles his strong arm across Mom's midriff, announces
to his blind wife, "I believe we have a derailment, Mary."
As for my dashing seatmate, I have no further memory.
What I remember is each slow-motion car
coming to rest at a random rakish angle, upright.
Dinky toys strewn between two tracks.

Our turn now. In the dome car we feel
only the wheels' strange grinding in gravel.
We stop on a slight slant.
What now?

Cars akimbo. Impossible to walk through, one to another.
We climb down from the zigzagged train, crunch along the snow
in shoes and bare arms—our boots and coats shed
in a sleeping car far ahead. The wind raw as our nerves.
We retrieve our baggage from a car so tipsy we feel drunk.
No way to let Uncle Ray know we are safe
as we wait in the cold for buses sent from Montreal.

His face bursts into a rare smile, when he spots us—delivered
to the train station two hours late.
The derailment already on the news—
worry rampant about serious injuries,
superficial cuts and pulled muscles the reality.
Aunt Joan's tearful hugs when Uncle Ray
lands us in their living room.
Cousins glad we can open gifts at last.

On Boxing Day the front-page banner headline.
Beneath it the first panoramic photo I've ever seen—
our train now a surrealist's canvas.

The reporter speculates the switcher forgot his task.
Lucky our train was on time, and the New York

express, all those joyful passengers
waving back Merry Christmas when we passed
on the double track, minutes before our derailment.

Christmas with Nanny

❄ Sue Campbell ❄

When I was a little girl, and by little I mean from babyhood to graduation, we spent every Christmas with my grandparents. Each Christmas was a new adventure for the three of us kids as Nanny has always been young at heart. Grampy would chop the wood, bring in the tree, laugh, and say, "Well, kids, this will be the best Christmas ever." With a sparkle in his eyes and a big bear hug, he would tease each of us, whispering little hints. Each year Nanny planned something different for us. We would try to guess, and ask Mom over and over what our surprise would be, and she would say, "Don't ask me."

It wasn't that far from Alberton to the family farm at Travellers Rest, maybe forty-five minutes. Away we went, just after lunch on Christmas Eve with the trunk secretly packed by my dad early that morning. The back seat could have lit up with electricity from the excitement and anticipation among the three of us.

Of the three, I was the only girl and the middle child. Actually, I am the only girl grandchild in the family and always will be. This put me in a very special place with Nanny and Grampy and I lapped it up, but it also meant that I was the "girl in the middle." Aunt Karen was Mom's only sister. She lived in Calgary with her three sons and they seldom came home, and never in my memory.

The old homestead never changed. Same white-shingled siding and black-and-white trim, which Grampy touched up every fall before he put up the storm windows. Same dark green kitchen tongue-and-groove lower walls with rose-and-vine wallpaper above. The living room and hallway were painted a flat beige and all bedrooms had slanted ceilings with the walls papered in patterns from years gone by, which had faded and almost disappeared wherever the sun reflected onto the wall through the windows.

Christmas at Nanny's was full of beautiful lights and the smell of homemade bread, meat pies, chocolate brownies, and apple crumb cake, and those memories made me smile as the bus wound through New Brunswick. I smiled again as I spotted the first sign for the Confederation Bridge or the "Fixed Link" as some still called it, including Grampy until he died about three-and-a-half years ago. I have always felt bad about not going home for the funeral. I was in the middle of final exams at Queen's and had maybe sixteen dollars in the bank. We never knew him to be sick. He was always full of fun and teasing, and right until the end he loved to make people laugh. Nanny said, "He just got tired, that's all." It is still hard for me to imagine them getting old and dying. In my memory, they would always stay the same as when I was six years old, but everyone gets old and all little girls become adults.

Finding myself alone this Christmas, I bought a ticket and boarded the bus from Halifax to Summerside. I was going home. Memories of each Christmas came to mind as the bus hummed along in the dark. One year we went out on Christmas Eve with a horse and buggy, complete with bells and blankets. We rode around Summerside to see the lights and hear the carollers singing from the steps of Trinity United Church and in the park on Spring Street. Another year, Nanny put on a treasure hunt, which led us all around the house, out to the barn, and even down to the road for a message in the mailbox, which said, "Okay now, kids, go up and look under your beds." There we found more presents than we could have imagined.

There were small snowflakes swirling in the headlights of the bus. The Strait was open water, but on the Island side the ground was covered with a skiff of snow. The sight of the red sandstone cliffs of the Island brought a lump to my throat. This will always be home, always part of me.

My life had turned upside down and backward lately and I needed my Nanny to tuck me into bed with a hug and kiss and tell me, "Dream beautiful dreams, sweetheart, everything will be fine."

Mom and Dad had split up four years ago. Mom moved with her boyfriend out to Kelowna, B.C., and Dad kept on whining, complaining, and drinking. Both my brothers had moved to Fort Mac for work and I was teaching second grade in Halifax. My live-in boyfriend, whom I foolishly thought I would marry, had left me for a married woman of fifty. We had all been close, but then it seemed the world got hold of us and, like scrambled eggs, our family was stirred up and chopped into little pieces.

The bus pulled into a gas station on the Island side. The driver announced, "We have no one for Charlottetown, so we will go right through to Summerside. Next stop, Read's Corner Esso and the last stop is the Summerside Irving."

I couldn't wait to see Nanny. What a surprise this would be. I took the little jewelry box out of my jacket pocket and opened it up. I had bought a gold bracelet with "Nanny" engraved in fancy writing. I knew she would love it. I could imagine Nanny opening the door to find me, her only granddaughter, the only one in the family with her blue eyes and blonde hair. She would say, "Of course you are beautiful, you look like your Nanny." I would have her all to myself. All of her love and warmth and delicious food. No one could cook like my Nanny. I could hardly believe it, Christmas Eve and I was home.

The bus pulled into Read's Corner Esso and the driver retrieved and handed me my suitcase. He asked if I was okay. I answered, "Yes, yes, I am home." In the gas station I got a large double-double from Tim's. Way too hot. The kid behind the counter looked too young to be out on Christmas Eve. I asked if he would call a cab for me. The cab was there within five minutes. As the driver put my suitcase into the trunk, I slipped into the back seat. I told him, "Go up through Travellers Rest and turn right at the second dirt road past the highway, please."

"You just home for Christmas? Do I know you? You look familiar."

"I don't think so. Danny and Marie Gallant—my grandparents? Grampy died over three years back. I'm home to surprise my Nanny."

The light at the highway turned green and once the cab was through the intersection, he pulled over.

"I should tell you, miss, your Nanny ain't there anymore. The farm was sold for taxes not long after Dan died and your Nan went a bit funny in the head. She's at the Manor now. What do you want me to do, miss? It's gone nine-thirty so there won't be no visiting hours until tomorrow. I could drop you at a motel—or a relative's house."

I couldn't hide my tears. "It's not far, could you take me out to the old place?"

"Sure I can. I'm sorry you're upset."

He turned down the second dirt road and there it stood, my

147

childhood sanctuary. No yard lights on, no Christmas tree in the front-room window blinking colours. No tracks in the snow on the laneway, or dogs bounding down to greet us. So sad.

"Yes, sorry, drop me at a motel, anywhere, I guess, as long as it's clean."

We went back into town and he took me to a motel on Water Street. He took my suitcase out of the trunk as I thanked him for his kindness.

I paid for two nights and the lady behind the desk wished me a Merry Christmas, handed me the key to number six, and went back to her TV show.

I trudged through the slush and opened the door to my room. Sitting on the edge of the bed, I had never felt so lost, cold, and alone.

Fully dressed, I locked the door, turned up the heat, and went to bed with the lights on. Surprising myself, I slept really well and woke Christmas morning to bright sunlight shining through the drapes. By the time I had showered and changed, it was nine-fifteen already.

I found the number for the Manor in the phone book so I dialed and it rang and rang until finally I got a lady who sounded out of breath.

"Sorry," she said, "we're on skeleton staff today, it being Christmas."

"Yes, of course you are. Is it okay if I come in to see Marie Gallant? I'd like to take her out and spend the day with her, would that be all right?"

"Well, dear, I don't know. How long has it been since you saw her last? Are you family?"

"Yes, I'm her granddaughter, and it has been a few years."

"Why don't you come on along and you can decide when you get here."

"Don't tell her I'm here, I want to surprise her."

I asked the cab driver to stop at Tim's and I picked up a coffee for each of us. I had never been in the Manor before and as I walked through the front door, the smell of turkey in the oven made me hungry. There was no one at the front desk so I wandered around until I met up with a nurse. I asked her if she could point me in the direction of Marie Gallant's room.

"Marie, I think, is out in the hall. Will you be staying to help her with her dinner? It's so good when family comes to help out as we're short-staffed to give as many as possible the day off."

I walked in the direction that she had pointed.

At the end of the hall, belted into a weird-looking high-backed wheelchair, was my Nanny with her head flopped over and sound asleep. I took her hand and said, "Nanny, Nanny, come on, wake up, it's me, Nicole." She didn't stir so I tried again. I kissed her cheek and tapped her shoulder, saying, "Nanny, I've come to spend Christmas with you, please wake up." Her eyes opened, the same deep blue as my own, and she looked at me and said, "Who are you? Why are you waking me up? I already had my pills, now go away and let me sleep."

My tears came instantly. I turned and there was the same nurse I had met on the way in. She hugged me and rubbed my back and, without saying a word, she led me to one of the chairs by the window.

"I am so sorry, dear. Marie has been here for a couple of years now. No one has come to visit. We didn't realize you didn't know she was here. Her days sway between not too bad to almost coma-tose. Sometimes she tries to feed herself and talks away about years ago. Other times she refuses to eat and just sleeps. It's okay, dear, it's all right to cry. Why don't you sit and talk to her for a while. Talk about when you were a little girl at Christmas time. Maybe she will remember you."

I sat and held Nanny's hand and talked to her about my bus trip and how good it felt to be home. I talked about the Christmas when she and Grampy took us on a buggy ride all around Summerside and we sat outside the hospital to watch the lights come on, and over to Spring Street for the carollers.

"Remember that? How about the year there was no snow and it was so warm out that we lit a campfire and roasted marshmallows at the top of the orchard." She squeezed my hand but she seemed to be sleeping. "Remember what little brats Joey and Mike were? How they would run around and drive us all crazy?"

"Oh, they were brats all right."

"Oh my God, Nanny, you remember."

Her eyes opened. "Yes, the little devils drove poor Grampy out of his mind with all the tricks they would play and y'know he was getting on, sometimes a bit short of patience. But that little Nicki is the light of my life. That little girl looks exactly like me. Y'know, I miss her so much. She would put her arms around my neck and tell me how much she loved me. Haven't seen her for quite a while."

A frown clouded her face and she said, "Who are you? Part-time help 'magine. How did you know my grandchildren? You must have heard me talking about them sometime. I do ramble on about them by times. Oh, that little Joey, so chubby I could just squeeze him and he gave the best hugs. Mike now was quite a bit like his grandfather. Didn't say or hug too much, but the devil was in him, you could see it in his eyes."

I asked if she would like me to take her for a walk. She shook her head and started dozing off again. About twenty minutes later a caregiver came by and told me that the turkey dinner would be here in a few minutes and asked if I would help with feeding Marie.

"Yes, of course."

My sadness had become heartbreaking. Here she was so alone in the world. No one came to see her. She must have felt abandoned. I didn't blame her for sleeping her time away. What else was there for her to do but feel her loneliness?

Her tray came complete with a plate for each of us with turkey, stuffing, mashed potatoes, turnips, peas and carrots, and a side dish with cranberry sauce and coleslaw. I was suddenly starving. I gently shook Nanny's hand. "Wake up now, wake up Nanny, dear, your turkey dinner is here."

She opened those vivid blue eyes and looked at me as if I were the enemy and in a sharp voice said, "Don't you dare call me Nanny, young lady. I don't know who you are, but my granddaughter is only twelve years old and I can feed myself, thank you!"

With that, she fell back to sleep.

"Oh, come on, Nanny, you must be hungry, it looks so good." I decided to get the nurse as Nanny wasn't stirring.

The nurse came over, winked at me and said, "Marie Gallant, wake up and eat your dinner, right now."

"All right, all right, you don't have to get cross, I will eat it."

I spooned her dinner to her in between eating from my own plate. The turkey dinner was so, so good. With summer savoury stuffing, just the way that Nanny used to make it, and now, sitting there at Christmas with my Nanny, made me feel so happy. Nanny didn't say much but kept smiling as if she knew me but couldn't place me. We ate our dinner and I made her a cup of tea with lots of milk and no sugar as I remembered.

"You are a good girl, I hope they keep you on here. You even know how to make my tea."

With that she dozed off to sleep again without even a sip of tea. I took the bracelet out of my pocket and put it on her wrist. She didn't even stir. The worker came and took the tray and I sat for a while watching her chest rise up and down. I kissed her cheek and left, thanking God that I still had all of my sweet memories of Christmas past.

The next morning I was back on the bus going over the bridge. I turned and took one more look at the Island and thought about how life could be so sad and yet so full of wonder and love. I vowed, God willing, that I would come back next year.

Little Banshees

✳ Margie Carmichael ✳

Catherine, Mary, and Patricia were the youngest set of sisters in a large Island farm family, like three steps of a staircase that climbed from 1955 to 1960. Together they were a complex unit, a force that filled their home with laughter, dramatic temper tantrums, and screeching that sliced through every nerve in the house. Their father called the three his "little banshees." They played well, fought well, and tattled on one another, and there were many two-against-ones. Their father was a better referee than anyone else—at least he could stop the screeching. Most of their kinks were sorted out by the time someone managed to put them upstairs into the bed they shared and make them stay there.

Catherine (the youngest) slept between Mary (the middle child) and Patricia (the oldest), who faced the wall. Mary fell asleep first, followed by Catherine, who curled up behind her, face nuzzled into Mary's fiery red hair. Patricia, back-to-back with Catherine, didn't fall asleep as readily, but once she did, she didn't shut up—according to her brothers on the other side of the wall.

They especially hated being put to bed in the wintertime, leaving behind the warmth and light of the parlour, jumping into bed in the dark, and trying to stay warm without suffocating the youngest in what she called "The Cafferin Sammich."

It was a different story in the weeks preceding Christmas. They knew Santa was watching! Often, they put themselves to bed. Once they got past their shivering, they said their prayers nice and loud to make sure their parents, God, and Santa heard them. They whispered, then, about Santa and presents and reindeer and dreams and fairies—interspersed with a pinch or a kick or a tickle or a cold foot walking up a warm leg—until they were asleep. Later in the night, when the fires were low, kitty cats padded into the room and fit themselves into empty spaces in the bedclothes.

Christmas was all about Santa and food. Momma Martha and Nannie Josie (their father's mother) ruled the house. Little girls weren't allowed in their kitchen when the squares, pies, and fruit-cakes were being baked. Normally, an older sister or brother looked after them, kept them entertained and out of everyone's hair, but on one occasion they were on their own. Momma gave them an important job—cleaning the parlour. They were to dust off the pump organ, wipe the baseboards and windowsills, tidy up the couches and chairs, and give the floor a good sweeping before their brothers got home from the woods with the Christmas tree.

Very little sweeping was done. They played horsy with the broom, drew pictures in the window-frost, jumped on the couch. Soon, though, smells of fruit and spice tormented them, making them feel especially hungry and testy, till all they did was bellyache and pick at each other, culminating in a three-way hair-pulling frenzy.

Into the middle of this drama came their father with an armload of wood, which he had to drop when they came running to his knees, crying and talking all at once. "She started it!" they said as one voice. "They forgot all about us—didn't feed us all day!" said Patricia, and all snotty fingers pointed to the kitchen. "That's w-w-wight!" Catherine sobbed. Mary rested their case with "We're too weak to work." They looked at their father and wailed. "Shhhhh!" he said. One by one he set the girls on the couch. He picked up the wood and walked through the parlour door into the kitchen, loaded the stove, then ran back out, laughing at the angry cooks as he swiped biscuits, cookies—whatever he could get away with—and gave them to his little banshees.

They were precious and fleeting, those years when they believed in Santa Claus, when they were too young to send to school, before they met the world beyond the end of their lane. One by one they entered this world, learned quickly, learned a lot—and wanted to. They also came to learn some disappointing truths, about Santa Claus, sin, and what the real playground rules were. Worst of all, they learned that they were poor. That meant Dirty. Smelly. Ugly. Alone. In this larger world they lost pieces of themselves. In all the confusion that followed, they couldn't find each other, not until they walked back up their lane.

In grade five, Patricia figured out Santa, and was relieved. She could not understand why Santa would give so little to her, and so much to a cruel bully like Frances who convinced their whole classroom that Patricia was poison, that if any of the others touched her or anything of hers, then they were poison, too, and outcast.

Now it all made sense to Patricia. Santa was never about being good. Santa was about not being poor. She shared this nugget of wisdom with her little sisters when the time came for them to not believe.

Family dynamics changed greatly as each year passed, and events marked each girl differently as they came to know bellyache hunger, anger, frustration, and fear. They would never understand the worsening drinking and fighting they witnessed among the adults. Home became a weary old house slowly caving in on itself, broken and full of holes. Innocence slipped through cracks in the walls.

Winters were the worst. The girls slept in coats and snow pants, hats and mitts. Snow blew in through shattered windows and holes in the roof—landed on the bed the kitty cats abandoned, it was so cold. Light was long gone from lamps, and from eyes of despairing parents. There were no animals left, nothing to eat—it was hard to find hope on this farm.

Yet, there was still Christmas, that faithful light that got them through the dark times. Sometimes it was all they had, the one time when they were certain that they were going to eat. For years, a beloved uncle gave their parents one hundred dollars before Christmas. As faithfully, an anonymous person had two huge boxes of groceries delivered right to their door, often from the same store that no longer extended credit to the family.

While hope barely prevailed, the sisters remained a unit that fit together differently as they grew up. They learned resilience and the value of a sense of humour, and became very resourceful. Catherine became adept at hiding cans and bottles she'd sneak out of the grocery boxes. When there was little left to eat but turnips, she would present her treasures to her parents, saving the family over and over again. To watch her smiling at her parents' praise was to see the sun come out.

One time, just at the end of the school year, Mary and Patricia were caught "borrowing" toilet paper from the convent school. Their mother was mortified and made them confess to the nuns and the priest, who let them off with an Our Father, a Hail Mary, and a Glory Be. Knowing they wouldn't see toilet paper again till they went back to school, they had to rough it. They came up with a brilliant plan, though, that would also solve one of their father's more vexing problems—and he wouldn't get mad at them.

It involved the boxes that came early every summer with visiting Boston relatives. There were always a few surprises for each one in the family, and they all had turns rooting through them, except for their father, who didn't have to look at all. He knew there was always a big box just for him, holding dozens of spotless, starched, white shirts. How he hated them!

He inherited the generational memory that resented those relatives who, for a hundred years at least, ran away from the Island to live in The States. Turncoats, all of them, and he saw the cast-off shirts as a deliberate boast of their citified success. He despised the shirts all the more when they required cufflinks. He wore them, though, for every dirty job he could think of. In no time at all they were stained from grass, mud, cowshit, horse lather, axle grease and all kinds of crop dust. He had piles of shirts to play with.

Mary and Patricia took away all of the white shirts that came in the boxes that same summer. With scissors, knives, and teeth, they cut off the cuffs and collars. Soon there were towers of three-inch square cotton swatches that were exclusive to the three girls. Since it was their job to empty the chamber pots on the manure pile, their little enterprise was undiscovered for a long time, though their father had his suspicions when he noticed little flags waving in the breeze over a frozen manure pile.

Credit must be given to Mary, who, inspired by the success with the shirts, devised an ingenious system of gift-giving at Christmas. Santa or not, there were few gifts under their tree. She explained the plan to the other two banshees, and they started their "shopping" after the Boston boxes had been rooted through. Throughout the fall, the girls swiped favourite things from each other. These treasures would be well-hidden, but given back to each other at Christmas. The next year, their older siblings noticed things disappearing, and blamed each other for taking them. Then, under the Christmas tree, as if by magic, brothers would receive lost combs, shaving brushes, and mates of odd socks, all lovingly wrapped in brown paper. Older sisters found missing bras, garter belts, beads, and stockings inside pretty purses made from wallpaper remnants. After that Christmas, all the siblings played the game. It was not about what was stolen or by whom. The thrill was getting something back and finding out who it was from.

The following summer when the boxes came, Momma Martha and Nanny Josie reached for the same lily-white corset at the same time. Nanny Josie won the tug-of-war and triumphantly declared. "It's way too small for you, Martha!" The hurt on their mother's face changed everything for the little girls. Shortly after that, the corset went missing from Nanny Josie's dresser drawer. She searched the house, especially among her daughter-in-law's clothes. The girls hid it well. Their father thought the old dog must've taken it for the bones.

The mystery was solved on Christmas morning. That corset was the best gift under the tree that year. It was wrapped in a nearly new red bib apron with white lace trim, and bow-tied by the straps. The carefully printed tag read "To Martha from Josie." Martha opened her gift, cried in gratitude, and smiled at her mother-in-law, who tightly smiled back. Behind that smile, Josie was raging. It couldn't be helped, some giggles got loose. Josie shot a look that went round the room and stopped at the little girls hiding behind their father. The jig was up. So was Martha, to put on her corset.

The rest of the day was full of play and good humour, sleigh rides, and a magnificent turkey dinner. Later that evening, everyone gathered around the organ and sang into the night. The little girls lay asleep on a couch, curled up like little kittens. Nanny Josie put a blanket over them and kissed each sweaty head.

Oh, Christmas Tree

❄ Carolyn Charron ❄

Every winter I dreamed of cash. Stacks of coins, piles of bills. Mom said we weren't poor, but we sure weren't rich. I didn't mind wearing hand-me-downs or not having all the latest toys. But there was something I wanted desperately—a real Christmas tree with its appealing aroma, dropping needles and leaving my hands sticky with sap. But they were expensive, ten whole dollars.

"Mom, please. Let's buy a tree this year!" My little sister Lori Beth and I started our yearly begging early in November.

"Joanie, I've told you, we can't afford it. Or would you rather I not buy Christmas presents this year?"

For a moment, I seriously considered her suggestion. Presents or a real Christmas tree—it was a tough choice. Lori Beth said "no" right away and then she poked me, shaking her head, until I agreed.

I wanted presents. I really did. But I wanted a proper Christmas tree, too. I loved trees. Climbing them, sitting in them, listening to them whisper in the wind. I loved watching for that faint green haze in the spring when you saw them at a distance. Seeing their leaves change colour in the autumn.

But the thing I treasured most about trees was their smell, especially evergreens. I could roll around in that fragrance and live there. My favourite hiding place was underneath the fir trees behind our house. A few of them had branches that dipped down to the ground and made little aromatic caves.

I wanted that smell in my living room.

We had this plastic Christmas tree that we dragged out every year. Not only was it artificial, it was so short even my twelve-year-old brother was taller. Every year it seemed smaller and more fake.

I didn't hate it. It was better than no tree at all, but I wanted a living tree, its scent filling the house, and I knew Lori Beth felt exactly the same.

We didn't have a whole lot of money between the two of us, so we tried to get our older brother and sisters, Marshall, Shirley, and

Marion, to chip in. Marshall laughed when we asked him and walked away, shaking his head. He didn't care about having a real Christmas tree.

Marion pulled out her wallet, but Shirley said Mom wouldn't like having needles on the living room carpet so she wasn't going to help us. Marion immediately agreed with Shirley and put her wallet away. I stuck my tongue out at Shirley for changing Marion's mind.

There was no way that we were going to earn enough money in time. Mom wouldn't let me get a job—she kept saying ten was too young—and we didn't get an allowance. So we had to find a tree that we wouldn't have to pay for. The first place we looked was the gully.

The gully was this huge valley right behind our house. We lived on the outskirts of a big city and our house backed onto a wild area. There were hills and a creek and a pond and, most importantly for us, evergreen trees. Lots and lots of them.

On the first Saturday in December we started our search, tramping around the gully looking at trees. It had to be the right shape and size. And have the right odour. Pine trees just didn't smell Christmassy enough so it had to be a fir. My nose was sticky with sap from sniffing so many trees and Lori Beth had started to complain about being cold when I finally saw it at the bottom of the hill below our house.

It was a perfect bushy green triangle. Full branches for hanging ornaments on. Tall enough that Dad would need a ladder to put the star on top. It was a fir and I crossed my fingers that it would pass the final test. The sniff test.

The needles tickled my nose as I breathed in. Its fragrance was amazing, Christmassy and woody and green. I could see it in our living room, sparkly with ornaments and lights.

"Let's get the saw," I said.

We ran back up the hill and snuck quietly into Dad's workshop to borrow a saw. I carried it carefully, since Dad was always drumming his "safety first" lecture into us.

Then we got to work cutting down our tree. It was a lot harder than it looked. I sawed and sawed and when I stopped because my arms were tired, I looked and couldn't believe how little I'd done. It was barely a scratch.

"I'll do some cutting, too," Lori Beth said.

"You're too little." She was only eight. I was two whole years older and much stronger.

"Am not. It's my tree, too." She held out her hand and waited. Her little lip was stuck out. She was very stubborn so I gave her the saw. I needed to catch my breath anyway.

She sawed and sawed, huffing and puffing. We could see sawdust on the ground now. But we had a long way to go. I put my arms around the trunk as best as I could through the branches but I could barely touch my hands together on the other side. Maybe it was too big? I shook my head—this was my tree now. It was coming home with me.

We spent the rest of the afternoon sawing at that fir tree. By the time Mom called us up the hill to supper, we were no more than halfway through the trunk. The next day was Sunday and we couldn't do anything until after we got home from church and then had lunch. We rushed down the gully as soon as Mom let us leave the table.

Our pile of sawdust got bigger. We were tired and sweaty, our arms hurt, and our hands were covered with blisters. Despite the cold air, we had to take off our coats. By the time it was too dark to see, we had cut through almost the whole trunk. I grinned at Lori Beth and she grinned back as we climbed up the hill to our house. We'd be bringing our tree home tomorrow for sure.

Neither of us had any problem falling asleep that night, we were so tired. I could smell fir trees in my dreams. The next day at school I had a hard time picking up my pencil, much less writing anything, my arms hurt so much. At lunch I sat leaning against the side of the school and Lori Beth came up to join me.

"Joanie, my arms hurt." She had tears in her eyes.

"Yeah, mine, too. But it'll be worth it, right?" I wasn't so sure anymore, and I wanted to cry, too. "Maybe we should finish tomorrow? Give our arms a rest? I don't know how I'm going to drag a tree up that hill when I can't even pick up a pencil."

Lori Beth nodded at me. She looked relieved.

At supper that night, Mom asked Dad to bring our plastic tree up from the basement and hose the dust off before we decorated it. Lori Beth and I looked at each other. We had to get our tree right away. No matter how much our arms hurt. But Mom wouldn't let us leave the house after supper. She said it was too dark.

The next day my arms felt a little better. They were still painful but I ignored it. The time passed so slowly at school that I was sure the clocks were actually going backward. I was desperate to get our tree before Dad took out that horrible fake one.

At last the bell rang. We ran all the way home to borrow Dad's saw again. This time Lori Beth dragged the wagon with us. We were determined to bring our tree home.

We were so sore that it was all we could do to keep the saw moving. My arms got tired much faster and Lori Beth couldn't work for more than a couple of minutes at a time.

"Joanie! Lori Beth! Time to come up for supper!"

I was under the tree and sawing as hard as I could when Mom called. I sawed faster.

CRACK!

Lori Beth screamed.

The end of the trunk went flying past my face and the tree came crashing down.

I scrambled to my feet and looked all around. "Lori Beth?" I couldn't see her anywhere. My heart was pounding like crazy before I finally heard her.

"Under here." Her voice was muffled but at least she wasn't dead.

I could see a bit of Lori Beth's dark blue coat under our tree, but the thick green branches hid the rest of her. "Are you okay?"

"I can't move."

I pushed and shoved at the tree, the smell of cut wood and sticky sap all around me until finally the tree rolled to the side and off my little sister. I looked for blood but didn't see any. Lori Beth sat up, shaking her head.

"Ow. That wasn't much fun." She had a few scratches on her face and her coat was dirty, but she was okay. Mom would have killed me if I'd hurt my little sister.

Now that the tree was lying down, I could see there was no way we were getting it in the wagon. It was taller than Marshall. Taller than Dad. Way bigger than our wagon. We'd need four of them to carry it.

"Let's put the cut end in the wagon. You pull and I'll lift this end," I said.

It was hard to lift the end of the tree. My fingers and coat sleeves were gummy with sap and the needles poked into me everywhere. But it worked, kind of. At least part of the tree was in the wagon.

"Joanie! Lori Beth! I said it was time to come up!" Mom sounded mad and we heard our back door slam shut.

"Coming, Mom!" Lori Beth and I looked at each other. We were going to need help to bring it up. But we couldn't leave our tree—it could get stolen.

I turned to my sister. "You ask Dad to help us. He'll listen to you."

"Well, if you didn't get into trouble all the time, he'd listen to you, too."

I made a face at her, and we trudged up the hill. I left the saw by the back door so Mom wouldn't see it, then I followed Lori Beth into the warm kitchen. Mom took one look at us, covered in dirt and leaves, and sighed.

"What have you been up to now?"

"We got a Christmas tree! Dad needs to help us bring it up." Lori Beth said, all excited.

"A Christmas tree? Where on earth did you find a Christmas tree?" Mom's mouth got all thin, like it did when she was about to start shouting. "Oh, no. You... you didn't. Please, tell me you didn't chop down a tree in the gully."

"Well, kind of. But we can't bring it up, it's too heavy," Lori Beth answered after looking at me.

This was not going the way I'd expected. I thought Mom would be excited and happy. She didn't look very happy.

"Arthur!" Mom yelled.

Dad came into the kitchen. "Supper's ready? Hiya, Joanie, Lori Beth." He smiled and then looked closer at us and back to Mom again. "What happened?"

"Your daughters cut down a Christmas tree. By themselves. In the gully."

I had a sick feeling in my stomach.

"You borrowed my axe? I've told you kids not to touch my tools. Hand it over."

Great. Now Dad was mad at us, too. I retrieved the saw we'd used and handed it to him. He held it for a moment, showed it to Mom, and said, "This... is what you used to cut down a tree?"

I looked at Lori Beth. She looked as confused as I felt. "Yeah. It's a saw, isn't it? I took the smallest one so we wouldn't cut ourselves."

"Joanie... Joanie, this is a hacksaw. It's for cutting little pipes. Not a tree." He started to laugh, and then Mom did, too.

"It's not funny!" I shouted, "I didn't know!"

"Is that why it took so long?" Lori Beth whispered to me. I shrugged.

Dad wiped his eyes, "Yes, it would have taken very little time with a different saw. How long were you cutting for?"

"Since Saturday morning."

Dad and Mom stared at each other for a long moment, then they started laughing again.

Marshall came into the kitchen. "What's so funny?"

Dad shook his head, unable to speak. Mom gasped for breath and finally said, "Joanie, show Dad where the tree is. Take Marshall, too. Since you cut it down, the least we can do is use it." She turned to the stove, still laughing.

I took Dad and Marshall back to our tree. The top of the fir lay on the ground and its raggedly cut trunk hovered over the wagon.

"Wow. That's a big tree! I can't believe you cut this down with a hacksaw." Dad turned to Marshall, "Go to my workshop and get me a saw. The big one with the wooden handle. Be careful with it."

"Sure, Dad." Marshall took off up the hill.

Dad and I were quiet, waiting for Marshall. By the time we heard him crashing his way back through the bushes, I was feeling kind of silly. How come I hadn't known what kind of saw to use?

As if he'd read my mind, Dad said, "Joanie, if you want to learn about my tools, come and ask me. I'll teach you. Don't just take them. You could get hurt."

"All right, Dad." I made up my mind to ask him what all his tools were for. I didn't want to look stupid again. I smiled at Dad although I still hadn't entirely forgiven him and Mom for laughing at me.

Marshall skidded to a halt in front of us and handed Dad the saw. It was a lot different than the tiny one I'd borrowed. Dad showed me the teeth. Huge and scary-looking. The hacksaw had tiny teeth on a small blade less than a foot long. This saw was longer than my arm and the teeth bigger than the teeth in my mouth!

Dad paced off the height of the tree. "Three, six, nine, twelve, fifteen, eighteen feet. You sure picked a big one!" He laughed. "Now our ceilings are almost twelve feet high so ten feet is good. That'll give us plenty of space to put the star. So we'll cut the end off, right about here."

It took him only a few minutes to saw through that tree trunk. I couldn't believe it. Then he cut off branches from the leftover bit and passed them to me. "No sense wasting these. Your mom will show you how to make a wreath for the door."

I buried my nose in the branches and sniffed. Marshall and Dad lifted the tree and carried it up the hill. We left it leaning against the house and went inside for supper.

The next day, Dad made a little wooden frame that he nailed to the bottom of the tree trunk and then he set the whole thing into a big bucket of water in the living room. Even before we decorated our tree, it looked wonderful.

I couldn't stop smiling every time I looked at my tree in the living room. It was the best-smelling Christmas ever.

Christmas Comes to Sable Island

❄   Don Scott   ❄

In August of 1960, I went to Sable Island to work on a weather station and spend the following winter there. My job, shared with two other operators, was to carry out upper air weather observations twice each day, using radio transmitters sent aloft on huge balloons. At twenty, I was the youngest of the ten people working on the island that year and this was my first Christmas away from home. In spite of that, I do not remember much about that day. It was just another working day for us as we were on duty seven days a week, in all seasons. What I do remember vividly is the delivery of the Christmas presents.

Our supplies and mail came by boat, three or four times a year. The last scheduled delivery had been in mid-September when we received our winter supply of fuel and food, including the Christmas turkey. Between boats, the occasional plane would come in with mail or equipment. The landing strip for these flights was the beach. This was not suitable for landing in the winter, so our Christmas delivery was going to be an air drop. The plane would fly over at a low altitude and slow speed and drop our mail and gifts.

Our friends and families had all been warned that any Christmas mailings should be sent before the beginning of December. These would be held in Dartmouth until delivery day. We were told that the delivery was scheduled for a couple of weeks before December 25, depending on the availability of a plane and suitable weather conditions.

The appointed day arrived with cloud and a low ceiling, but we received a message that the flight was coming as scheduled. The drop zone was to be in a valley about half a mile from our station. We finished up our morning balloon flight and were all up on the hill, out of harm's way at the appointed time. The DC3 came in from the west, down out of the clouds, and flew over at what would have been treetop level had there been any trees. Just as it passed opposite where we were standing, a door opened and several big grey mailbags were dropped. The plane circled around, made another run, and several more bags came down. Seeing it continue on and disappear up into the clouds once again emphasized for me the isolation. We knew then that, barring an emergency, this would be the last flight before spring.

Back at the station, the mail was sorted and the packages distributed. Two items among my packages were blueberry jam and a large box of cookies. The jam was wrapped in a plastic bag. My initial thought was that my mother had been very clever in packing the jam in a plastic bag to avoid breakage. Upon closer examination, I realized the jam had been in a bottle that had been so badly smashed, that without the metal lid, it would have been hard to tell it had been in a bottle at all.

The cookies were an old family recipe called "German Spies." They were always decorated with three large sticky raisins, positioned to look like eyes and a nose. At one time during the war, my grandmother had served them to a visitor who said,

"Look, German spies," and that became their name. The biggest pieces of the cookies that remained after the drop were the portions stuck to the raisins. The rest of the cookies were dust.

My coworker, Len, fared better than I did. His mother had sent him a bottle of rum. She had packed it inside a bread loaf. The bread had dried out in transit and the impact had reduced it to crumbs. The rum, however, survived the drop.

Say Cadillac!

❄   Louise Burley   ❄

New Orleans is a long way from Prince Edward Island. But my son Liam and his new wife Emma were living there and invited my husband Bill and me and our younger son Martin to spend the Christmas holiday with them. This was only a year-and-a-half after hurricane Katrina had smashed New Orleans to smithereens. What would we discover? I find flying terrifying at the best of times. On this flight we came into New Orleans on the tail of a storm. We descended, bucking and lurching like a white water raft, with stabbing ear pain for me, and the pilot warning us not just to fasten our seat belts, but to fasten them tightly as we were encountering "severe turbulence."

Even a year-and-a-half later, the wreckage of Katrina was still obvious everywhere—smashed roofs and caved-in porches. What people refer to as "the storm" seems mainly to have fossilized the poverty that was already there, the endless sweep of tiny dilapidated houses that surround the city like a shabby moth-eaten cloak. The whole city is below sea level, a big bowl waiting for water to come rushing in. How wide the Mississippi River is there, and Lake Pontchartrain is huge, with that long low bridge stretching twenty-four miles across its expanse. Katrina must have licked her lips when she saw New Orleans.

Though it was raining the first few days we were there, and though it was winter, I felt the sleepy heat of the deep South, not as a temperature but as an atmosphere. There was that gap between the surface and what's underneath, which I associate with the south: a mixture of violence and gentility. On the highway into the city a billboard advertised a gun show and was positioned just above a sign for "The Nativity Story": Mary and Joseph bent over baby Jesus. Palm trees lined the streets, and massive live oaks with their gnarled roots and tangled branches conjured the wilderness of Louisiana's past.

In Liam and Emma's neighbourhood people sat on their stoops and hollered across the torn-up streets to each other. Broken-down neighbourhoods butted up against the plantation-style grandeur of St. Charles Street where you could look through the glass panes of a giant door and see a sweeping Scarlet O'Hara staircase. The French Quarter streamed with people, and jazz trumpets blared from bars the size of small kitchens. Preparations that started last summer for February's Mardi Gras were now intensifying. It seemed the "Big Easy" was getting back on her feet.

One night all five of us went to a late-night bar called "The Half Moon." The floor was part dirt, part concrete. Liam and Bill partnered against Emma and Martin for pool while I watched. A boisterous group of people were having their Christmas party at a nearby table and welcomed us to share their feast. But Emma had to get up early for work the next morning, so we smilingly declined.

We were saying any old thing to each other as we left the bar, when out of the alley staggered a man in a shabby sports jacket, who pompously bowed before us and announced, "I'm a professional!" We stopped as he approached, and he showed us that he had a Polaroid camera. He told us he would take our picture for three dollars. It seemed pretty fishy—just some drunk from the alley looking for a buck, so we started to move away, but eighteen-year-old Martin, always generous, dug in his pockets and came up with a dollar and change.

"Come on now, pony up," said the professional to the rest of us, growing eager when he saw Martin's gesture. "You won't regret it. I'll make y'all look *great!*" Someone else found a couple quarters.

"See that Cadillac there?" He pointed to a beat-up old heap that had run aground in the alley he had emerged from. "That's my ride. Yessir, I'm a professional photographer. Tell y'all what. I'll take y'all's picture for $2.50." He looked at me, his eyes bleary. "You's the mother, aint you." It was a statement, not a question. "We all come from mothers," he said reverently, as though I were the Madonna herself. To the others he said, "You gotta respect your mother, y'all!"

I asked him if he was going to spend Christmas with his mother. "Maybe not," he said, momentarily sober, almost sad. "But I'll phone her."

"Now, is everybody ready?"

We nodded. Humour the guy, what the heck.

"Say *Cadillac*!" he commanded.

"Cadillac!" we shouted, and then laughed. He clicked the camera. Flash!

When we went to hand him our change, he shook his head, rocking unsteadily.

"Not until I know you're satisfied."

We dutifully examined the picture until it swam into focus and, lo and behold, there we all were, surprised into something strangely joyous. The "professional" then took our change and stumbled off, dropping his camera in the street with a clatter. Had he noticed the camera fall? Would he come back for it? Or was his mission accomplished? He wandered off into the dark and did not turn back.

We all had the funny feeling that something wondrous had just happened. The "professional" had made ordinary us look great, our best selves, as though the one who loved us most had held up a mirror. As though the shabby man was not what he appeared to be.

Christmas morning arrived in a grainy mist. The day before, we had decided to go to a small Baptist church just outside New Orleans, with Liam and Emma's neighbour, Miss Rose. Liam and Emma's car was in the garage; our only other transportation was the tiny hatchback Bill and I had rented. Liam drove. Miss Rose sat in the front, dressed impeccably, head held high. Emma, Bill, and I squished into the back seat, our hip and rib bones jamming into each other, while tall skinny Martin folded himself like an accordion and climbed in through the hatchback.

At the little clapboard church, with its broken step and peeling paint, we were conspicuously white. We were also conspicuously tall. My sons, Liam and Martin, are over six feet and I'm pretty near that myself. We sat up close to the front with Miss Rose, stern and inscrutable, at the far end of the pew. We were a little uneasy but ready to listen. The deacon was the first to get up. A graceful, elderly man in a dove-grey suit, he welcomed "our visitors" with a slight nod in our direction, then bowed his head and said, "Dear Lord, thank you for your touch on my face this morning and thank you for letting me wake up in my right mind."

Now the choir came step-step-stepping down the aisle, giving last-minute tugs to their robes, and singing cheerfully. The preacher came to the pulpit in a suit that flashed purple and blue and silver. He looked around at the small congregation as though searching for someone. Then, in spite of our eager smiles, he said sharply, "Ain't your birthday!" All of his teeth, at least the ones I could see, were gold, so that when he smiled he seemed as fierce and unpredictable as a pirate.

No, it was not our birthday. Yet sitting in that little church on the outskirts of a city drowned almost to extinction, I could see that a special birthday was still possible. There were, after all, angels in the alleyways, and shepherds with gold teeth, and a ragtag choir rocking side-to-side singing "Joy to the World."

Beht-le-hem

❊ Renée Blanchette ❊

She looked at his back as he led the delicate way through mud hillocks and gouges in the earth. Hands deep in the pockets of an old army jacket, shoulders slumped slightly, his neck bent in thought, he knew the way by heart and foot. He had walked it many times, most often late at night. This was only her third time.

Earlier they had disembarked at the last bus stop at Avenue de la Paix but there was a considerable way yet to walk. They left the concrete slab apartments behind them and turned toward a desolate midwinter field of long grass, leafless trees, and a deep-cut ravine. Darkness shrouded the spaces beyond the last haloed streetlights and there was an orange glow on the horizon. Charged with the burden of history, the air was damp and cool. It was her turn to hold the groceries they had bought and the thin plastic handles bit into her fingers. He had a slender bottle of wine in one of his pockets. It was Christmas Eve.

Her thoughts ran to the Second World War scenes she had seen in film, replete with the imaginary boom of artillery in the distance and the squelching of their boots. She put in the dotted line of a rifle slung over his shoulder, and his resigned slouch, she thought, was a measure of his battle fatigue. It was comforting to have a destination even if distant, and although it had been a long day of wandering in La Centre Ville, and her legs felt wooden and mechanical, she was prepared to follow as far as need be. He was thin, rueful and very, very kind.

Edging the field, they could make out the cement edifice in the fog that he called home. Bunker-like and unadorned, it was a functional collection of tiny apartments in the outskirts of Besançon, France, suitable for student life. With care, they had purchased a few items at the huge supermarket a few kilometres away. It would be an elegant but simple meal, prepared by candlelight likely, as the electricity had been cut off days ago.

Key in the lock and the heavy metal door swung on hinges as though into a prison. To the immediate left was a second door which led into a charming bathroom kitchenette ensemble, walls a yellow grey paper over cement, including a toilet, small shower and sink, propane cook stove, and tiny fridge. Suddenly, he straightened his back, leaned into his heels, knees bent, and pealed with laughter.

"What the hell are you doing?" he said with amusement and surprise, hands in open supplication.

His roommate, Ali, was sitting on the toilet, seat down. He was fully dressed in pale shirt and dark, tightly belted pants as though for a sunny game of backgammon. She could just see him there, in the light from the hallway, small and wedge-shaped, his stomach and hips wider than need be. As he leaned forward, his eyebrows knitted. They appeared to her peaked in the middle like a black letter M, squashed down to cover the entire width of his brow. His expression showed deep concentration and piety.

Large lips pouting seriously, he said in French, no doubt for her benefit, "I like to sit in the dark and contemplate obscurity."

This brought hoots of laughter from the host, his friend, and a small smirk from her.

"Move out, we are going to make a meal here," Kamal ordered and Ali slumped out into the bedsitting area to wait for his dinner and continue his quiet ruminations.

"*Falaheen*," Kamal whispered to her in Arabic as they removed damp coats and boots and manoeuvred their way into the tiny space to put away the food.

"Country bumpkin," was how she chose to translate "peasant." Both men were Muslims, but Kamal was from an upper-middle-class family in Damascus and Ali from a small village in the south of Lebanon.

They were down on their luck but Ali more so due to a diminished capacity with human relations, and Kamal felt sorry for him. They were students of translation. Ali had the tenacity of a bulldog with the details of syntax and gender subtleties, but had been kicked out of his residence for some reason and Kamal had taken him in. Then the money from his brother in Dubai had dried up suddenly and now it seemed that Kamal, so obviously the captain, might, too, go down with the ship.

He had seen action in southern Lebanon, first as a pilot and then, strangely, back for more in the infantry, and he had the war wounds and nightmares to prove it: two small bullet holes in his back and slightly damaged vision.

They had first met at a party, of course, she passing through to visit a friend for the holiday season, and he for the free wine and food. She was on a post-university tour of Europe, from the east coast of Canada. On another occasion they met by accident in the dark, stone-arched student café. By that time his war stories, loosened by three or four French beers, had a warm grip on her naïve heart. She had felt compelled to listen and to hang out, maybe to help. It was her embarrassment that had his attention. She was so apologetic about having no idea where Syria was, and confessed to only a vague idea where Lebanon might be, which came from quick exchanges with immigrants in corner stores where she was from. Her polite chagrin completely disarmed him, being all too used to the brash, honest, but often racist French. Her friend had suddenly decided to go skiing for Christmas and she was unhappy about staying at the hostel alone so he had invited her to his place. They had spent the better part of a week together, both not sure what would happen next.

The meal consisted of charcuterie, minus the pork, of course. Kamal drew the line there, enlightening her with details about the immorality of raising pigs in desert countries and pork's similarity to human flesh. Nose wrinkling in disgust, she chose duck paté, cheese, and bread and they settled on two dozen frozen escargots. They were sold in large trays and were pleasantly inexpensive. These they slurped down with great gusto while Ali picked and minced his way through the meal and placed his pudgy hand over his glass whenever she offered the Cote du Rhône. She had squirreled away a second bottle of red, some twelve francs worth of Christmas fun, and said happily, "All the more for us!" Ali shook his head slowly but good-naturedly, muttering in Arabic that his friend was most assuredly going to hell.

Later, stretched out on the two couches in the bed-sitting room, they rested full bellies. The humidity from cooking had steamed up the large window on the east wall, and their eyes, accustomed to the light from the street and candles, could see each other's shadowed faces well enough. Ferouz singing Christmas carols on an ancient cassette player and Ali intoning phrases from the Koran about Joseph and Mary in Bethlehem (*Beht-le-hem* or house of the Butcher, in Arabic, and sounding quite a bit like a clearing of the throat). Soft chuckles and insults came from Kamal's drowsy figure.

She passed out presents.

A small package of socks for Kamal and writing paper for Ali.

Ali put his hand on his heart and frowned with pleasure. "Thank you, sister. *Shoucran. Shoucran.*"

Sisters and brothers. They referred to each other so casually like a clan of familiar faces. A thin trace of genes from everyone leading back to the same place.

A few days before, an older man had come to the door while Ali was out and Kamal invited him in to sit. He had steel grey hair and large hands and sat with his long legs bent at a sharp angle in the low chair and his hat in his hands between his knees. He was an Algerian from down the hall, *un pied noir,* as some French were known to call them, and he was illiterate. While they waited for Ali, Kamal took out pen and paper and began to write down the old man's news to family back home.

He had the brown eyes of a golden retriever and such potential strength wrapped in soft humility. He was grateful and said so many times. The sound of hot sweet tea pouring into glass tumblers, its red-gold glow so warming.

When Ali arrived they had already written two pages and Kamal blustered about how Ali would do a better job. "*La, la!*" Kamal insisted in Arabic. "No, no! You must stay and write it again with him." She had been admiring the straight lines of perfect curlicues from right to left. He had spent some time teaching her the alphabet. If moon snails could write they would write like that, she'd thought. He had just crumpled it up and thrown it in the dustbin.

"Why would you make Ali do it all over again? What a waste of time! Yours was perfectly good," she said to him later in the kitchen.

He shrugged as though she could not possibly understand but smiled at her and said with a kind of sadness, "I knew he was lonely and didn't want to go. Why send him away so soon?"

We are not like that back home, she thought. The sooner gone the better, she realized, that meant more time to spend alone or with one's own family, one's own books. She felt a strange awe.

"Ssshhhh! It's midnight!" one of them whispered. For some reason they all felt compelled to look outside into the black night. She cleared the steam from the window below the silver rope of tinsel she had childishly draped from the curtain rod. The three of them kneeling on the couch, the warmth of their shoulders barely perceptible, they looked out at the moon and lines of charcoal trees trimming the hills beyond. Each of them contemplating, as drops of water chose their paths down the window to the moldy sill. Briefly, they were as one, their eyes searching for meaning in the dark. Breath fogging up the window, by turns they used their hands to clear away the mist, wanting to improve their vision, wanting to see more.

a christmas carol in afghanistan 2001

❄   Lee Ellen Pottie   ❄

A country crooner sings the sentimental tune,
another in the long list of songsters
reminding me this Christmas Eve of

the night when columns of combative boys
sang *Stille Nacht* across   no-man's-land, shook
hands, played a little ball, brief

brothers until midnight when shooting
and strafing started again. Who
will write this war's holy-night song if

no one touches, if Christmas is just a day
when retailers, with a twelve-hour respite,
add up their profits while the no-person's land

is in the sky, rockets launching
and bombers desperate to flatten
mountains, not move them?

At War

❄ Sarah Glassford ❄

Early November, 1917. Jean MacLaughlan shivered under her heavy woollen coat, adjusted the parcels in her arms in order to free one hand, and rapped sharply on the wooden door of the Henley farmhouse. Beside her, the afternoon light hit the glass of the front-room window at such an angle as to transform it into a mirror. Jean shifted her weight onto her other foot, caught sight of her own reflection, and frowned. There didn't used to be so much grey in the dark hair peeping out from under her hat, or so many creases around her eyes and across her forehead. Worry and winter winds did nothing to improve a forty-two-year-old woman's appearance.

The door swung open just enough to reveal the large eyes and shy smile of Louise Henley, age six.

"Hello," said the girl. She did not appear inclined to open the door further.

"Hello, Louise. I think you know my daughter, Miss MacLaughlan," said Jean kindly. "She's the teacher at Silver Bay School."

Louise's eyes lit up in recognition. She opened the door a few inches wider.

"I've come to pack Christmas boxes for our soldier boys," said Jean, failing to suppress another shiver as the Island wind whipped around a corner of the verandah and hit her full-force. "Do you think I could come in?"

Louise nodded and began to pull the door open when, behind her, a woman's voice called out in annoyance, "Where is that draught coming from?"

Anne Henley bustled over to the door to see what her youngest child was doing. Her figure suited her personality: everything larger than life.

"Oh my goodness, Jean MacLaughlan—come in out of the cold this instant. Louise Henley, you haven't got the sense God gave a mouse. What are you thinking, leaving Mrs. MacLaughlan out on the porch like this? Come in, come in!"

Louise was unceremoniously pushed aside, and Jean pulled into the front hall, relieved of her coat, scarf, hat, and parcels, then bundled down a hallway hung with needlework samplers of indeterminate age. Anne Henley, a farmwife in her mid-forties like Jean, kept up a steady stream of chatter.

"You wouldn't think it by the way she behaves sometimes, but my Louise is a bright girl, and she's taken to your May like butter on bread. Every day after school, I swear to you, it's 'Miss MacLaughlan this, Miss MacLaughlan that.' I think it's just splendid of May to have taken the position. It takes a firm hand to keep the pupils in order, and I sometimes wonder how a little slip of a girl like that can possibly keep the children in line, but she seems to be doing quite well—but, of course, you would know that, wouldn't you? I expect you're glad to have her back home again after her course at Prince of Wales College. A year in Charlottetown might turn some girls' heads, but I can't see that it's done your May any harm."

Jean inhaled and exhaled slowly—the best way she knew to restrain her annoyance at her neighbours' tendency to judge her daughter's morals and manners.

The two women found the kitchen bright, warm, and bristling with activity. Six other women bustled about setting piles of chocolate, chewing gum, hand-knit socks, and other small home comforts along the length of the wide, well-worn wooden tabletop, and on the adjacent sideboard.

"Mrs. MacLaughlan," said a diminutive wrinkled woman whose head was crowned with snow-white hair, "we thought you might not make the trip in this weather. It's a long walk from your place."

"Hello Mrs. Leggatt," said Jean. "I would have walked twice as far, if necessary, but it's only a few miles when I cut across the fields."

"Still, it can't be pleasant in this wind," said Mrs. Leggatt. "Big Cory and Ella McLeod kindly brought me in their wagon." She pointed toward the kitchen doorway. "Big Cory's in the front room with Dan Henley, keeping out of the way."

Jean looked in the direction of the older woman's hand and caught sight of her parcels, which Anne Henley had placed on the sideboard.

"I've brought the cigarettes with me," she said to no one in particular.

"Excellent," said Hannah Williams, a well-dressed doctor's wife in her early thirties with a stunning head of glossy black hair. "I knew we could count on you, Mrs. MacLaughlan." Her voice took on an official tone as she turned to address a slimmer, bespectacled version of herself standing beside her. "Are we ready to begin, Madam Secretary?"

Adelaide Arsenault, spinster, church organist, and younger sister of Hannah Williams, stood poised with pen and minute book in hand. "All present and correct, Madam President."

"Then I hereby call the third annual Silver Bay Women's Institute Christmas parcel-packing meeting to order. I propose we dispense with the usual formalities and get right down to work. Let's have members with sons or brothers in France pack their boxes, and divide the rest of the local boys equally amongst the group. All in favour?"

"Aye," chorused seven female voices.

"Let the packing begin," said the President.

"I know Mrs. Leggatt thinks she's a bit much with her 'Madam Secretary' and such, but I always think Mrs. Williams adds a certain dignity to our W.I. meetings, don't you?" whispered Ella McLeod, a long curl of her unruly red hair slipping out from its pins and falling across her forehead as she passed Jean a box. She tucked the curl up again with a practised hand, scarcely registering that she did so. "We're lucky to have someone so capable to lead the Institute."

Jean caught Ella's eye. "No one would agree with you more than 'Madam President' herself."

Ella playfully slapped her friend's hand. "Behave yourself."

Jean smirked and began moving from pile to pile around the room, fitting the various comforts into her box like a jigsaw puzzle. Her thoughts drifted.

I wonder if this box will actually reach Tom Simpson in France? They say German U-boats sink so many ships as they cross the ocean. Will he be glad to get it? The boys all say they want cigarettes and socks and such, but maybe they're just indulging us. Wouldn't—

"Jean?" It was Ella McLeod again, her eyes twinkling. "Jean?"

"I'm sorry, Ella, I was thinking about the war."

The sparkle left Ella's eyes, and she placed a supportive hand on the small of Jean's back. "I just wanted to tell you that when you pack Andrew's box, I have a special fruit cake set aside for him. No raisins."

"How sweet of you to remember."

"He was in my Sunday School class for several years, as a boy—do you remember? I can still hear him saying, as we talked about the

Last Supper, 'If there were raisins in anything, I sure wouldn't eat a bite.' He must have been seven or eight at the time."

"Yes, that sounds like my Andrew," admitted Jean, amused. "Thank you for this. He'll be so pleased when he receives it."

"I'm glad you think so. I often think of the little boys who passed through Sunday School, now fighting in France. I know it's only fruit cake, but when I think of all they're doing without, over there…"

Jean squeezed her friend's hand, then moved away to finish filling Tom Simpson's box.

Across the table from Jean, Adelaide Arsenault and Hannah Williams began to quietly hum "The First Noël" together. The raven-haired sisters' voices, one a sweet alto and the other a richer mezzo-soprano, blended into a pleasing harmony.

"Good heavens, it's only the start of November," protested Anne Henley in her over-loud voice. She rearranged the contents of Chester Smith's box to make room for a pair of woollen socks. "It's too early for Christmas hymns."

"Nonsense," replied elderly Mrs. Leggatt in an unusually firm tone. "We're packing Christmas boxes, aren't we? We should sing carols as we work. That way we'll send a dose of good cheer and the spirit of home along with trinkets and cake."

Mrs. Henley looked duly chastised, and raised no further objections. Mrs. Leggatt added her tremulous soprano to the sisters' duet.

Jean had just finished packing her third and final box when Louise Henley timidly sidled up to her and tapped her hand to get her attention.

Looking down at the little girl, Jean noticed that Louise's brown eyes were round with concern. "What is it?" she asked, leaning down toward her.

Louise looked nervously around her at all the women bustling about in the kitchen, then whispered, "A lady's crying on the stairs."

Just then Anne Henley caught sight of her daughter. "Off with you! You'll only be in the way!" Louise scurried out of the kitchen.

Jean took a mental roll call of the women around her: Mrs. Henley, Miss Arsenault, Mrs. Leggatt, Mrs. McLeod, Mrs. Williams. Where was Mrs. Prince?

Jean slipped out of the kitchen and walked down the narrow hallway to the front of the house. Through the closed door to the front room she could hear Dan and Big Cory guffawing.

At the base of the staircase, she found the newest member of the Institute, Alma Prince, seated on a step. With her head leaned against the wall beside her, Alma's bright golden hair made the faded yellow roses on the wallpaper look shabby. Her eyes were closed, her pale cheeks wet.

Jean sat down on the step beside the young woman, the floor creaking underneath her feet as she did so. Alma opened her eyes and hastily wiped her face with a damp white handkerchief embroidered with a pink rose.

"I'm sorry," said Alma, once she had composed herself. "It's foolish of me, I know. Everyone else is so... *stoic*. But sometimes I just can't pretend everything's all right."

"No need to apologize. Were you thinking of your husband?"

Tears welled up once more in the young woman's eyes. "As I filled his box, I realized that the next hands to touch the contents would be his." She sniffled and dabbed at her eyes with the handkerchief. "I just wish *so much* that he was home again."

"I've forgotten how long you were married before he left. Was it a year?"

"Six months. I've known him most of my life, but..."

"But six months is not nearly long enough to be with a new husband."

Alma sighed. "We've been apart much longer than we lived together."

"Odd, isn't it," mused Jean, "how we can be so proud of a man for doing his duty, and yet resent him for it at the same time."

"This isn't the life I imagined, when I agreed to be his wife."

Jean rubbed Alma's back in slow, soothing strokes, the way she used to do with her children. "The war is hardest on young people, I think. Our May is seventeen this year, and she's so serious it almost breaks my heart. She should be going to dances and walking on the shore with her beaux under the moonlight, dreaming of her future. Instead, she's spent the past three years writing letters to her brother in France, and rolling bandages or collecting money for the Red Cross... even while she was studying for her teaching certificate. I'm proud of her, but it isn't what I wanted for her."

"Or for your son, I imagine," ventured Alma.

"No," agreed Jean, her voice heavy. "This is not what I wanted for my son."

They sat quietly together until they heard someone softly clear her throat nearby. Turning toward the sound, they saw Ella McLeod standing in the dim light of the hallway. The same stray lock of red hair tumbled across her forehead as she smiled in apology.

"I'm sorry to intrude. Some of the ladies wondered where you had gotten to."

"Not at all," Jean assured her friend. "We just needed a quiet moment, didn't we?"

Alma nodded.

Ella sighed. "It's all so trying, isn't it? We do our best to carry on, of course." Her voice wavered ever so slightly, and the two women on the staircase knew she was thinking of her nephew Cameron. The full extent of his injuries remained unclear, but the whole village knew he was lucky to be alive. "We're blessed to have one another to lean on."

"I agree," said Jean, pulling herself back to her feet with the aid of the smooth wooden banister beside her, "and the best cure for gloominess that I know of is to throw myself into a job that needs doing."

"My mother had twelve children," said Ella, tucking up her hair again as the three women walked down the hallway to the kitchen. "I remember my Aunt Caroline once asking her how she kept cheerful with so many to care for. 'When I feel like crying,' said my mother, 'I scrub hard, instead.'"

"I do like to keep my hands busy these days," Jean concurred. "I never much cared for knitting until Andrew enlisted. Now it's a wonderful distraction. It gives me such a firm sense of purpose."

Back in the kitchen Hannah Williams had produced brown paper, glue, and string with which to wrap the boxes. Mrs. Leggatt sat at the table, her white head bent over white paper labels onto which she copied names and regimental addresses, ready to be pasted onto the finished parcels.

Jean wasted no time in preparing two of her boxes: with her customary efficiency she double-checked their contents, sealed the boxes, wrapped them in brown paper, and attached the appropriate label to each one. When she came to Andrew's box she stopped. Cigarettes. Socks. Special raisin-free fruitcake. Chocolate. Chewing gum. Writing paper. Pencil. One by one she removed the items and held them each in her hands, imagining Andrew opening the parcel and examining its contents in much the same way.

Where will he be when he opens it? Will it arrive before Christmas?

Will he think of us celebrating without him, on the twenty-fifth of December?

And then the awful, unavoidable question: *Will he still be alive by then?*

Jean consciously redirected her thoughts to the task of assembling the parcel. Such speculation always led her to a dark place from which she found it difficult to return.

She placed each item back in the box and added a piece of plain white card upon which was written, in Miss Arsenault's elegant hand, "With fondest wishes this Christmas from the Silver Bay Women's Institute." On the back Jean had added, in her own distinctive handwriting, "Packed with love by Mother. Place set for you at Christmas dinner."

The latter phrase—a tradition by this point—had begun as a promise, scribbled at the bottom of early letters and packages sent to Andrew overseas. She hoped it would reassure her son that his safe and swift return remained her constant prayer.

"It's a topsy-turvy world, to be sure," said Mrs. Leggatt, apropos of nothing, as she finished copying out the last label.

"Why is that?" asked Alma Prince, affixing the label to her husband's parcel with a deliberate caressing motion.

"This war, of course," said the septuagenarian. "Queen Victoria's descendants—God rest her soul—fighting like a pack of school boys. Family should meet around the table at Christmas, not throw mortars at one another."

"I believe one shoots a mortar, rather than throwing it," corrected Miss Arsenault.

"Shoot, throw… they could be juggling them for all I know about it," replied Mrs. Leggatt, nonplussed. "But they certainly do make a mess with the things."

The other ladies smiled to themselves and finished their wrapping. When the last of the parcels had been addressed, the group sang "God Save Our Splendid Men" and adjourned for tea with the two men in the front room. The afternoon was growing late and the sun set early at this time of year, so no one stayed for a second cup.

As she walked home across a frozen field, retracing the path she had cut through the shin-deep snow earlier that day, Jean marvelled at the stillness of her surroundings. The first significant snowfall of the season always had that effect: it sat like a blanket over the

182

rolling hills of the farms, stretching down to the cold grey-blue water of the not-yet-frozen bay, cloaking the browns and greens and rust-reds of the earth with white and hushing the thousand-and-one sounds of autumn. A single-file line of spruce trees ahead of her were darkly silhouetted against the dusky-mauve sky. She sighed with contentment, thankful for the loveliness of home.

It's strange, she thought, *the idea of not being in Silver Bay. I might have followed my sister to Boston and gone into service, but then Adam proposed and a year-and-a-half later we were married with a baby. I knew my children might have to leave the Island someday. When Andrew was little he used to talk about following his cousins out West on the harvest excursions. But... France.*

Jean found it hard to wrap her mind around the fact that a child she had carried in her womb and brought into the world was far away across the ocean, fighting a war in a foreign land. She had lived her whole life in Silver Bay, and although she had been to Charlottetown three times, she had never left Prince Edward Island. Her entire history, and that of many generations of her people, was tied up in this small community. She had known most of the women at the W.I. meeting that day either all of her life, or all of theirs. She expected to watch their children and grandchildren grow up, and there was something reassuring and solid about that. Now she had postcards on the mantelpiece in her front room from Halifax and London and Paris. Images of the Citadel and the Houses of Parliament and the Arc de Triomphe. On their backs: Andrew's brief message and signature. Each time she looked at them, she struggled to make sense of it.

That night, as she sat on the edge of the double bed she shared with her husband Adam, brushing and then braiding her glossy but greying dark hair, Jean's thoughts returned to the W.I. Christmas parcels stacked in a neat pile atop Mrs. Henley's sideboard. Adam came into the bedroom and changed into his nightshirt, then pulled back the patchwork quilt and bedclothes on his side of the bed and eased himself under the covers. He let out a weary sigh as his head came to rest on his pillow. The sound pulled Jean back to the present, and she turned to look at her husband.

"You need more help with the livestock. You'll get sick if you have to keep working this hard."

Adam murmured noncommittally. It was a conversation they had held many times since Andrew enlisted. Adam said what he always said: "Andrew is doing his part, Jean. I have to do mine."

Jean nodded. She blew out the candle on the dresser and climbed into bed beside Adam. She thought again of the Christmas boxes. Beside her, Adam's breathing began to slow as his body relaxed in the direction of sleep.

"Do you think the boxes do any good?" asked Jean, in the darkness.

Adam grunted in confusion. "What boxes?"

"The W.I. Christmas boxes. Do you think they do any good?"

Adam was silent. Jean waited.

"Well, they aren't machine guns."

Jean's heart sank. He was right: socks and cigarettes were useless. Worse than useless, even—they were trivial.

She pictured the postcards on the mantelpiece. She imagined another Christmas with Andrew's empty place at the table. She thought of May's long hours at the Red Cross sewing rooms, and of Adam's endless round of farm chores with no son to help him. She wanted to hurl the Christmas parcels into the bay and watch them sink under the surface of the cold water. Shout in anger at the sky and shake her fist at God. But above all, she wanted the steadiness of life in Silver Bay to return. Something had come unhinged in 1914 and Jean could no longer discern the familiar outlines of the future she had always expected. Some days she could not even find names for the fears that assailed her.

Adam shifted beside Jean, and repeated himself. "They aren't machine guns... But I expect a boy likes to know his people are thinking of him at Christmas, all the same."

Jean rolled over onto her side, took her husband's hand in her own, and shut her eyes tight against the darkness.

Wartime Christmases

✳ Florence Vos ✳

"Santa Claus will come tonight, riding on his sleigh," we'd sing to each other on Christmas Eve, to the tune of "Jingle Bells." My five-year-old sister had told me, a year younger, that Santa did not exist, a revelation that I accepted as fact. How could he visit all the children in one night? For confirmation I asked my mother, who said, "Your daddy's your Santa Claus." That made much more sense. But we kept up the pretense for the sake of the younger children.

In spite of the lost Santa illusion, Christmas was always an exciting time, even with the war and the lack of things suitable for gifts. Sister Joyce and I barely remembered the time before the war, but the conversation often included the expression "prewar" when, we felt, the world had been loaded with treats and toys. Maybe it was, but our family had certainly never been in a situation to take advantage of the bounty.

It was in September 1939, when the war started, that the Government evacuated thousands of children from London, England—among them my sister, brother, and me. Our mother came with us, our father being in the regular army. The town we were sent to in Kent was not far enough to avoid all the war action and there were many air-raids, but also many unforgettable good times.

The big house in Ashford, where a kind family had taken us in, was full of life and gaiety. Our hostess, Mrs. Wise, or Auntie Crisis as we called her, in keeping with the situation, was warm and welcoming and the house seemed to be full of guests coming and going all the time. No need to wait for Christmas for fun. A vivid memory is of our hostess laughing heartily and slapping her knee. There were games and constant laughter in the house, with the participation of both adults and children.

My main memory of Christmas early in the war is the stack of packages that came in the mail and was piled against the wall. No giftwrap in those days, just untidy-looking brown paper and string, but who knew what magic they contained? Although I was aware that few of them would be mine, gazing at them was enough.

Joyce and I, aged five and four, walked to school together, well-trained in how to react to air-raid sirens en route: crouch down by the hedge, cover your head with your hands, and wait for the all-clear, when you get up calmly and go home. There were air-raid sirens at the school, too, and we'd all troop into the brick shelters and sing songs. Santa Claus's visit was exciting during one air-raid. He had a big canvas bag with a sweet for each of us in the bottom.

The joys and, what must have been for the adults, the stress of life in Ashford came to an end when my father decided we'd be safer in Scotland with my mother's family. So we headed north to Musselburgh where it was more peaceful and where we stayed for the remaining four years of the war.

Christmas in Scotland was not such a celebration as it had been during those heady days in England. Hogmanay, or New Year's Eve, was the big Scottish celebration. On that day, after the house had been cleaned from top to bottom, there was traditional food: black bun, fruit cake, shortbread, and, maybe the only night of the year that it might appear, the precious bottle of whiskey. For the younger set there might be homemade ginger beer. Friends and neighbours went from house to house for a short visit and refreshment. After midnight everyone waited for the "First Foot," the first person to enter the home, preferably dark-haired and carrying a piece of coal, some bread and a drink, all to ensure warmth, food, and drink for the coming year. All very entertaining, but not geared towards the youngsters.

We were fortunate that our mother liked Christmas and did her best to make it enjoyable for us. The preparation started well ahead of time, with the making of the Christmas cake and the plum pudding. This depended heavily on the availability of dried fruit. Early in December a small supply might be in the shops and the word went around, "raisins are in this week," and there was a rush for each family to get their small supply. Some weeks it was oranges or canned fruit or two eggs each instead of one for the week's ration. How it was all appreciated!

The ingredients assembled, we children would take turns stirring the mixture in the dish pan, that being the only large enough container, while making silent wishes and then throwing in the lucky "favours." Those were tiny silver thimbles or rings and the smallest coin we had, threepenny bits, all wrapped in wax paper, later to be discovered in the serving on our plates on the big day.

The Christmas dinner was not special to me, disinterested eater that I was. Meat was rationed and in short supply. I know we did not have turkey or even chicken, but whatever it was would be nutritious and satisfying and had to be eaten before the glorious plum pudding.

One year Joyce and I went Christmas shopping with a small sum of money we'd saved. The chemist nearby won all of our business. There was a facecloth and soap and probably toothpaste for the family members. It was a maturing experience, being in control.

We had a tree, a small one in Grannie's tiny crowded house. It had no lights and, of course, there were none outside during the blackout when every chink of light from the houses had to be covered. We were delighted with it, not knowing any difference. Paper chains were easy to make, although the paper we had was thin as newspaper. A streak of watercolour paint did little to enliven it, but we found the effect perfect.

For me, the main thrill was opening the presents, limited though they were. One aunt always sent a pair of hand-knit gloves and a five-shilling money order that went straight to the bank. Books were a popular choice.

My mother was quite imaginative. One Christmas near the end of the war, she got a friend to make two wooden boxes with lids and lots of little compartments. She varnished them and added to the insides needles, threads, and other sewing necessities. At eight and nine years, my sister and I felt quite flattered with such a grownup gift. Brother Tom got a wooden fort. It had only one wall, but with battlements and a drawbridge. He spent many an hour with his tin soldiers winning battles. Little Elizabeth was enchanted with a baby crib made from an oval wooden fruit basket, draped in apricot silk cut out from an old dance dress of my mother's. We felt as fortunate as the young Princesses, Margaret Rose and Elizabeth.

In those stressful, austere war years, probably of least concern to the adults was making a fun-filled holiday. But the energy and enthusiasm of our mother ensured exceptionally warm and joyful Christmas memories for my siblings and me.

Why I Still Believe in Santa Claus

❄ Elaine Breault Hammond ❄

I come from a prairie farm family. My parents lived through the poverty of the Great Depression and it marked them for the rest of their lives. History tells me that the war years of the 40s, when I was a child, were prosperous ones in this country. I still don't know if we lived in poverty then because we really didn't have money or if it was because my traumatized parents lived in constant fear of the Depression coming back.

We went to church each Sunday, not for religious reasons but because the church was the heart of the community and my parents were big supporters of community and neighbourliness. By Christmas time the roads in those pre-snowplow days (I was born in 1937) were usually packed with snow, so cars were left in their sheds and the horses were brought out for transportation. We didn't travel far from home in the winter and only at times of necessity. So there was no church at Christmas and I don't remember any emphasis on the Christmas story, except at the school concert where the big kids dressed in bathrobes, and with towels on their heads acted parts of the old story.

But my parents made sure that we kids knew about Santa Claus. They loved their children and made sure the stockings were full Christmas morning, unlike their own experience in even harder times of getting nothing. I had few books to read, but a family friend, a lawyer from Winnipeg, gave me an illustrated copy of *The Night Before Christmas* when I was two and I fell for the story with huge delight. The magic was wonderful and imagination-expanding.

That year, when I was two and my sister was a baby, Christmas sneaked up on my hard-working parents and they were caught without any shopping done on Christmas Eve. I hung up a clean brown-ribbed stocking and another for my baby sister before I went to bed. I heard the rest of the story years later, perhaps when I was twelve or thirteen.

Dad and Mum told me that they discussed their options that Christmas Eve. Dad couldn't hitch the team to the sleigh and go to town because a prairie blizzard was sweeping the land and there was too much danger of getting lost and freezing to death. They could postpone Christmas but that wasn't really an option because, even though I was small, I knew that tomorrow was THE DAY. Dad was the one who suggested the option they finally chose.

We had a very intelligent horse whose name was Beauty. She had a highly developed homing instinct. Dad would ride her bareback to town, five miles away, shop for Christmas, and get home safely before I woke to check the stocking. He was sure Beauty wouldn't get lost even if there was no visibility at all.

Mum watched while Dad found a sack to carry parcels in, tied it over his shoulder, and made his way to the barn through the blowing snow. She must have been terrified for his safety; she told me, all those years later, that she got no sleep that night.

Dad remembered a long cold ride to town through sub-zero temperatures, and finding the one store locked and dark, the owner and his wife home because it was Christmas Eve. He told of pounding on their door, of the couple's looks of horror at seeing this half-frozen snowman on their steps, and of their offering hot drink and food, but he didn't have time for that. He first put Beauty in the Livery Barn and gave her food and water, then he and the storekeeper went to the store. He filled his sack with Christmas candy, a few decorations for the little spruce tree planted in a pail of sand in the corner of our "big room," and a toy each for Pat and me. He put grapes and Japanese oranges in a package inside his coat, close to his body so they wouldn't freeze. He tied a piece of twine around his waist so the package wouldn't fall out, then was back on the trail. The night was black dark, temperatures were falling, and the snow was still blowing so he couldn't see any landmarks, but Beauty, true to her reputation, got them both safely home.

I have no recollection of that Christmas morning. I don't know what was in my stocking. I suspect I felt a thrill that the magical elf had come down the chimney and transformed the flaccid stocking I'd hung at night to one full of lumps and bumps and wonderful mystery in the morning.

That story became a myth in my mind, which gradually merged with the Santa Claus myth. Like all powerful myths it represented values and emotions I felt deeply then, and still do. That myth connotes family love, and putting someone else's needs before your own. The character of my hard-working, loving father, a man who lived his principles, is a vital part of this mixture. This is why I still believe in Santa Claus.

The Shoppers

❄　Beth E. Janzen　❄

He shows up at Sears
dazed amidst the glitter,
the old man
in the faded blue ball cap,
married 40 years.

She never asks for anything
but she wants a waffle maker this Christmas.
I don't even know what waffles are.

I lead him
to the waffle makers
and point to the images
of crispy, brown waffles.

We had a waffle maker once,
a wedding present.
But the waffles used to stick
to the small, teflon squares
and come apart
when we lifted the lid.

These days, I'm just one
more woman in retail
going through divorce,
bustling around,
assisting the shoppers.

Like them,
I still dream
of coming home
with the perfect gift,
the one that atones
for so much.

A Quarter
(for Pat)

❄ Malcolm Murray ❄

Poverty and loneliness are made worse by comparison to others' abundance. At no time of the year is that contrast more salient than at Christmas. To the deprived, giftwrap glitter is more vertiginous than promising, and festive lights are a kind of taunt.

When his cousin called to invite him to Christmas dinner, William accepted. He was not particularly charmed by his cousin's wife, and vice versa, but the lure of eating turkey and gravy and mashed potatoes swayed him. Ample food and its aroma, but also the sound of children, the adorned Christmas tree, the warmth of a fire, the softness of carpeting: these gentle images evoked in William a past glory, a time when Christmas was a happy occasion, when the future was kind—scars of an era lost. He stared out the window into the dusk and wondered whether the children would recognize in him, their maudlin relative lurking in the shadow of their parents' generosity, a *momenti mori*, a clue to how the magic of Christmas is simply an old conjurer's trick. Had William been able to invent a credible excuse, he would have called back to decline. The lonely prefer to forgo than intrude.

A general rule: guests are not to arrive empty-handed—especially at Christmas. William explored his barren flat to see whether any treasure may be found there. A book of stories by O. Henry he had once cherished might please the children. Or would they see merely its dust, its age, the musty odour of decrepitude stuck in its pages? To maintain the illusion of Christmas, he realized, gifts must be newly purchased. He counted his money, and then recounted in case he had overlooked a bill or a dime. Leaving aside enough coins for the bus, he could perhaps afford a candle, to represent light, and bread, to represent a bountiful harvest. Of his few presentable shirts, he chose a white one to match the purity of that unfamiliar sentiment roused in him by gift-giving with forethought.

In the dark outside, a maritime dampness seeped through thin coats and white shirts, and bore into marrow. Snowbanks had melted in the streets, and William stepped gingerly across puddles of brown slush pooling on the sidewalk. A woman, in well-soled boots, came toward him carrying two large presents tightly wrapped in red and green and gold. William stepped into a puddle to let her pass. "Merry Christmas," she said, for she was gay, giddy at the prospect of giving and receiving. William could feel cold liquid seeping through the sole of his right shoe.

After studying the wares in the gift aisle of a pharmacy, mainly pewter angels and ceramic puppies, William selected a vanilla-scented candle that seemed affordable. He approached the woman at the cash register to ask about gift-wrapping, but she was talking to another clerk about a boy named Roger, who was seeing someone else they knew, an Emily. Certain actions this Emily had committed illustrated how unworthy she was of Roger. What Roger saw in Emily, they could not fathom. "Excuse me," William interjected, and the clerk, before turning to him, said, "Perhaps she doesn't have to work for minimum wage on Christmas day." She was unable to wrap his candle.

Bakeries were closed, as he should have anticipated, and the convenience store's selection of bread was scant. He wanted a hearty loaf of bread. A freshly baked bread, at the least. As a concession, he bought two chocolate bars for the children. The compromise, to give something for the children, seemed to him, at least briefly, serendipitous. By the time he reached the bus stop, a doubt grew. Perhaps his cousin's wife would not approve of gifts to her children made of sugar. Convenience store bread would have been preferable. If not preferable, less offensive.

William waited for the bus. During the periodic lull in traffic, he could listen to the serenity of a winter's night, but mostly he heard only the fricative noise of tires on wet asphalt. Vehicles with heated interiors speeding to their joyous destinations. William's damp foot was cold. Would his cousin's wife mind his one wet sock traipsing through her home? He rued losing the upper button on his fraying coat.

As he stood with his unwrapped gifts in a plastic Bargain Drugs bag, William wondered when the bus would come. He refused to consider whether it would come at all, even when he knew that Christmas had a way of interfering with schedules. A self-help book he had once read convinced him that doubt is the seed of depression, and so he managed to adjure himself to be patient. In that pursuit, he idly counted the coins left to him from his purchases and discovered that he was twenty-five cents short of bus fare. While he wondered how his miscalculation had occurred, a pedestrian approached. William was envious of the man's thick, well-buttoned overcoat, and of the man's impermeable boots. "Excuse me," William said. The man's expression did not alter, nor his pace slacken. A woman, pulling the mittened hand of her son, followed a few metres behind. "Excuse me," William repeated. "I'm a quarter short for the bus." "Sorry," the woman said, and tugged harder at the boy, who seemed to want to say something.

William listened to the drone of tires in the black night and wondered whether he could board the bus without full fare. He had so many nickels, for example, given to him when he bought the chocolate, that the odds of the driver knowing how much he deposited were slight. Surely the sound of a quarter was indistinguishable from a nickel. A young woman in a tan coat and a matching tan hat approached. As she neared, he marvelled at how smooth were her cheeks, how thin and pointed was her nose, how long her eyelashes. Something was alluring about her tan coat as well, a newness, perhaps, that he wanted to feel pressed upon his palm. "Excuse me," he said to her. "You wouldn't happen to have an extra quarter, would you? I need it for the bus." The woman raised her head, looked at William with magnanimous brown eyes, and said, "No, sorry." She continued walking.

The bus turned a corner two blocks away and headed toward William. A man and a woman also approached. With arms interlocked, they laughed gaily in a mood of generous good will. Had they failed to give each other a lingering kiss, they may have reached William ahead of the bus. Instead, the bus arrived first. Its doors opened. William stepped on. While the driver cleaned the grime-smeared side window, William's coins rattled into the metal fare box. He remained standing, uncertain, guilty. The bus driver turned to him, wondering, perhaps, whether he was waiting for a transfer. William confessed: "I only had two dollars. I was a quarter short."

"Why did you put it in the coin box, then?"

The few passengers looked forward to see who was causing their delay. "I was hoping two dollars was sufficient. I have to get to my cousin's."

"Can't. Company policy."

"You mean I have to get off the bus?"

"Yes. That's what it means."

"Can't you let it go this once? It's Christmas."

"Not up to me, Christmas or not. Do you think if such matters were up to me, I'd schedule myself to drive a bus on Christmas? I got places to go, too, you know."

The driver's point was sound. William had contributed money, however. That was worth something, one would think. He asked the driver, "Can I go part way? I paid part of the fare, after all."

"Not possible," the driver said.

"Can I get my two dollars back, at least?"

"Sorry," the driver said. "I don't have access to the box. Imagine if drivers did? Everyone would rob us." William remained standing for a moment longer. The passengers fidgeted in their seats. One looked at her watch. A small gesture from the driver propelled William to step back off the bus. His left shoe alighted in a puddle. The driver closed the door, and William watched him say something, most likely apologetic, to the riders, and put the bus in drive.

That woman who was swathed in a new tan coat came running back up the sidewalk toward William. When she arrived, panting a little, she held out her gloved hand to him, and on it was a quarter.

"Here," she said. "I thought of you when I got home. I had some change in the dish I keep by my door."

William stared at the proffered quarter.

"Please, take it," she said.

William took the quarter and thanked her.

"My pleasure," the woman said. "It's Christmas, after all."

William nodded his assent. She had uttered a true statement. Made merrier from her act of benevolence, she turned to walk back to her warm house, a house with spare coins in a dish by her door.

"Merry Christmas," William replied.

Hanukkah / Godot / Christmas

❄ J.J. Steinfeld ❄

The house was already full of people when Joel walked through the front door, looking for Noreen. There were two mistletoes hanging over the door, to go along with the two Christmas trees he could see, a ceiling-touching one in the living room and a much smaller tree in the dining room, and he wanted to try out the under-the-mistletoe kissing tradition with Noreen. He had already told her he loved her and she had told him to cool his amorous jets. Bad enough his declaration of love had been on the first day of Hanukkah, four days ago, and he had neglected the candle-lighting observance that night, but she was engaged to be married; and adding to the unruly infatuation mix was that she was going to direct him in an amateur production of *Waiting for Godot* in the New Year. At least, Joel thought, she was lukewarm about her fiancé and more than a little derogatory.

Noreen had a glass of wine in her hand when he found her in the rec room downstairs, where a group of people were dancing to "Jingle Bell Rock." He smiled at the memory of his maternal grand-mother singing that song in Yiddish, one of the many Christmas songs she had translated. His grandmother, dear Bubbe, actually liked Christmas songs, especially the ones written by Jews, and she knew at least a dozen of those Jewish-penned songs. Joel remembered watching the musical *White Christmas* on TV with her one Hanuk-kah, she singing along merrily with Bing Crosby to Irving Berlin's "White Christmas," except in old-world Yiddish. His maternal grandfather, equally dear Zayde, had passed away by then. He was no fan of the holiday season, Joel recalled, sometimes commenting in his old left-wing Yiddish-accented way that Santa Claus was the patron saint of capitalism.

After Joel took off his winter coat, Noreen said with delight, "That T-shirt is quite different."

"I wore it especially for the occasion. Designed it myself."

"Samuel Beckett and Anne Shirley together at long last."

"Platonically posed, of course."

"Interesting literary juxtaposition, Joel."

Looking around the festively decorated rec room, with yet another Christmas tree, this one artificial, Joel said, "You and I are the only ones here under forty, I'd bet all my Hanukkah *gelt* on that," and then explained the tradition of giving small amounts of money to children during the eight days of Hanukkah. Noreen had warned him that he might not like this party; most of the people would be in their forties and fifties; her fiancé was fifty-three. She was thirty-four, though Joel, twenty-two, at first thought she was no more than two or three years older than he. Turning toward the people in the rec room, he asked, "Which one of these lucky gentlemen is your fiancé?"

"He's upstairs. Discussing some business with a friend. You two will not get along, trust me, Joel."

"Conflict is the heart of theatre."

"If anyone wants to know who invited you, say you're my cousin. I always wanted a cousin."

"Call me baby cousin. I can play the part, Noreen."

"Have a beer and enjoy the Christmas spirit. Up in the kitchen fridge."

"Introduce me to your fiancé, Noreen."

"Make some new friends first. Socialize, baby cousin. Tell them about your brilliant playwriting and fledgling acting career."

"I will have *two* beers and get quasi-drunk on the Christmasness of it all," he said, as he headed for the stairs. "I warn you, I can't hold my liquor, cuz…"

Noreen had met Joel a week before, during a community theatre audition for *Waiting for Godot*. She thought he would be perfect for Lucky, although he would have preferred playing Estragon. They had gone to the same high school, a decade apart, his parents moving to the Island the year Joel started high school; they had moved back to Toronto last year, with Joel staying to finish his fourth year at UPEI. He had somehow managed to charm her and wrangle an invitation to this Christmas party, even though her fiancé would be there. Yesterday, they had spent an hour at a downtown coffee shop discussing the practical, sensible reasons they shouldn't fall in love.

Upstairs, Joel opened the refrigerator and took out a beer. He moved near to the stove and stood watching the activity in the kitchen.

"Have you been naughty or nice this year?" one of the nearby women asked the large-headed man who passed by her at the entrance to the kitchen. The woman held her glass awkwardly, choking it, and attempted to look serious. She was posing the lighthearted Christmas question to people who wandered into the kitchen's sanctuary. It was an untidy kitchen but not as crowded as the other rooms in the house.

"Naughty, naughty, naughty, sweetheart," the man said, upsetting the woman with his lewd squinting, and she chased him away with a scornful, "Get lost before Santa erases you from his gift list."

"We've never met," the woman said, offering her hand.

"Noreen's cousin. Distant cousin. Long-lost reunited cousin."

"I'm Laura. You have a name? Or should I call you long-lost cousin?"

"All my friends call me long-lost," Joel said, and the woman turned away. He wondered if any of the men who were in the kitchen or passed through getting a drink was Noreen's fiancé's.

"By the way, I've been as naughty as Godot," he said, his reply helped along by a Christmas song, "Sleigh Ride," on the house's impressive sound system. "Another Christmas classic written by a Jew," he said to no one in particular.

Joel left the kitchen and went first into the living room, finishing his beer and putting the bottle down on a bookshelf, then into the dining room, attracted by the crowd of people. He wanted these people to be in the audience, watching him perform. He took a stick of celery from the ample supply of snacks, twirled it through the dip, and climbed up onto the table that was pushed into a corner of the dining room, careful not to step on the bowls of snacks.

"What are you doing?" a woman called up to Joel, his head nearly to the ceiling. Noreen came up the stairs and saw Joel on the table. She hurried through the crowd.

"Either play-acting or being exceedingly crazy. I'll leave the determination to you," he said, his hands fumbling with his belt buckle. "My grandmother would say *meshugge*, but she'd say it with affection for her grandchild." He pulled out his belt and pressed it against the ceiling. "Genuine tooled leather I have here. An unappreciated artisan toiled seven thankless weeks on it before he went mad…" Joel declaimed, speaking to the back rows of some huge theatre. When he saw Noreen, he said, "Front row centre for the elegant woman. Tell the ushers you know me."

Noreen knew Joel was being facetious, but he spoke earnestly, and his expression was grave.

"What did the artisan go mad from?" she asked, wanting to steal Joel from his performance.

"The commercialism of the modern world," he shouted.

The chattering people in the room looked at the man on the table, waiting for something terrible to happen. "Who is this guy?" a man with drinks in both hands asked.

"Godot," he enunciated slowly, dropping his belt to the floor at Noreen's feet, "and your long wait is over."

"That your first name or last?" a man wearing a fake Santa beard asked.

Joel started to smile, but altered his expression: "Middle name."

"And a fine middle name it is," Noreen said, eager to keep the conversation going, but Joel appeared to be angry, twisting his face for emphasis.

After another Christmas song, "Santa Baby," started playing, and Joel proclaimed it also written by a Jew, the owner of the house rushed into the dining room. He had been informed that someone—described hastily as a nut case and dirty drunk—was standing, and stripping, on his most valued piece of furniture, contaminating the snacks.

"Get down, you idiot!" the owner yelled as he made his way toward the man on his dining room table.

"I claim this table in the name of sanity and all unrecognized Canadian craftspeople."

Noreen's fiancé entered the room and moved toward her.

Joel removed his T-shirt and threw it at the infuriated owner, who let it drop to the floor. "That shirt used to belong to Samuel Beckett, not that he ever saw our adorable Anne at the Confederation Centre. He wore it night and day while he was writing *Waiting for Godot*. You can have it in trade. It's worth a dozen paltry tables." Joel still had on a sleeveless white undershirt, boxer shorts, running shoes and socks, modelling his outfit without a trace of self-consciousness.

As the owner attempted to get Joel off the table, the performer continued: "What is your favourite Christmas song written by a songwriter of the Jewish persuasion?"

With people calling out the names of Christmas songs, and arguing which ones were written by Jews, Joel began to do a little dance, whistling in accompaniment.

"Don't make me call the police," the owner threatened. "Get down!"

By then everyone in the house, close to forty holiday revellers, had squeezed into the dining room to view the spectacle of the disrobing stranger. People asked each other who the man was, and the word got around that he was Noreen's cousin. Her fiancé said that he hadn't known she had a cousin, and that she told him he recently moved from Toronto and they had never been close. Despite the confusion, the crowd's mood was festive, except for the house's surly owner. Growing even more perturbed, he again threatened to call the police.

"I'll call my muscular Muses," Joel said, "to eradicate you and your nit-picking, kill-joying, sleep-inducing kind. The cops versus my Muses, hardly a fair contest." After he had spoken, Joel bowed courteously to his audience.

A few hands reached up to pull Joel off the table but he moved evasively, scattering bowls of snacks and shaking the old table, seeking balance, spraying cutting glances at those who wanted to dislodge him from his stage.

"Leave him alone!" Noreen called out, startled by her outburst in defending Joel. It was just not like her to act this way.

"If he's your friend, Noreen, take him away," the house's owner said.

"He's her cousin," Noreen's fiancé explained.

Noreen collected the discarded clothing and held it close. To her, love at first sight was so much delusive garbage, the creation of sentimental movie-makers, yet she wondered if she had fallen in love with Joel the moment she had seen him at the audition.

The house's owner finally managed to get hold of Joel's leg, and pulled him roughly off the table. Joel landed on his feet, bumping into a woman who had been waiting for the boxer shorts to drop. She spilled her drink and swore at Joel. As he started to apologize, the owner punched him in the stomach, Joel grasping his abdomen with a yell of surprise and pain. He straightened up and attempted to look unhurt.

"You didn't have to hit him," Noreen said, stepping between Joel and the owner as he tried to hit Joel again, a hockey enforcer denied his calling.

"Let's get out of here. This is no place for Mr. Godot," Noreen said to Joel, the people around her losing shape, their voices indistinct and far-off.

She turned to her fiancé. "I have to make sure my cousin gets back to his room. He doesn't know Charlottetown." She grabbed her coat and bag containing the notebook in which she had written notes about the young playwright, actor, and university student she had met less than a week ago.

"Like Lot, I will lead you from this disgusting Gomorrah." Joel took hold of Noreen's free hand. "If you look back you'll be turned to boredom." He pulled her out of the house.

As Joel finished buckling his belt, a police car drove past them and parked in front of the Christmas party house. Joel clapped his hands in exaltation. "Our exit timing couldn't have been better."

With the cold December air caressing her, Noreen felt her mood change. Joel confused her and she wanted to ask questions, to know all about him, but she became timid, her crowded-party mask lost in the dark night.

"If you want to dare the unknown, we can read from a play, in exchange for you having helped me," Joel said. "That is, if you but venture home with me, harmless Godot, even if I will be impersonating Lucky."

"I thought you lived on stage."

"A tiny, cramped, one-bedroom apartment in an old dingy building, but with a beautiful antique menorah. You can help me light the Hanukkah candles. It has to be before midnight."

"How far is it from here?"

"Twenty minutes if we walk with rapidity. Or in a more leisurely twenty-five minutes we can summarize our lives to each other, maybe debate the relative merits of celebrating Christmas or Hanukkah."

After unlocking the door to his third-floor apartment in downtown Charlottetown, and grumbling that he had forgotten to buy some Hanukkah mistletoe, Joel lifted Noreen and carried her inside, she protesting only mildly. He kept holding her while he stood in the middle of the room, she looking at all the radios, not caring if her feet ever touched the ground again.

"I, as you can see, live simply. Radios and an antique menorah are my only extravagances. All of the radios work, by the way. Inherited them from my grandfather, who repaired electronic stuff for a living, a lifetime before the days of iPods and flat-screen TVs." There were extension cords and multi-plugs throughout the room. "Each radio is in the proper place. Later I will give you an audio treat unlike any you have ever heard."

He put Noreen down, and instructed her to wait, not to allow any jealous dybbuks or foul-breathed golems into the apartment. Joel complained that the dybbuks and golems, along with a few critics, were out to get him, and he disappeared into the bedroom.

He returned to the room, waving two copies of a script.

"Situate yourself comfortably on the floor," he said, and led her to the centre of the cluttered room. He handed her one script and kept the other. "My latest unproduced play. This is the one I'm working on. School keeps getting in the way… and auditions."

Joel opened the script and told her a little about it, how he imagined his grandmother as a young woman in Poland falling in love with his radio-collecting grandfather as a young man, before coming to Canada, and then they started reading lines from Joel's latest play. It did not take her long to get into the mood of the play and they performed three scenes from the play as though an audience was present.

"That is a poignant and intense play," Noreen said when they had finished their reading.

"I haven't felt even close to relaxed in months and it feels great," Joel said. "Catharsis à la mode. One great bowel movement of the soul…" With an affectionate smile he kneeled next to Noreen on the floor and added, "I love a gorgeous, talented co-star, especially on Hanukkah."

"I almost forgot it was Hanukkah. Too much Christmas spirit tonight."

"We better light the candles. It's the fifth night," he said, as he took six thin candles out of a small cardboard box and put them into his menorah, explaining the significance of the five Hanukkah candles and the sixth one, the *shamus*, which was kept in the middle elevated holder in the nine-pronged candelabrum and used to light the others.

Joel lit the candles, stumbling over the blessings he used to say at Hanukkah growing up in Toronto. Lighting the Hanukkah candles was the one Jewish tradition his parents brought with them when they moved to the Island. Neither one was ever comfortable living on the Island, and after six years they returned to Toronto to get divorced, leaving the family's old menorah with their son.

"You want to read from another unproduced play of mine or make out? Or we could improvise a play about an actor about to play Lucky in *Waiting for Godot* getting lucky with the director and singing Christmas songs in Yiddish and lighting Hanukkah candles."

Joel pulled her gently to his level, and they kneeled near each other. When Joel began to undress her, Noreen became tearful, he feeling responsible for her tears.

"You're the most beautiful human being I've ever seen," he said. "I thought if I didn't stop yapping I wouldn't have to confront that. Nothing intimidates more than beauty."

"I hate being called beautiful," she said harshly. "I hate being told how beautiful I am. So what, so what…"

"Shut up, you ugly clump of deformity," he shouted, falling backward from his kneeling position, but regaining his balance quickly and nestling close to Noreen.

Her tears abated and she smiled, holding Joel tightly. Noreen relaxed into Joel's arms. He stroked her face, searching for a flaw, a telltale mark or small scar, but found only serene beauty despite her former disquietude.

Joel stood up and turned on some of the radios, setting them to the same classical music station. "This occasion calls for eighteen radios playing simultaneously." He rejoined her on the floor.

"I've never listened to eighteen radios simultaneously."

"Eighteen is my lucky number."

"I don't have a lucky number."

"I give you eighteen. *Chai.*"

"*Chai?*"

"The Hebrew word for life. Add the numbers of the Hebrew letters together and you get eighteen. My Christmas-song-singing Bubbe right up to the day she died gave her grandchildren eighteen coins or dollars on their birthday, depending on their age. When I was young it was eighteen nickels… then eighteen dimes… eighteen quarters… and when I became a man at thirteen, eighteen bucks. She died when I was fifteen, but left me $1,800 in her will."

In the living room and with only the Hanukkah candles burning, the eighteen radios playing in symphonic harmony, Joel continued to undress Noreen. He felt unsure and more than sexually aroused.

He knew that he cared for this woman, trying to block out thinking of her as a potential character for a play; so many of the people he met were just that, potential characters, material to be mined.

"I should take my engagement ring off," she said, and took off the ring.

"That's probably worth more than my writing grant from the Council of the Arts."

"All I want for Christmas is a broken engagement."

"What a wondrous present. A true gift of the Magi."

"I shouldn't do it over my clever little smartphone, should I?" she said, holding up her phone.

"That wouldn't be very Santa-like, would it? Better to get back to our romantic script."

"I need to tell you something, Joel," Noreen said, a worried tone rustling her words.

"I am not averse to using the latest in contraceptive latex," he said, taking the ring from her and balancing it on his head.

"Please, Joel. My stomach is awful-looking." She lowered her head and stared at a coffee stain in the carpet.

Joel felt saddened by Noreen's revelation but showed a wide smile. "Want to buy a diamond engagement ring?" he said, holding it up in the air. "Nothing about you, my friend, is less than pulchritudinous." He lifted her chin so that she was facing him.

"I sure hope that's an insult," she said, attempting to turn away, Joel refusing to allow the lovely face to leave his sight.

"A pretentious compliment. Pulchritude is beauty and it's you, Noreen."

Noreen closed her eyes so hard that her head throbbed. After a pause during which she heard the rasping echo of memory, she moaned, "The scars," as if it were a song of grief for what had happened many years ago.

"I fell out of a tree when I was a teenager. I fell by accident. I have to believe that. I don't want to believe a seventeen-year-old girl wanted to die. When I fell out of the tree the branches ripped up my stomach and legs."

He stood up and shut off the lights, only the Hanukkah candles illuminating the room.

She kissed him passionately, and he finished undressing her, she then helping him take off his clothes. In the dimness of the room, he could faintly see the scars along her stomach and legs, and he touched them, kissed them, as if her very beauty resided within them.

Later, while they were lying together on the floor, she said, "You never told me what your favourite Jewish-written Christmas song is."

"'White Christmas.' Just like my dear Bubbe…"

Joel started to sing "White Christmas" in Yiddish as the Hanukkah candles burned down, and Noreen tightened her embrace of him.

Christmas Gift!

❄ Sally Russell ❄

In our household we followed an old Southern American custom called "Christmas Gift!" According to this custom, on Christmas morning, you greeted everyone by crying, "Christmas Gift!" The goal was to get in before others. You had to be specific: "Christmas Gift, Daddy! Christmas Gift, John!" or it didn't count. If you said "Christmas Gift!" first, technically the other person had to give you a gift. The contest got hotter and hotter as the morning progressed.

I do not recall gifts being given, with one exception. Our bachelor uncle, Dick, the eldest son in my father's family of thirteen siblings, was rumoured in his youth to have been the most ambitious Christmas gifter of all. Uncle Dick kept silver dollars in his pocket, and to each niece and nephew who got him on Christmas Gift! he'd give a silver dollar. There was no evidence of any ambition to win, because he never tried to outdo you. He just wanted to hear you say, "Christmas gift, Uncle Dick!" I still treasure three of those silver dollars, and the shining memory of Uncle Dick enjoying the music of this game.

My father was the youngest son and number twelve of his lively and boisterous family. He wasn't an eager game participant. Sandwiched between a brother older by a scant year, who was a fast talker and would become a famous preacher, and a charming, loquacious baby sister two years younger, he'd developed a slow, studied speech that didn't suit the speedy needs of Christmas Gift! Which isn't to say Alex Russell did not enjoy the contest.

Christmas in general was a favourite time of year for this youngest son, who became a medical doctor. His holiday mood was deliciously mellow, partly thanks to gift bowls of eggnog, well-laced with bourbon, offered by grateful patients. For twelve days of Christmas such a bowl might grace our dining table. Back in the late 40s, Doctor Russell was known for extravagant gestures at Christmas. He'd buy a giant candy cane, manufactured down at the candy plant in Athens, stash it in the boot of his car, and wherever he went on house calls, he'd take a hammer and knock off chunks of peppermint candy for patients and friends. He was an arch supporter of the American Legion toy drive, and anyone in town was welcome to come shoot his fireworks on Christmas night in our front yard. Georgians loved fireworks in those days, and numerous friends and neighbours would gather for the pyrotechnic racket.

Years passed. We all grew up, the candy plant closed, fireworks were outlawed. But we continued Christmas gifting on Christmas morning.

Sometime in the early 1970s, my father showed up at my house unexpectedly on Christmas morning. We were to gather later for a greater-family party, so I was surprised to see his stocky frame getting out of his weary, worn-green Volkswagen bug. He was a little arthritic by then, grey, slightly stooped. Daddy had cows on the farm next to ours, so I figured he was out to check on them and enjoy the frosty, sunny Georgia morning. He loved to be outside as much as any man I've ever known, and would rather have been a farmer than a doctor. He had chosen medicine over farming because he figured he could make a better living as a doctor, but he indulged his farming longing with constant projects. We had a milk cow for many years, and often grew a large garden, a wide field of peas, or a hillside of watermelons. For several years we raised laying hens and boxed a few thousand eggs a week for the nearby hatchery. The boys got to sell watermelons by the highway, and we girls got to weigh and clean eggs.

This Christmas morning I hid behind the kitchen door, knowing he never knocked, and jumped out to Christmas Gift! him. Two granddaughters, aged five and eight, followed suit before he could catch a breath.

Smiling, he tousled their blond heads and said, "Well, I don't mind if you've got me because I've come to give you a Christmas gift."

Alex Russell was still known for uncommon generosity, and he had been generous with grandchildren, from calves to coats and cars, not to mention doctor visits, but somehow I knew a story was coming. We all went into the living room and sat by the fire and the shining tree to hear Granddaddy's tale.

"The week after Thanksgiving," he began, "I was about to go out when a patient drove up in the yard and asked to speak to me about a private matter. It was Mrs. Beulah S——. Sally, you'll know who she is. I invited her in and we sat at the breakfast table. She told me that she was in need of a little money, that she'd got behind on her bills and work was slow at the sewing plant. If I could loan her a little, she'd be able to pay it back, she thought, after the first of the year."

This was a familiar story with Dr. Russell. A few patients sometimes asked my father for loans of this type, and he had been willing to help. He never charged interest nor kept any record. I once asked him if he'd been paid back.

"Not one hundred percent," he'd said, "but close enough that I'm satisfied. I figure they paid what they could."

"So how much did Miss Beulah ask for?" I said to my father that Christmas morning.

"She wanted thirty-five dollars, and I gave it to her. She's a hard-working woman with four children in school and I'm sure she never sees much of J.W.'s paycheque, though I've never heard her say a word against him."

I could see my father, familiar with the plight of this country woman married to a hard-drinking, poker-playing husband, quietly taking out the wad of cash, mostly dollar bills, he carried in his pocket to make change at house calls, and peeling off thirty-five dollars.

"She probably takes home thirty-five dollars a week from the sewing plant," he went on. "She's never asked for money before."

"So she's paid it back early?" I guessed. "Maybe J.W. missed his poker game?"

"Doubt he'd have missed the poker game," Daddy allowed, ducking his head. He loved a good poker game himself.

"Yesterday morning she was back at my house," he said then. "I confess I thought, 'Uh-oh. She's needing more money.' But, in fact, she brought in a leather handbag that she had found and she thought I might know who it belonged to. Well, it wasn't leather. More like genuine Naugahyde.

"'I found this handbag in the parking lot up at the new mall, late yesterday,' Beulah said, 'and it has pill bottles in it with your name for the doctor. From the driver's license I see it belongs to a coloured lady down at Statham. I figured you might know where she lives.'

"One look at the name on the prescription bottle and I knew the bag belonged to Louvinia D——. You know her. She works for your sister, Susan."

I smiled. Daddy had already told us about Louvinia when a year or so earlier she had started to work for Susan, keeping her four-year-old son two afternoons a week so that Susan could teach piano lessons. Daddy had pointed out proudly that Louvinia and her sister, Iola, two old maids, lived on their own farm. Their father had managed at the turn of the twentieth century to buy his own land and to farm it successfully. Alex Russell noted this was no mean feat for any man in Georgia at that time, black or white, but would have to be rated a remarkable accomplishment for a black man. Their brother had also farmed the land, and when he died, it came to Louvinia and Iola. They prized their land, kept the taxes paid, the house painted, and the barns standing. They worked as house servants, and in 1976 they were paid better wages than in the past because they were innovative. By working for several different families, rather than for the same family all week, they could charge each one a more nearly fair wage. Susan, in fact, could not afford Louvinia to clean house, only to take care of little John. They also insisted that their Social Security be paid.

"I told Mrs. S— that I know Louvinia—I've been her doctor for nearly thirty years—and that I would be glad to return the bag," Daddy continued. "That farm is hard to find out in that country, and it's a good piece from where Mrs. S—lives.

"'I'd be right grateful to you for that, Doc,' she said. 'I know she'll be glad to find it agin.'

"So I decided I'd take the purse right on to Statham. It was Christmas Eve. A lost purse is bound to be a heartache, more so in circumstances like these where the spectre of want is ever near. I could tell from the well-worn bag it was a treasure. And to tell the truth, I was mighty curious to find if anything went missing. I didn't inspect the bag, though, just dropped the pill bottle back inside.

"Louvinia and Iola were surprised to see me. 'We ain't called no doctor!' they exclaimed. But they invited me into their little kitchen and we sat down at the table. I'd held the bag down like it was my doctor bag, and I put it up on the table saying, 'Something you've lost has been found.'

"Louvinia's face lit up like the prettiest Christmas tree you ever saw. She grabbed up the purse, laughing. 'Lawd, lawdy! My purse!' She held it to her chest and danced around the table. You know how she can be sort of crazy like that. 'I been sick all night and day 'bout it, sick to my stomach thinking how I'd left it on top of the car.'

"She looked at Iola, who was smiling, too, then back at me. 'Where on earth did you find it? I done drove back to the mall and looked and looked and asked all around and nobody'd seen it. So I wuz tryin' my best to accept it wuz gone for good.'

"She opened it and started going through it. I waited to see if any grief would result from the exam. For careful minutes, she sifted through a few papers, three pill bottles—she has her ailments—a lipstick, an envelope or two, a handkerchief. Finally she took out the wallet and counted the bills in it and the change in its change purse. She looked up and announced, 'It's all here! Every penny!' Then she looked at me, laughing and blushing, 'Oh, doctor, I didn't mean I thought you'd a took anything.'

"'Louvinia,' I said, 'a patient of mine found your purse and your pill bottles led her to me. She asked me to bring it to you.'

"Her face lit up again. 'Will you tell that lady how much I appreciate it? I is happy as the day I was born!'

"I assured Louvinia those thanks would be conveyed, and then I confess I had to ask her how much money was in the purse.

"'Thirty-five dollars!' Louvinia exclaimed. 'Everything I've saved since summer.'

"Iola, the quiet one, hadn't said a word until then. 'We was wondering how we was gonna pay our taxes. I tells Louvinia not to carry her cash around in that bag, but she will do it.'"

Now my father looked at his two granddaughters and said, "I hope someday you'll understand why being part of this story is such a gift to me and why I'm giving it to you. Things happen to all of us to destroy our faith in human nature. Then we learn about something like this, and we feel happy to be human."

I have never forgotten that story or my father's quiet pleasure in it. We still tell it at family gatherings, too, not always at Christmas. "What about Daddy and Louvinia's purse?" someone will say and then the story is brought out, a shining Christmas gift! payment more to be treasured even than Uncle Dick's silver dollars.

Mrs. Higgenbotham's Red Hat

❄ Glenna Jenkins ❄

Some say Blind Billy Fortune was sweet on Martha Kavanaugh because he always cut her wood first. Martha maintained they had merely struck a deal: she owned a woodlot and they both needed firewood. So, Billy agreed to fell two dozen trees and cut and split them in return for keeping half.

The early December sun had barely risen when Billy pulled up Martha's drive with his axe and his two-man crosscut saw. Mist drifted off the frost-tipped grass and into the damp morning air. Martha's oldest son, Larry, waited in the yard. Billy's near-blindness meant he depended on the boy to guide his trusty Percheron, Maggie, through the woods.

"We're after the old growth, Larry. Less brush there."

"Ma said to remind you about the meeting."

"Right," Billy said.

Billy whistled and sang as the wagon jostled down the grassy slope. Larry urged Maggie down the pasture toward the woods. When they reached tall spruce, he whoa'd up the horse. "Looks good here, Mr. Fortune."

Billy climbed down from the wagon, reached a hand out for a tree, and looped the reins around it. "Pick us a good'un."

Larry found what he thought to be a twenty-five-year-old spruce. Billy tested its size with his thick calloused hands. "Which way, d'ya figure?"

Larry picked a fall line and stretched out a hand. Billy swung his axe and chipped a "V" into the thick trunk. He and Larry each grabbed an end of the saw and placed its toothed blade into the open wound. Larry followed the older man's rhythm, felt the pull on his shoulders, and his hands begin to blister.

When they piled the last tree onto the wagon and fastened the load, Billy climbed into his seat and grabbed the reins. Larry led

Maggie toward a turn in the path, then home. The Percheron's barrel chest bulged under the strain, and the wagon jostled behind her. Billy sat up tall, his ruddy cheeks catching the chill air, his toque sitting low over his broad forehead. His hands made thin strands of the reins.

When they reached the edge of the woods, Billy whoa'd up Maggie. "Whad'ya say we cut a Christmas tree for your mother?"

"That's a grand idea." All of fourteen, Larry already sounded like a grownup.

Billy handed him the axe. "Not too tall. You don't wan'it scrapin' the parlour ceilin'."

By the time they had finished, Martha was waiting in front of her modest white farmhouse in her navy-blue coat and matching gloves. Her turkeys free-ranged around her. "That's some load of wood."

Billy turned an ear to her voice, directed Maggie toward her, and removed his cap. "Where d'ya wan'it, Martha?"

"Better offload it for now, Billy. We'll be late for the meeting."

Larry heaved the Christmas tree off the wagon and held it up.

"It's perfect," Martha smiled.

By the time they reached the church hall, the meeting had begun. Father Mulally sat in front of the near-packed room. He had heard the Murphys would attend and had chosen a vantage point from which to maintain civility.

Daniel Murphy stood in the front row, red-faced, gripping a sheet of paper on which he had written a long list. His brother, Tobias, sat beside him. Father Mulally's housekeeper, Mrs. MacGee, sat directly behind them. Martha knew Tobias had come to support Daniel and that Mrs. MacGee always helped with the Christmas concert. But when she saw that a parish council member occupied almost every other chair, including the council president, Archie Jamieson, she suspected the Murphys had spent the previous evening on the party line. Three empty seats remained along the back row. Martha, Billy, and Larry sat there.

"That's parish council business, Daniel," Father Mulally said. "We're discussing the Christmas concert today."

"It concerns the Christmas concert, Father," Daniel said.

Billy stood up. "If it's the concert you're talkin' about, you talk to me."

"Well, I'll tell you then," Daniel said. "Since you're finally here."

"Sit down, Daniel," Father Mulally said. "Council meets tomorrow."

Daniel pursed his lips and eased into his seat.

"The concert's my business, I want to hear about it," Billy said.

Daniel shot to his feet. "Youse is robbin' the church."

"Who's robbin' what?" Billy said.

"What's this all about, Daniel?" Father Mulally asked.

"It's like I said, Billy's takin' church money to play for the concert." Daniel pounded a finger to his chest. "I'll play for free."

Father Mulally put a hand on his chin.

"He's after dippin' into the collection is what I'm sayin'," Daniel continued.

Billy pulled his shoulders back and stretched out his six-foot-three-inch frame. "A man has a right to a living."

"Not from the church he don't," Daniel said.

Billy stepped toward Daniel. Martha touched his arm.

"Leave it for tomorrow, Mr. Murphy," Father Mulally said.

Daniel shook his head and dropped into his seat.

The Murphys had been in a snit over Billy Fortune and his *St. Peter's Church fiefdom* for months. They had brought motions before the parish council. Their wives had gossiped over the party line. *I hear tell he's askin' for twenty dollars a month now, 'fore you know it, it'll be thirty.* They noted the number of mouths that fed and how Billy wasn't the only one suffering from the potato prices these days. But what bothered the Murphys most were the ten dollars the widower was paid each month to direct the choir and the additional twenty cents he received for each Mass and thirty cents for each wedding and funeral.

Tobias Murphy stood and pointed at Billy. "He's robbin' the church is what he's doin'."

"Is that true, Billy?" Martha asked.

Billy turned beet red.

"That's church money youse're takin'," Archie Jamieson chimed in.

"I earn every penny," Billy said.

"If Billy's already bein' paid to conduct the choir, shouldn't that include the Christmas concert?" Daniel asked.

"Mud 'n your eye, Daniel Murphy," Billy said.

Father Mulally turned toward Billy. "Daniel has a point. Perhaps we should consider that Billy's stipend includes the Christmas concert."

Heads nodded.

The near-blind man scanned the low wooden rafters and searched for words. "You're askin' for more of my time, Father. There'll be twice-weekly practices, more as the date approaches."

"If it's too much, then what's the problem with Daniel's offer?" Father Mulally asked.

"He can't read music, that's why. He can't work the pegs. He stomps on the pedals. He's... he's bloody awful."

Daniel turned toward Billy. "Youse can never get enough, can youse, Blind Billy Fortune. Youse're damn greedy."

The parishioners sat in hushed silence.

Billy stormed to the front of the room and jabbed a finger at Daniel. "You can't play but three-note hymns. *Tunes* you even call 'em, that's what you know."

Daniel's Adams apple travelled up and down his skinny, stubbled neck.

Tobias stood and shook his fist. "Squeeze every last penny out, you would. Skin your own dead mother for a nickel."

"That's enough," Father Mulally said. "We'll discuss the matter tomorrow."

But it was too late. Billy swung a brawny fist at Tobias, who ducked and fled for the door, and Daniel followed him, Father Mulally, and Billy. Martha hurried outside after them. Larry got up and stepped toward the window. Some of the council members ventured toward the now-open door. Others crowded around Larry and the window.

Father Mulally turned to Martha. "Get back inside."

"I will not." She circled around Daniel, who now lay splayed out over the frozen lawn, to where Billy prepared to take down Tobias, who edged toward the priest. And just as Billy moved to land a fist across Tobias's face, Father Mulally stepped in and took the blow. Bright red blood began to flow.

Billy stood back, horrified.

Tobias escorted the injured priest up the lawn toward the Glebe. Daniel roared after Billy. But the widower refused to brawl any more. Not after striking the priest. His thoughts moved to the confessional, where he would face the injured party. He dashed to

213

his wagon and urged Maggie toward Northbridge Road, cursing the Murphys.

"Damnation to the lot o' youse."

Maggie rounded a corner and pounded up St. Michael's Road. Billy reined her up to his barn, unhitched the horse, put Maggie in her stall, and fed and watered her. Then he crossed the pasture behind his house, entered the familiar path through the woods, a forearm fending off branches, found Dirty River, and navigated its icy bank to the Higgenbothams' back door.

Later, he sat by his cook stove and cradled a teddy of hooch. At midnight, he telephoned Martha. "Les'see how they do wishout me, then."

After Billy hung up, Martha thought she heard breathing on the other end of the party line.

Martha rose early the next morning. The shadow of yesterday's debacle hung over her household and her stomach ached from the overnight fast she observed before taking Sunday communion. She stoked the fire in the cook stove. "We'll have oatmeal pancakes and maple syrup after Mass," she said as Larry headed out to tend the livestock. She was referring to Mr. Higgenbotham's maple syrup, a product of one of his two legitimate enterprises, the first being fox farming, which he insisted he pursued for their pelts. But the entire community knew the Higgenbothams depended on the creatures' strong, musky odour to hide their more lucrative enterprise down by Dirty River.

Larry soon returned, wiping back tears. "The turkeys."

"No!" Martha bolted out the back door and stood on the stoop. "Mother of God!"

She raced across the yard and stopped and stared at what would have been her Christmas gifts to Father Mulally and Billy Fortune and their own Christmas feast.

Martha had carefully tended those turkeys, buying them as chicks and starting them in a spare stall in the barn. Soon, they were big enough to free-range by day and were herded back into the barn at dusk. When the weather cooled, she fed them warm molasses mash. And as December approached, she watched for Mrs. Higgenbotham's red hat at church, a sure sign the hooch was ready. She would purchase her supply and stash it away. During each of the four days before Christmas she would add a cup of moonshine to her molasses mash. The flavour would soak through the meat and make it moist and succulent. It would add a bite to the gravy that smothered the blandness of her mashed potatoes; it would add a tang to her plum pudding.

Larry swallowed hard. "Sorry, Ma."

Martha didn't assign blame. "We were tired last night."

"Was it a fox?"

"Something slinked out of here around dusk." Martha thought she saw the Murphys' dog.

The Kavanaughs' pew was toward the left front of the church. Mrs. MacGee sat directly behind them. The Fortunes sat in front of the Kavanaughs and just behind the Higgenbothams, who always marched through the main double doors and up the centre aisle to the front pew, no doubt to make a "red hat" day seem like any other.

Martha noticed the two empty pews in front of hers as she and Larry took their seats. She knelt and thought about the choir without their organist. She wondered whether Billy was forcing his children to miss the first Sunday of Advent, making them commit a venial sin. And Hannah, his youngest, had been excited about lighting the first candle on the Advent wreath. Did Billy's late-night call mean he was quitting the church altogether?

The main doors opened. A cool breeze drifted in. A short stout woman marched up the centre aisle, the telltale red hat perched above a mass of grey hair.

The men perked up. The women muttered their disapproval. That red hat meant they could count on three weeks of nasty drunkenness. But, at least, the harvest was in.

Mrs. MacGee leaned forward. "I s'pose our Billy paid the Higgenbothams a visit last night, pie-eyed that he was."

Martha suspected someone had been listening on the party line the night before. Now she was certain the whole community knew about the misdirected fist, the uttered curse, and Billy's alcohol-induced decision.

The Higgenbothams slid into the front pew. Mr. Higgenbotham stood towering over his wife, his black suit jacket and trousers hanging loosely over his scrawny frame. Four altar boys swept out of the sacristy and up to the altar. Father Mulally followed, his head bowed over the bright purple alb that announced the holy season. He usually greeted the congregation with a vibrant smile. This time, he turned his back to them, faced the altar, and ploughed through the Mass.

When it was time for the Gospel, he moved to the pulpit and embarked on St. Mark's fiery rendition of the second coming of Christ. When he placed a finger on a passage and raised his battered face, the congregation drew a collective breath.

"Saint Mark tells us to take heed, lest our hearts be overburdened with indulgence."

He closed the Book. His blackened eyes searched the pews. "What is community, can anybody tell me?" He waited, though he knew laymen were forbidden to speak during Mass. "The dictionary tells us it's a people living in one place. Isn't that us?"

The congregation stared back, silent.

"The dictionary also tells us it's a people of the same religion. Now, I know that's us. But where it says it's a people with things in common, I'm not so sure we'd all agree." He stared at the Murphys and their two respective families, lined up in their pews, dressed in their Sunday best.

When Father Mulally stepped away from the pulpit and moved to the centre aisle, the congregation wondered at this unorthodox approach to the liturgy.

"Can anybody tell me what we have in common, here, in St. Peter's Parish?"

The parishioners shifted. Somebody coughed. A baby began to cry.

"On Northbridge Road?" He faced the Higgenbothams. "Prince County, Prince Edward Island?"

Mrs. Higgenbotham stared at her skirt. Mr. Higgenbotham took in the statue of Mary, in her long sky-blue robe, and the serpent that was wound at her feet.

The priest tossed a final, disgusted glance at the Murphys, then returned to the pulpit. "We all need each other. And whether we like it or not, we're bound together. Sometimes, some of us forget."

The Murphys hung their heads. The rest of the congregation wondered which version of the Fortune-Murphy story Father Mulally was referring to and how any of it had to do with them.

The priest raised a finger. "Council meets directly after Mass. I expect every member to attend."

After the Blessing, Father Mulally moved down the centre aisle toward the main wooden doors, which now stood open. The congregation followed him out under a mid-morning sun that had barely risen above the woods across the road. Frost still clung to the leafless shrubs that edged the grounds.

As each parish council member filed past him, Father Mulally gripped a hand. "You're coming to the meeting then?"

Some smiled and nodded their heads. Others shrugged, their eyes darting toward where the Higgenbothams boarded their jaunting wagon. Women mingled in groups and wondered at *the gall of them and why they didn't just flat-out advertise their wares in the parish bulletin*. Mrs. Higgenbotham gripped her red hat as their wagon rolled down the church drive. A stream of wagons immediately followed. When the council president joined the convoy, a woman pointed a finger. "Where's Archie Jamieson goin'?" Another marched toward her own wagon, glared up at her husband, and jabbed a finger toward the Glebe.

Father Mulally shook his head as the procession rolled down Northbridge Road.

"You go on home, Larry. I'm going to that meeting," Martha said.

"But it's a parish council meeting, Ma!"

"I know what that meeting's about and I'm going."

Martha followed Tobias Murphy across the lawn toward the Glebe. She waited for him to disappear inside the colonial-style house, then approached the front door.

Mrs. MacGee opened it. "Father's at a meeting." Behind her, Tobias Murphy followed five other men into the parlour.

"That's what I'm here for," Martha replied.

"The women are meeting next week." Mrs. MacGee moved to close the door.

"They're talking about Billy," Martha said.

"I'll get Father." The housekeeper left Martha standing in the porch.

Seconds later, Father Mulally appeared. "Martha, dear, there are no women here today, you know that."

"They want to take Billy Fortune's job away, don't they?"

"You'd better come in." He escorted her to his study and offered her a chair. "I'm afraid our Billy has shown his temper once too often. And I'm not just talking about yesterday."

Martha considered the priest's battered face. "I suppose the whole council's against him."

"It doesn't look good."

"Is there nothing you can do, Father?"

"I've one vote and the list of grievances is long." The priest thought for a moment. "You come with me."

Heads turned as Martha followed Father Mulally into the parlour. Six men occupied the only available seats. They each held a copy of the list of grievances Daniel had brought to the previous day's meeting. Someone rose and offered the priest his chair. Father Mulally directed Martha toward it and then stood and leaned against the mantel behind her.

Tobias pointed a finger, "What's *she* doin' here?"

"Mind your manners, Mr. Murphy," Father Mulally said.

"Right, then," Tobias said.

"Where are the others?" Father Mulally asked. "Where's Archie Jamieson? He's president."

The men glanced at each other. Tobias shrugged. "Other business, likely."

Tobias's neighbour, Ben Creed, raised a hand. "I'll stand in for Archie."

"Let's get to it, then," Father Mulally said.

Ben moved to the mantel and stood beside the priest. "We all know what we're here for."

"I don't," Martha said.

Ben held up his sheet of paper. "Says right here."

"Where's my copy?" Martha asked.

"And mine?" the priest asked.

Ben checked the mantel and the coffee table in front of the settee. "Looks like we're out."

"Perhaps we could have a look." Father Mulally took Ben's copy, passed it to Martha, and leaned over her chair. Martha put a hand to her face as she read.

Ben Creed cleared his throat. "First, there's Billy's wages. That eleven dollars and forty cents a month is church money, innit?"

"Wouldn't it be nice to get paid for somethin' you loves to do," Tobias said.

"Bloody fortune," another man said.

"Billy works hard," Martha said.

Father Mulally turned to Tobias. "What do you do for a living, Mr. Murphy?"

218

"I'm a farrier, Father."

"And you enjoy your work?"

"I do."

"And you have some training?"

"My father learned me."

"You take pride in it?"

Tobias struggled to see the priest's point. "Yes, Father."

"How would it be if your customers decided against paying you?"

"But, I've a family, Father."

"So, despite Billy's training and the hours he spends choosing the repertoire and practicing with the choir and maintaining the organ, he shouldn't be paid because he enjoys the work?"

"But, it's for the church!"

"So, you mean to say that I shouldn't be paid either."

Tobias raised his eyebrows. "You get paid, Father?"

The other men sat up and stared.

"You're shocked?"

"Well, I never thought."

"Good, then. Work is work, right? Whether you like it or not. And how are we feeling about Billy Fortune, now?"

"But the money's from the collection," Tobias said. "It's for the poor. It's to run the church."

"You don't give up, do you, Mr. Murphy?" The priest shook a finger. "Well, I'll tell you something. We keep a list of the poor, here, in my study. And every family on that list gets eight dollars a month and fifty cents extra for each child. So, Mr. Fortune gets twelve dollars a month for him and his children and not the eleven dollars and twenty cents you're complaining about."

"I never seen no list," Tobias said.

"No," the priest said. "Because it's none of your business. But since you think it is, Billy refused the money. Said he'd rather work for it." The priest turned to the now-silent men, at a defeated Tobias Murphy, and at Ben Creed, who was now edging away from the mantel. "So I gave him a job. And that's nobody's business either." He crumpled up his paper and tossed it into the fire. "Who wrote that list?"

Tobias hung his head. "Daniel did."

Several members folded their papers and placed them on the coffee table.

"Where's Daniel now? And Archie Jamieson? And the rest of them?"

219

"Down Northbridge Road, likely," Tobias said.

Father Mulally smiled for the first time that day. "Seems a red hat stole your quorum."

Billy Fortune played for the Christmas concert that year. He played the organ and conducted the choir at midnight Mass on Christmas Eve and again on New Year's Eve. Then he walked out of St. Peter's Church and never returned.

Mimi, Maman, et Père Noël

❄ Laurel Smyth ❄

Mimi's first impression of her Seniors College Writing Class was not at all what she had expected—but then, things seldom were. She had a lifelong habit of imagining in advance how things would go and often suffered disappointments as a result. Partly in an attempt to channel her imagination into something more constructive, she had decided to try her hand at creative writing. It seemed a panacea for the unanticipated boredom of retirement, preferable to becoming one of those red-hatted women attending gallery openings and theatrical first nights in a clump of rouged cheeks and clouds of oppressive perfumes.

To her surprise, the instructor, an amiable woman with glasses, greying hair, and a sardonic glint in her steely blue eyes, issued a list of recommended reading as well as a first assignment that sounded like something from grade school: "My Favourite Christmas Memory." Jeesh! Not exactly the "Guide to Perfecting Haiku" or "Secrets to Life Writing" Mimi had imagined. Still, Mimi gamely bought (second-hand) the first book on the list as an early Christmas present to herself. It was a very popular twelve-week course designed to "free up the Inner Artist," full of writing exercises and other fun stuff like making collages and taking oneself on an "Artist's Date." This latter was supposed to be a time set aside for some form of self-indulgence that might encourage creativity. Hmm. Mimi decided to leave that for now and concentrate on having something in hand for that first assignment. She dutifully cast her mind back to a time when Christmas still held a promise of magic and marvel—and landed with a bit of a thump in Toronto, 1959...

That day, Mimi awoke huddled under the old brown silk quilt which had once been the pride of Maman's bridal bed, curled up in a tangle of fast-growing, ten-year-old limbs. With a start of guilt and an audible *pop!* she pulled her thumb out of her mouth and anxiously pressed back against her front teeth to counteract the buck-tooth effect her mother often warned her about. She kept the comforter pulled up over her head to keep out the wintry drafts from the rattling windows in the attic room she shared with one of her older sisters. The other half of the bed was already cold, so Val had been up for a while.

Funny, she hadn't heard Maman call up the stairs, "Valerie, bathroom's free!" which was the usual start of Mimi's mornings. Through the patchy stuffing of the quilt she could hear her sisters arguing almost amiably down at the breakfast table. Maman scolded, "Hurry, don't be late for school!" Mimi giggled softly. Maman was forgetting to call her to get up; she'd have to send her to school with a note of apology to the teacher if she didn't get going soon. Snug in her silken cocoon, Mimi listened to the bump and bustle as the girls dressed for the cold, their calls of "Where's my hat?" and "That scarf's mine!" accompanied by the long zip of ski jackets being closed, the bang of the front door, the sudden silence that followed their departure. As she listened, her feeling of smug glee was slowly replaced by one of dismay. Maman had forgotten all about her.

How could she? By the time Mimi got to the kitchen, her dismay had become a hot balloon of righteous indignation that made her chest ache. How could Maman forget? Mimi bristled in the doorway, fists clenched, scowling, angrier with her mother than ever before. How *could* she? But Maman turned to her with such a soft, open, loving look that it pierced Mimi's heart, burst the bubble of anger, and caused her to wail, "You forgot you had me!"

Maman clucked and chuckled and enfolded her in an embrace. "*Mais non, chérie, c'est impossible!* How could I ever forget my little Mimi? You're my baby. I just thought I would let you sleep in a little because today I have something very special planned just for you and me."

Maman pulled back a little, kissed away the tears, made a French *moue* at Mimi to make her smile, and started dancing her around the kitchen, singing, to the tune of "Mary Had a Little Lamb," "We're going downtown to see Père Noël, Père Noël, Père Noël. Just me and my littlest gal, we're going to have some fun!" until Mimi grew giddy with wonder and excitement.

That morning, Mimi's world was turned upside down as Maman proceeded to break all the rules. Sleep in. Skip school. Sunday clothes on Wednesday. Before Mimi knew it, she was all dressed up in the amber-coloured velvet dress she'd finally grown into, thankful that neither of her sisters had ruined it while it was theirs. Even better, her mother had decided that this year Mimi could

wear the camel-hair coat with the real fur collar that rich Tante
Marie had sent up from the States. Like the dress, it was a hand-
me-down from her cousins but coveted nevertheless.

Mimi almost felt like a princess as she boarded the streetcar behind
Maman, obeying her whispered injunction to "Scooch down" so
that she appeared shorter than a line etched on the metal pole to
define those too big to pay only children's fare. Maman shot her a
look of pleased complicity as she dropped the two tickets into the
glass box.

"Red and green, just like Christmas. Two transfers, please, M'sieu!"
she sang out with a dimple to the driver, who, like most men, was
too disarmed by her pretty smile and soft Acadian accent even to
notice the tickets. Maman could have dropped bay leaves or
potato peels into that fare box and still have gotten her transfers.

"Going downtown today, ladies?" the driver smiled back.

"Yes, to see the windows, and Santa Claus, of course." Maman
winked. She was such a flirt! Dad always said, "You'll drive the poor
guys crazy, Toinette!" but Mimi could tell he was crazy-proud of
her.

All the way downtown, Maman was in the highest of spirits. "Isn't
this fun, Mimi? I feel like I am the one playing hooky. I've got the
whole day planned out and you are going to love it."

And, of course, Mimi did. Everything that day was pure surprise,
unsullied by expectation. As the streetcar lurched its way into the
heart of the city, shop windows became increasingly brilliant with
lights and trees, beautiful giftware, and clothing. Maman was like
a big kid.

"Look at that snowman, Mimi, he looks drunk. And those little
gnomes, so cute. Oh, see the fairies? Everything so beautiful, *si
beau...*"

When they finally got off at Yonge and Queen, they squeezed
their way through the crowds in front of Eaton's corner windows.
There, in animated miniature, was Santa's workshop, complete with
pointy-eared elves hammering on wooden toys or painting dolls'
cheeks a rosy pink. Little trains ran on shining elevated tracks
around the perimeter, through tiny mountain villages and forests,
into tunnels and over trestles. A sleepy Santa was nodding over his
Nice & Naughty list. Beyond the little panes of the workshop's
windows, tiny skaters twirled in time to calliope carols, snow falling in sparkles all around. It was another world, a world where

Christmas and merriment ruled, where plenty was the norm, where troubles were forgotten. As they inched, arm in arm, along the gleaming bank of wondrous windows, Mimi and Maman paused to marvel at each element, pointing out special features to one another, smiling until their faces hurt.

Maman squeezed Mimi's arm as they stood before the final window.

"You know, Mimi, that first year your dad and I were in Toronto, before you girls were born, was great… until it got close to Christmas. Then all of a sudden I felt so homesick for the Island, I thought I'd die. I was almost sorry I'd married my handsome Air Force pilot and followed him to Ontario. How could I have a happy Christmas without my family and friends, all the kitchen parties and sleigh rides? Well, I was still just a girl, really, even though I was a married woman. I was only seventeen, just three years older than our Lainie is now. I felt so blue…

"Then one evening your dad brought me here and let me look and look, just like now. Oh, we laughed and pointed at all the pretty things, and ate hot chestnuts from a street vendor. One thing we never had in Abram's Village was windows like these. I decided I'd better give Toronto a chance to let me love it. And now I do." Maman shrugged. "Still, each Christmas I do think of home, and wish to be there again. We were planning to go back this year so you girls could have a real *Joyeux Noël* with *Grandpère et Grandmère*. But then they shut down the Avro Arrow and now Dad doesn't have work, so…" Maman's voice trailed off.

Mimi turned her eyes away from the kitten peeping again and again out of Mrs. Santa's knitting bag and really looked at her mother. In that moment, Maman seemed so sad behind her smile. It was strange for Mimi to think about her parents before she was born, of her mother as a girl homesick for her childhood home. Hearing Maman share her feelings made her feel almost grown up. She wanted to say something to make things happy again, but she didn't know what. So she just pressed closer to Maman's side and the two of them stood there in silence for a while as the early winter dusk set in. It began to snow, big fat flakes that stuck to their hair and eyelashes.

Suddenly Maman was laughing again. "Mimi! We're turning into snow girls. Time to go inside."

They headed for the Annex Tea Room to warm up over cocoa and currant scones, trying on hats along the way, giggling over their reflections in the counter mirrors. Maman gave Mimi ten whole dollars to spend on presents. She spent it all on a pair of gloves for Dad, so he wouldn't keep his hands shoved deep in his pockets. She'd already hidden a tiny bottle of Evening in Paris in her bedside table for Maman, which she'd bought at the corner drugstore with money from pop bottles collected on the way home from school.

After cocoa, it was time to see Santa Claus. Mimi felt a little foolish in the lineup; all the other kids were shorter and younger than she was. In truth, Mimi was no longer so sure about Santa. All her friends no longer believed. Val and Lainie had rolled their eyes when Mimi gave Maman her letter to Santa to mail, although Maman seemed happy enough to do so. And she seemed happy again now, fussing over the angle of Mimi's beret and smoothing her ringlets so she'd look good in this last picture with Santa. For her mother's sake she kept quiet. Somehow she had come to understand that this day was more about Maman than it was about herself.

So as she perched on Santa's knee, she dimpled like Maman to make him go "Ho Ho Ho!" and gave her best smile for the camera elf. And for Maman, who stood smiling and a little bit tearful.

"You looked so beautiful up there, chérie," Maman said proudly as Mimi stepped down. "It will be a wonderful photo."

And so it was.

Now Mimi lifted it out of an album to accompany the story as she wrote it for class. Maman had managed a minor miracle—a photographic record to send home to her family, showing her girl posed on Santa's knee and looking as pretty and prosperous as a princess. Maman had kept up appearances to save face, her husband's pride, and their relatives from worry. That was their last winter in Toronto; the next summer they moved back to the Island so Dad could work at the airfield in Summerside. From then on, they always had a *Joyeux Noël*.

Somehow writing about that time deepened Mimi's understanding of her mother's actions that day. How wise of Maman to surprise her that way; she understood her girl too well to let imagined pleasures take the shine off real ones. She realized that Maman had given herself—and Mimi—an "artist's date," an experience to acknowledge the creative, magical sense of wonder inside each human heart.

Angel Missing

❄ Dianne Hicks Morrow ❄

On December 15 I awake in a funk. All I want for Christmas is Michael's angel down from our attic to give him, now that he has a son of his own, almost six months old. But these days, in my late sixties, I'm a Nervous Nellie about dangerous things like climbing up into the attic. Just yesterday a friend sent me an email listing the four most common causes of accidents: #1 Rushing #2 Inattention #3 Fatigue and #4 Over-Confidence. Confirmation of the wisdom of this list came earlier this week when both my husband Andy and I tripped. I wrenched my ankle, and he, his knee and wrist—thanks to #1 and #2 and #3.

But I've learned my lesson. I'm not rushing, I'm paying careful attention to what's required to safely pull off this caper, and I've had a good night's sleep.

When son Michael was a December newborn, one couple gave him a *papier mâché* Christmas angel. Most friends brought flowers to the hospital, impossible to bring safely home in the worst winter storm in years. At the time I was surprised by this angel gift, but over the Christmases of our firstborn's life I've loved seeing it among our annual decorations. It always reminds me of Michael's first Christmas, just two weeks old, tucked under the tree, in the doll cradle Dad had made for me as a child.

This time last year, with Michael and his wife Kathy expecting their first child, I'd cajoled Michael into bringing in the tall, teetery wooden ladder from the shed and going up into our mice-and-bat-poopy attic to find the box containing his angel. In recent years, I'd stored most of the decorations on the back stairs so Andy and I wouldn't have to deal with the attic, but somehow the angel was missing.

Michael had grumbled a bit about having to go up in the attic, but humoured me. As I'd stood at the foot of the wobbly ladder, with my weight on the bottom rung to keep it steady, he'd called down, "It's gross up here. What does the box look like?" Which I couldn't recall any more. So he passed down several. I was optimistic about a brown box, but it contained the golden angel that usually topped the big, ceiling-high trees of our youth. I was puzzled and disappointed not to find Michael's Angel in white, standing in her sweet-grass basket, surrounded by tiny candles. Somehow he must have missed it. Or maybe, as it turns out, I should have been just a little clearer about what I was looking for.

This Christmas I'm determined to pass on our firstborn's angel to his firstborn. So today's the day. I've bought a particulate mask at the hardware store to protect me from breathing in pink fibreglass insulation slivers and bat guano. I've found the headlamp and have my gardening gloves at the ready. Yesterday, before the snow forecast for today, I lugged the wooden stepladder into the sunporch. Now, all I need is Andy's help to tote the ladder up the stairs without knocking family photos down from the wall, and to firmly anchor the ladder while I climb.

Together we haul it up the stairs. He recalls exactly where to place the ladder, one leg needing a half-inch-thick book to balance the opposite leg. I put on my breather and gardening gloves, much to Andy's amusement. I get halfway up the ladder before I realize I've forgotten the headlamp. Without it I'll see little, given there's only one tiny window up there, and this is a dreary day. Of course Andy can't let go of the bottom of the ladder, so back down I gingerly come, pick up the headlamp, figure out how to fit the three straps around my head, turn it on, and climb back up.

The ladder shakes enough to make me wonder if I've committed the #4 cause of accidents: overconfidence. But I make it up to the second top rung and successfully push the heavy trap door—laden with thick fibreglass insulation—up and off to one side. Now I have to climb onto the flat top of the ladder to reach across droppings-dotted insulation to each of the five cardboard boxes that remain up here. I open them in turn, and discover my late parents' large frosted tree lights, a bonus. I know Michael and Kathy will appreciate adding them to ours, passed on to them last Christmas.

I find other decorations from my parents' home but no sign of Michael's angel. I had feared I'd find it damaged by marauding mice, but it never occurred to me I'd not find it at all. Grumpily I climb down the ladder, note the bemused look on my patient husband's face. Now I'm wondering if the angel has been in one of the boxes on the back stairs all along and am annoyed with myself.

I resolve to check the back stairs one more time. But the phone rings. It's Michael to ask about a recipe. I decide to confess that I've been up in the attic—yes, I admit to a feeling of bravery as I tell him this, and I detect a note of admiration in his voice as he asks why. I'm now wishing I'd gotten Andy to take a photo of me in my regalia.

"I wanted to find your angel so baby George can have it his first Christmas, just as you did when you were a newborn."

To which he replies, "Then you're almost six months late!" Then he adds, "Didn't I find that last year? Didn't we have it here last Christmas?"

In that moment I can picture it in the centre of their coffee table.

I'll now add another item to the list of what causes accidents: #5 Memory Lapse.

Operation Santa

❄ Philip Macdonald ❄

As it turned out, Christmas 1953 was a turning point for me. I was in third grade at Dalton School in the careful custody of Mother St. Mary Justin.

The weeks before Christmas were, of course, the penitential season of Advent in which the nuns worked to prepare us for the coming of the Christ child. I confess I was quite distracted from their efforts by the anticipated arrival of that other seasonal visitor—Santa Claus.

That Santa would come bearing wonderful gifts was as much an Article of Faith to the kids in grade three as was the arrival of the Baby Jesus. Unlike the Son of God, however, Santa was not all-knowing and had to be told what gifts to bring. And so, around the middle of November, my friends and I began what we came to call "Operation Santa."

The first stage of the campaign involved listing all of the most desirable toys and games we could think of. We pored over our primary sources—the Christmas catalogues from Eaton's and Simpson's—and listened to "The Sleepy Town Express" on CFCY to get additional ideas from the letters to Santa from children in far-off places, such as Charlottetown or Montague.

The local stores also provided opportunities for research. In a storage space above their main floors, the Tignish Co-op and Morris & Bernard created "Toyland," a veritable trove of childhood delights. These Toyland displays offered a wonderful chance to identify new items for our wish list and, if the clerk could be distracted, do a quick field test of some of the more novel offerings.

Our lists grew over the several weeks of research and, after review in recess-time focus groups and with nonchalant advice from parents, we achieved the final selections by the agreed-upon deadline.

The letter to Santa had to be sent by mid-December, just like the catalogue orders to Eaton's or Simpson's. It was painstakingly composed, drafted and rewritten many times. Finally, it was ready:

sealed in its envelope, addressed to Santa at the North Pole, and added to the family Christmas cards to be stamped and mailed.

The letter having been sent, our attention could now focus on the next stage of the campaign: the visit from Santa.

Santa's visit was announced by a telegram delivered to the school. The message was written on the telegraph form used by the CNR and in the handwriting of the Station Agent. This allowed me a brief prominence among my classmates since, as son of the Station Agent, I could vouch that the message was authentic.

That telegram must have bothered those who had come to question the very existence of Santa. For some inexplicable reason, that doubt seemed to have something to do with growing older (like the changing voices of the boys, the changing shapes of the girls, or pimples). The children beyond grade six were mostly nonbelievers. But the CNR telegram must have shaken their unbelief. Santa had sent us an actual wire from the North Pole. And he was coming to visit us in person.

Fortunately Santa's visit happened on a Saturday, when we were free of Mother St. Mary Justin's surveillance, and took place at the Legion. The chairs had been pushed aside in the hall, which welcomed us with the lingering aroma of old popcorn and stale smoke from the Friday night movie. A big chair, obviously for Santa, had been set up in front of the movie screen.

Santa arrived right on time, emerging from the cab of the village's fire truck. Members of the Legion and the Village Council, deputized as Santa's helpers, herded the ragtag mob, struggling under toques, scarves, mitts, and parkas, around the hall towards Santa's throne. We were noisy, frisky, and nervous.

We were nervous because, while the meeting with Santa was very exciting, it was not without danger. There was the pressure to remember exactly what had been listed in our long-ago letters and there was the embarrassment of voicing those requests aloud. There was the fear that you might be thought greedy and be reproved by Santa or—perish the thought!—that your friends, surveying your gifts after Christmas, would know that Santa had refused to give what you had asked for.

When I arrived at his chair, I was lifted onto his comfortable knee and greeted with a great many "Ho Ho Ho!'s." His head was encased in a red stocking cap and his lower face was covered by a fleecy white beard. He wore a red suit, still smelling of fumes from the fire engine, and a wide black belt with matching black gloves. But rather than boots, he wore overshoes like my father's, even down to the patch on his left instep.

Leaving the Legion, my friends eagerly recounted, over and over, the details of their encounter with the Great Man and planned the treats they would set out for his real visit on Christmas Eve.

Somehow, I didn't feel like joining in their plans. In fact, the 1953 campaign was my last Operation Santa.

Once Upon a Christmas Morning

❄ David McCabe ❄

once upon an empty
christmas morning
we walked an antiseptic
hallway
two brothers, silent
save the callous echo
of leather heels
on yellowed waxed
linoleum

shuttered
by oily smooth
elevator doors
the hard cold rumble
of steel on steel
sealed from our father
abandoned and stark
on cold crisp sheets

all fires out
masks fallen away
father and son
twisting and turning
to find one another
to connect
over all that distance
and time
would not return now
to the green grass bank
below the bridge
where the river philip bends
and slips softly to the sea

at a parking lot door
my brother turns
face contorted
and tears
"you're a hard man"
he says

but by then
my head had turned
to other things
the business
of death
finding a christmas morning doctor
signing papers
shipping a corpse
by freight

and my escape
to sanctuary
with two small daughters
in my arms
before a tinseled christmas tree

I Keep Looking

※   Kathleen Hamilton   ※

My mother hasn't spoken to me for most of my adult life. She finds me unacceptable, always has. I'm past fifty now. The first time she disowned me I was fifteen. I had run away from home and she told my younger sister to walk past me if she saw me on the street. But you could say she abandoned me long before that. Over the years, we've tried, a few times, to be family to each other, but our recon-ciliations never last. She doesn't break up with me exactly, she just stops taking my calls. She has no contact with my children. My fourteen-year-old wouldn't know her.

It's not that I don't have my ways of coping. You know one thing I do? At Christmas, I order books for myself on Amazon, and I fill out the gift card. Then, when the package arrives I open it and there's a note that says, Happy Reading, Love Mom. I know I sent it to myself but it still makes me happy.

In my first memory of Christmas my mother figures promi-nently. I would put my age at six years old, which would make it 1967. My mom had been a teenage bride, and tragically widowed at twenty, so by the time I was six, she had taken herself to night school, had trained to be a secretary, and was working full-time to support me and my younger sister.

What I remember about this Christmas is that Mom told me, enough times that it stayed with me all these years, that "Santa is not made of money, so don't expect much" and "there'll be a few things under the tree, but only a few."

I was young enough that I didn't have expectations, although I suppose I would have been influenced by the toy commercials on TV, as would my mom. The oldest child of a single parent, I was a mature, serious girl. I had already gleaned that parents were Santa, and since my dad was dead, and my mom "worked darned hard" for her money but didn't earn much, I knew that presents would be in short supply.

On Christmas Eve I went to sleep calmly in the bed I shared with my sister, believing there would likely be two presents each for her and me. I told myself not to hope for an Easy Bake Oven and a doll, since Mom probably had to get us clothes.

In the morning, I padded out to an alarming sight: an ocean of presents, what looked to me like millions of presents in drifts around the tree. I remember Janet was thrilled, literally dancing with glee, and my mom's eyes were all shiny and her voice husky.

It was shocking to me. I remember I felt uneasy, almost sick. How had she paid for all this? Why had she? I felt unworthy.

We opened the gifts and found the Easy Bake and not one, but several dolls, and pick-up sticks, and etch-a-sketches and barrels of monkeys and slippers and musical jewellery boxes with ballerinas that turned, crayons and colouring books and I can't remember what else. A crazy amount of stuff. Janet kept exclaiming and kissing Mom and diving for the next present; I was overwhelmed by the sheer quantity of it all, the odd mixture of feelings bouncing through my body.

But I also got that my Mom felt proud of her accomplishment, and I admired her—was awed by her.

What I didn't understand when I was six was anything about the shame that must have filled my 1950s-era mother at her teen pregnancy, and the resulting obligatory marriage to my father. But I could sense that our circumstances now were somehow shameful. The moment my dad died, my mother became a widow and was stripped of power in society. We, as her children, although technically not illegitimate, became less than other children, as the kids in our apartment playground were quick to point out. "You don't even have a dad" were words I didn't have to hear twice. What I knew was that we weren't considered a real family, and I was starting to notice the effort it took for my mother to hold up her head. Making an extravagant Christmas was a way for her to fight back, to rise for one day above stigma and poverty.

Christmas was always my mother's big event. I can't not think of her at Christmas time. I remember her when I decorate my house. She always had a real tree, as do I. She was gently particular about where the decorations should be placed, that each be displayed to its full advantage. Lights were not just lights, they were there to show off the decorations—balls should be placed so that they *reflected* the lights—a ball without a coloured light shining on it was a ball *misplaced*. And tinsel, well, tinsel must never just *hang* there, it must be carefully draped from branch to branch to achieve a *cascading* effect, like a waterfall. One should not see the *end* of a tinsel. My mother shared this with me in the warmest, most confiding of tones when I was young. So ingrained is her teaching that in years hence, when I saw that most people had not the patience for such labour, and instead threw tinsel at the branches and let the strands catch where they may, I decided to forgo tinsel altogether so as not to offend her memory.

Christmas was when my mother was at her most peaceful and yet animated best. Even my stepfather dared not mar the event. Christmas was sacred to her.

She showed it in many ways. Her handmade chocolates, created for the Christmas candy tree my sister and I helped her to assemble each year. The branches were dishes that each held an exquisite handmade chocolate and formed the centerpiece of her holiday dessert table.

In the basement, her freezer was stacked with Tupperware containers of Christmas baking—I know there must have been a variety, but all I remember are the shortbread cookies, of which I will never in my life be able to eat enough.

One night near Christmas when I was barely in my teens, I found my mother sitting alone in our darkened living room beside the Christmas tree. The lights glowed, competing with those of the town below.

"Come in," she said in a hushed tone, as if I'd come upon her in church. She patted the seat beside her. "I like to sit and admire the tree."

I felt as if I was being invited into a womanly enclave of heavenly peace. I sat quietly near her.

"What are your favourite ornaments?" she asked me, and I got the feeling this wasn't small talk.

"Um, the birds?" I ventured. I was pretty sure she liked the birds.

She nodded. "Those were Mer's," she said. Mer had been my great grandmother, remembered now through the antiques she'd left Mom in her will. "They're old, but I wouldn't dream of throwing them out."

The birds were tiny and metallic, painted in shimmering colours that reminded me of the puddles at gas stations. They had extraordinarily long tails, delicate and pretty.

She sighed with what seemed a deep contentment, the way I sigh now when I settle into my chair at the beach. That's how right with the world she seemed that night.

"I love looking at the presents," she said dreamily, "the beautiful wrapping."

"Yeah," I said companionably.

"Look at that one there." She pointed below the tree. "See the one with the velvet bow? Isn't it pretty? I wonder what could be in that one."

"I don't know," I admitted.

She reached in among the presents and retrieved it, something I hadn't known was allowed. She turned it over in her hands, most reverently. I don't remember whom the gift was for or from. I don't think that was important. What mattered was the beauty and the mystery, and my mother found that in the gifts and ornaments of Christmas.

I'd all but gone off Christmas by then.

It made me feel crazy, the schism between my mother's expectations of Christmas and the reality of our home life. Not only did I have my usual fear of being caught for some real or manufactured infraction of my stepfather's rules; not only was there the daily possibility of being beaten and humiliated; but in December, overlying my usual fear was the special holiday fear of such an event ruining Christmas for my mother.

Unbearable for me was the pressure of performing, of pretending for a full day that our home was a happy one, and yet having no control over the outcome.

Christmas was a time of craziness condensed. Highly pressurized fear. I'm not sure I can describe it. You know how feelings about family get heightened and amplified at Christmas? If you're lucky those feelings are love and good will. The usual emotional climate in my family, at least for me in those years, was fear. So, at Christmas, it was my apprehension that was intensified and multiplied, my anxiety and dread that mounted, and it took great effort on my part to contain it, to put on a good show.

But even though I hated being a fake, even though it made me feel angry and insane, I was still willing to do it to please my mom.

A few years—but really a lifetime—later, I return to my mother and stepfather's home in Terrace, B.C., and spend Christmas with my mother for what will be the last time. I've just turned eighteen and have flown in from Ontario to appear before a judge at my divorce hearing. (I *know*.)

As it turns out, my sister Janet, fifteen years old by this time, has run away from home (not for the first time) and my mother is sad that she isn't there for Christmas. I don't want to be in my parents' house without my sister. This is selfish of me, entirely. There is no benefit to Janet in this, but, on Christmas Eve, I leave my mother's mansion on the hill and track my sister to her refuge in a trailer across the tracks.

What I'm doing is unconscionable, really. I have attained freedom. I have a life in Ontario and need only stick out a few days over the holidays, appear in divorce court, and be on a plane out of here again. Janet has somehow propelled herself out of our parents' house with god knows what effort, and after what provocation. Another beating? Threat of death? But I'm not thinking reality. I am thinking beauty and mystery and Mom will be so happy. I am thinking, *Mom's eyes will be all aglow.* I am thinking, *I have the power to make my mother happy at Christmas.*

So I go to the trailer of the friend where Janet is hiding, enjoying the rights of teenage runaways everywhere: to drink beer and chain-smoke cigarettes, and stay up all night with the Eagles blasting on the eight-track. We haven't seen each other for over a year, and we sit with our arms around each other on the couch, and we sing "Take it to the Limit" over and over, and when we are full of the Christmas spirit I convince her to go back with me.

We awake hungover the next morning. Mom cries and hugs Janet, but my stepfather does not bother to hide his anger.

"Why the hell did you bring her here?"

"Mom wanted her."

"Christ, that's all we need."

The glamour of Christmas, my mother's wishes for all to be calm and bright, the glow of alcohol, none of it is enough. We try to fake it, one last time, but we've lost the ability.

Now I make my own Christmases on the opposite side of the country, in PEI. It's been thirty-five years since I lured my sister back to the home of our abuser, to please my mother on December 25.

My mother and I have spent most of those years estranged. We've had a few Christmases "on," but mostly "off." Christmases we're on, she sends her exquisitely wrapped gifts with expensive treasures inside (a jewelled turtle, brass manicure set, baccarat serving dish), and her presence is tangible. Christmases we're off, as we have been for ten consecutive years, her love of the season is still with me.

This year, on Boxing Day, I arrive at the home of Susan, a woman I know only slightly, through a larger community of friends. She is away for the holidays and I'm borrowing her home as a writing retreat.

The first night at Susan's house, I'm flooded with memories of my mother, her spirit, her tastes and sensibilities. I can see her full, painted lips and smell her Estée Lauder perfume. Susan's house in rural PEI reminds me of my mother. I'm not sure why. Perhaps because it's full of beautiful belongings, perhaps because it's lavishly decorated for the season.

My mother likes nice things. That's probably the only thing I could say about her that she'd agree with. I haven't been to her home for thirty-five years (although I know she's moved to a condo), but I imagine the décor is not dissimilar to that in Susan's house, where lovely Christmas vignettes vie for attention on every polished surface, and where I hunt the cupboards for dinner plates that aren't rimmed in gold and where the plain white pasta bowls are Royal Doulton.

It's my custom when I go on retreat to explore the space before I write. I need to get familiar with it, make friends with the "stuff," and I've done that here, but still, when I look up from my notebook, and away from the winter wonderland outside the glass patio doors, the graceful tamaracks, branches glistening with ice, snowflakes dancing by, when I look up and let my eye wander, it invariably lands on some *objet d'art* I haven't noticed before. Just now it's a bold acrylic of whimsical daisies. How could I not have seen it before?

In my late teens I went to weekly therapy sessions—the sessions continued for about two years until I moved away. Then, sometime in my twenties, I returned once to visit my former psychologist at his office. When I complimented him on his stylish new furnishings and exclaimed over the photographs of his family now hung on his wall, he smiled and said, "They've always been there." At first I refused to believe him. I'd sat in his office over a hundred times. How could I not have seen what was right in the room with me?

239

In a case like the whimsical daisies, the answer is simple. It's well understood that when we sit in a different chair, we get a different view. We say, "from where I sit" this is how things look. At my psychologist's office, I must have been too focused on the crises I was living to notice the décor. When my circumstances had changed, I was able to see more clearly what was in my environment. We see what we're able to see.

What I see now that I didn't see before: my mother's lies. It was her lies, perhaps even more than my stepfather's brutality, that made me feel crazy. Never more than at Christmas time.

For adults, living with lies is crazy-making. For children it is catastrophic. Our perceptions tell us one thing, and the person we love most in the world tells us another. It makes us feel insane, for longer into our adult years than we care to admit.

My path to sanity was twofold: 1) stop believing the lies, and 2) stop pretending to believe the lies.

The truth in my family is that my stepfather was a violent abuser, a sociopath; my mother's lie is that he was a great guy who loved us. The truth in my family is that my mother knew about, approved of, and sometimes helped him "punish" us; the lie is that she didn't. The truth in my family is that my sister and I acted out in response to the cruelty; my mother's lie is that we were bad kids who got inexplicably worse, no matter how hard my parents tried.

We have some strange ways of talking about Christmas. We say Christmas is coming. Christmas will soon be here. As if it's an event that arrives with its own suitcase to unpack. But Christmas doesn't just come. Christmas is made. By people. Often by moms.

In my household, my husband and son and I are aware of making Christmas for ourselves and each other. We choose a series of experiences: the tree, the guests, the food, the gifts. I like to acknowledge this "making" in small ways. This year, we hosted a small party at our home on Christmas Eve, and when all our preparations were ready, when our house was clean and our party table set, we took a moment, the three of us before the guests arrived, to raise our glasses and toast each other. "Merry Christmas," we said. It was a gesture of good will and celebration, a way to say: we are a family making Christmas together.

Here's what I know. My mother doesn't love me. I try to be okay with that. It's mostly at Christmas that I feel the loss of her.

I know my own Christmases are far more meaningful and magical than any she was able to make, despite her desire, because mine unfold in a home where the family members love and respect each other, and where no one is afraid of anyone else.

It's scary, writing about my mother. It seems disloyal. It seems "How could you?" "How dare you?" "Who do you think you are, young lady?" and "You're getting too big for your britches."

Over the years, as I've grown older and healthier, I've become strong enough to speak certain truths to her:

I don't enjoy phone calls from "Dad" on my birthday and Christmas.

I forgive you for not protecting me.

Thank you for putting me on a plane out of Terrace.

To the extent that I lay claim to my truth, my mother recoils from me as though from attack. In her refusal to take my calls, to meet my eyes at family events, she is protecting herself. I know that.

I knew the danger when I decided not to participate in the lies. I knew the risk when I decided to speak up. So I'm living with the consequences. I get to tell the truth and have a voice. I don't get to have a mother.

Sometimes I think I'm over her. But I know I'm not.

In the afternoon, I venture into the basement of Susan's house. I'm not sure why. But when I see it I know. The freezer.

In the basement of my mother's house, too, there was a freezer. I go straight to it. Lift the door. Ah, the Mother lode: a stack of Christmas tins that can contain only baking. I reach in for the top tin and pry off its lid. Oh, the love. Shortbread cookies. The tin contains dozens of plump, perfectly shaped cookies with just the right number missing so that two more will not be missed.

I trot back upstairs with my treasures. Just as they did in my mother's house, these frozen shortbreads offer delicious resistance as you bite and chew, so the flavour lasts longer. Plus, you get the contrast of the initial cold, giving way to melting warmth as sugar and butter yield to mouth and tongue. And, of course, the thrill of the illicit, the illegal.

This is as close to my mother's love as I'll come.

For whatever reasons, this house is strongly evocative of my mother. I find myself visited by sense memories of her, and all my writing circles back to her. Everything reminds me of my mother. Why?

Because I keep looking for her. If I tell the truth, there's a part of me who still loves her, who still wants her mother, or at least my dream of who she might be, if only she were different. If only she were strong. And true. If only she treated her children with reverence and saw in them beauty and mystery.

I'm looking for that mother when I bite into frozen shortbread, when I unwrap my Christmas ornaments and tell my son to be sure the bulbs are reflecting light onto the balls.

When I realize I really do like the birds best.

An Abundance of Spirit

※　Liam McKenna　※

I had always loved music, but it wasn't until I went away for high school that I decided to dedicate myself to it fully. I stopped attending classes, preferring to sit at home with my friend Brodie, himself a truant, and we'd smoke and he'd play his guitar and I'd sing. I started to play his guitar, too, and he taught me, and I thought this to be vastly more valuable than the lessons I was learning in class. It seemed a much more accurate representation of the life of an artist, this not caring about the world outside – we were dedicated to our art, intent on studying it seriously.

My parents, though, were paying for a school I wasn't attending, and I didn't tell them of my plans to become a musician because I couldn't even say it to myself without realizing how silly it sounded.

My grades had plummeted. I was but mildly concerned about this; I was the only one of the four children in my family to go away for high school, and although I had expressed my concerns and desires to my older brother Kyle, I knew my secret was relatively safe.

The school's registrar, Valerie, lived on my parents' street. It so happened that on Christmas Eve my parents were out walking when they ran into dear old Valerie, who happily informed them of my academic troubles. I had gone from star pupil to academic pariah in a hurry, and as I lounged unawares in our family home on the biggest holiday of the year, Valerie was dutifully explaining to my parents my status on the day of the year when it was perhaps the least convenient.

My brother approached me midmorning, before we went out to my grandparents' house for our traditional pond hockey game. "Mom and Dad know about your school," he said, "and they're pretty mad."

Now, my mother had something of a reputation in the neighbourhood. Vocationally, she looked after children, running a pre-school from our home. While a visitor to our home might see our daily routine as a sort of controlled chaos, in reality my mother was pointedly aware of everything that went on in her home and with her children. I was a fool to think I could keep such a significant factor from her; any boy who thinks he can keep the details of his life from his mother is.

My mother's reputation, then, was one of a staunch disciplinarian who teetered on the brink of despotism. In matters academic, my father was concerned and was often the primary source of helping me with learning; however, my mother was responsible for enforcing the policies of homework and application of effort. Having both my parents enlightened about my academic status was terrifying; that I had kept the secret from them for the duration of an entire semester was doubly damning, and I was certain of my doom.

"They're going to kill you," said Kyle helpfully.

I opted for a strategy of careful ignorance. I assumed that the holiday would prevent my parents from addressing the issue for a while, as long as I could keep my contact with them public, in front of my other relatives. I schemed, but even that embarrassment was preferable to the lashing I'd receive from my parents. relentlessly – I would travel to my grandparents' with Kyle and my younger brother and sister, Darcy and Megan. We'd reminisce and fight the whole way out, sure, stopping on embarrassing moments from each of our childhoods, but even that embarrassment was preferable to the lashing I'd receive from my parents.

The moment I stepped on the crowded ice, the problems of the day were forgotten, and as often happened my cousins and brothers and I buried ourselves in the game of hockey. I was feeling particularly good that day, imagining that my girl was watching from the side of the pond. That year, the pond had been particularly well-tended to, as my cousins oversaw the construction of a smooth ice surface through careful flooding, and from my first strides and the delicious carving of the skates on fresh ice I was a whirlwind. I skated confidently and handled the puck deftly, moving among the other skaters with fluid grace and artistic skill. My father would later comment on it, having watched amidst the soft glow of Christmas candles from my grandfather's house. It was rare for me to skate so well.

Brimming with a confidence grown from my dominant abilities that day, I strode up the ice with the puck in tow. Kyle approached and I amazed even myself, putting the puck between his legs and retrieving it on the other side of him. His immediate reaction was to lash out at the puck desperately with his stick, which missed its target and struck my own stick, riding up the shaft and striking me between my eyes. Before I knew it, I had turned on him, my stick clattering to the ice, my gloves cast aside. I grabbed a handful of his jacket with my left hand and met his jaw with a hard right cross, drawing my fist back with the warning of another punch.

"There's a lot more where that came from," I snarled. What occurred next became the stuff of familial legend. The other children gathered around to watch what would happen between their two older cousins. In the house, the gentle chime of silverware and the polite laughter ceased. Kyle and I stood, both in disbelief at what I had done, my right fist still drawn back ready to strike, Kyle's own hands casually by his side as he processed the offence.

In an instant, I was under a barrage of blows. For as much as I had felt like an artist playing hockey, Kyle orchestrated a beating that was nothing short of masterful. It was a symphony of fists, each note coming on top of the last, building to a powerful and percussive crescendo that left the audience to my pulverizing impressed and empathetic. Afterwards, I lay a crumpled heap on the ice, and, both inside the house and out, activity resumed. My six-year-old cousins skated around my bloodied figure.

I dragged myself off the pond, spitting into the snowbank. I gathered my stick and my gloves, put them back on, skated aimlessly on the outskirts of the action. That my beating was so well-deserved left me bearing no ill will towards Kyle, and for the rest of the day, any time I touched the puck, I passed it quickly and harmlessly to another player. Kyle had sent his message, loud and clear. When it came to our parents, we were on the same side. Academically, he knew I could best him. But when it came to hockey, the message was this:

Don't even.

We left in the early evening, after a casual dinner of Christmas ham and seafood chowder, which we continue to enjoy every year at my grandparents' house. The informal nature of Christmas Eve meant I could duck my parents in the crowd of our huge family, and I cowered among drunken uncles and the ever-opening doors. Kyle signaled it was time to leave, and the four McKenna children piled back into our little car for a nighttime trip home.

Darcy and I had a plan; although Kyle was old enough to buy us beer, he refused out of what he claimed to be fear of our mother finding out. Kyle's lifestyle, however, did little to showcase much fear of anybody, and it was always our suspicion that the reason behind his refusal to supply us with alcohol was that he believed we should be challenged with finding it, as he had been.

The natural result of this was that Darcy and I conspired to find booze, most often at the expense of our father. At the time, Canadian beer companies had made much fanfare of miniature kegs that held around thirty beer, and the convenience of the offer was not lost on our father, who abhorred drinking from cans and couldn't abide the mess of bottles. The convenience wasn't lost on us, either. Our father had three kegs which had been stowed downstairs for months, and Darcy and I had monitored them carefully. Our father was forgetful – a trait he had passed to me – and Darcy and I saw fit to take advantage of this by squirreling one of the kegs into a kitbag for furtive consumption over Christmas Day. Given the overhanging likelihood of my punishment for my failures at school, I saw myself as protected by facing the maximum sentence already. Also, I could blame Darcy if we were discovered.

He and I set to work as soon as we were home. We turned on our video game console and started a game of virtual hockey, which we played to a halfway point, and then paused. We went into the downstairs pantry, selected the keg our father, by our judgment, was least likely, and took it to my room. We opened it and drank a few glasses to ensure its quality. Emboldened, we wrapped it carefully in a sweater, and gingerly placed it in my schoolbag, which was normally next to my dresser on my bedroom floor.

The driveway lit up with headlights. My parents were home. Darcy and I sat casually in my room, faces glued to my television, resuming our game as though we had never stopped. The front door opened. Along with my father and mother, we heard additional voices – their friends and my uncles and aunts, eager to continue the festivities.

Eager to consume miniature kegs.

My father came down the stairs boisterously, retrieving the first keg from the pantry without fanfare, and returned upstairs. Darcy and I looked at each other, the relief apparent on our faces, and continued our game. The next hour flashed by before my father was downstairs again and we held our breath as we heard the pantry door open. Dad paused.

"I thought there was another keg in here," we heard him say to nobody in particular. He called upstairs to my mother. "I thought there was another keg in here!"

My mother replied that *she* hadn't drunk the beer. "Wayne, *you* probably drank it."

"No," said my father. "I was saving them. There were three in here."

He rummaged again through the closet before our bedroom door burst open, as we now knew it would.

"Have you boys seen my keg? I'm missing a keg of beer." He sounded accusatory. Darcy, as always, was quicker than I was:

"*You* probably drank it, Wayne," he said, without looking away from the game. I hated it when he called Dad by his first name, and so did Dad; but I knew better than to say anything given the delicate nature of my situation, and Dad was too focused on the recovery of his beer to care.

"I didn't," said my father. He did the worst thing I could imagine. He came and stood directly between us and the television, his foot mere centimeters from my school bag where the beer sat. It was the size of the moon. It was incredibly obvious, like hiding a bowling ball in a snake.

"If you boys see it," he said, "Let me know." He left.

We didn't touch another drop until Boxing Day.

Christmas morning, coffee was distributed and presents were being opened. It was the least fun I'd ever had at Christmas, the guilt growing ever larger inside me as the inevitable conflict approached. My parents knew, and by now they realized that I knew they knew, and that I was aware the consequences were going to be very bad. I wondered if I would have to switch schools, or if I would simply be killed outright. I didn't know which I'd prefer; I needed to know the method of execution before I could decide.

The presents were all open, the floor littered with wrapping, another Christmas over. My mother said, "Liam – go stand over by the far wall. We've got something special for you. It's a surprise."

This is it, I thought. I stood against the wall. I was to be shot. I wasn't ready for this. I'm a coward. If it's going to be done, I hope it's over quickly. A single shot to the head would be best.

My father came into the room with a guitar.

I accepted it with teeth gritted, fighting back tears, my shame overcome by this miraculous generosity. They had learned, disconcertingly, no doubt, that my interest in school had declined, but for them to feed my artistic passion rather than punish my lack of scholarly focus overwhelmed me. I hugged them both.

I held the guitar. It was heavy with my guilt and the crushing emotion of the holiday.

Damn it, Christmas, you'd done it again, and not even my teenage angst, my artist's withdrawal, could hold you at bay.

Later that evening, I lay on the couch, full of Christmas dinner and watching the specials on television. My mother came into the room and sat behind me in a chair. I was half asleep. She began to sew quietly, and after half an hour she spoke.

"So things aren't going well at school, are they?"

"No."

"Are they going to get better?"

"Yes. I promise."

She didn't say anything else.

I learned to play the guitar ably, and I finished school. And when I pick up that guitar, I think of my education, inside the school and out; and I think of being caught and being let go, and of when sins are punished, and when they are forgiven.

My Shepherd

❄ Orysia Dawydiak ❄

In spite of the deep cold and snow of northern Ontario winters, December and January were my favourite months of the year. As the daughter of Ukrainian immigrants, I got to celebrate Christmas three times—Saint Nicholas's birthday, English Christmas, and Ukrainian Christmas over two days in January. Make that four times, with three separate opportunities for gifts, special food treats, and extra days off from school. Many years later I realized my good fortune to be raised in a post-World War multiethnic community. Before I could speak English I learned to converse with the neighbourhood kids in Italian, Croatian, Polish, German, and French. Apparently, my mother once overheard me demand in Ukrainian that my little friends must speak *my* language when we played in *my* yard. And they did. I must have been some bossy-pants pre-kindergartener.

The Saint Nicholas pageant opened the doors to our Ukrainian Christmas season on December 19. A short play began with three children in a peasant home, sitting at a table and complaining about school homework. Suddenly, their door banged open and a lizard-like creature burst into their home. Dressed in black, face crimson red, sporting a forked tail and horned head, the devil crouched before them. He was hunting for naughty children, and he had found his prey. Oh, no! He chased them around the table while they stifled their giggles and squealed in pretend fear. The parents in the play stayed out of the way, shaking their fingers, saying, "I told you so!" At least that's how I remembered it.

The audience booed the devil and cheered for the children, who were finally saved by the bell. Several tinkling bells actually, and sweet soprano voices singing in Ukrainian, "Oh who, who, loves St. Nicholas?" Two rows of winged angels pranced in through the entrance, followed by Saint Nick to banish the devil. A coveted role, the angels. All of us girls wanted to wear the stiff sparkly wings and white gauzy gowns trimmed in tinsel. With the devil vanquished, they helped Saint Nick hand out oranges, candy, and the gifts a few parents had provided him ahead of time. The devil made a final curtain call, however, to pursue certain adults in the audience with whipping switches. The older children cheered; the younger ones wailed in terror.

A few days later, December 25 was celebrated with a decorated Christmas tree and gift-giving, though I don't recall any special dinner on that day. Our real Christmas Eve was reserved for January 6 when we were supposed to fast all day and begin our twelve-course dinner only with the appearance of the first evening star. Fortunately, children were not required to fast, but we ate very little in anticipation of the Christmas Eve feast, our *Sviat Vecher*. This Holy Supper was a meatless, dairy-free meal, which began with kutya, a mixture of whole wheat, honey, poppy seed, and walnuts. Then we had beet borsch with beautiful braided egg bread called *kolach*, perogies, cabbage rolls, sauerkraut with peas, pickled fish, mushroom sauce, and a variety of pastries and sweets. Afterwards, the adults and older children were off to church for Midnight Mass. The next day we went carolling from home to home where we were offered more food and drink. Or we stayed home to host the frostbitten carollers and listen to their greetings and songs and share in gossip.

I don't recall any of those Ukrainian Christmas Eve meals as being more memorable than others, except for the time a male guest tossed a spoonful of sticky *kutya* up to our ceiling. My mother, a fastidiously fanatic housekeeper, protested loudly; we kids laughed with delight. It was an ancient, agrarian custom to predict the wheat harvest for the coming year, a bit like reading tea leaves, but messier. Since my dad was a chemical engineer and we lived in a city, it wouldn't have been much use to us, even if we had known how to read the speckled pattern left behind.

No, my most memorable Christmas was the night of December 24, 1961. I don't remember how I ended up at my Aunt Stella's that day, a reprieve from my hectic household with three younger brothers aged six months to eight years. As the only girl, I was often invited to spend time with my sophisticated cousin Jean, a teenager with one foot already in the adult world. But she tolerated me well enough. Perhaps she felt sorry for me, encouraged by her gentle mother, my Aunt Stella, to give me some time away from my frazzled, rough-handed mother. Or perhaps I amused Jean, like the time we played strip poker in her bedroom, and unbeknownst to me she had stuffed her fluffed up hair with bobby pins, an inside-out porcupine. Each time she lost a hand of cards, she removed a pin, while I shed clothing until I hid shivering beneath the covers, buff naked. To the end she remained fully clothed, smirking at me, with hairpins to spare. I declined a second game. Come to think of it, I've never been keen on cards, possibly scarred by my early overexposure.

Perhaps I was visiting that Christmas Eve because Jean was giving my pencil-straight hair a perm. She loved to play with hair—colouring, perming, straightening, and teasing hair into cotton candy beehives when that style was all the rage. She's the one who streaked my brunette tresses for my high school graduation. I returned home late that night and when my mother poked her head into my room the next morning, she awakened me, shrieking in Ukrainian, "Who are you? Where is my daughter?" Jean had gone overboard so all my mother saw were solid platinum blonde bangs. I rather liked the look, once I got used to it.

Jean took me to matinee movies when no one else would go with her. *The Day of the Triffids* and *Village of the Damned* were especially notable for the months of nightmares that followed. Maybe she wasn't the best judge of movies for children, but I adored her. She was cool and she actually acknowledged my existence.

Aunt Stella was married to my mother's brother, a man cut from the same coarse bolt as his sister. Even so, my mother looked down on his drinking, smoking, card-playing ways and rarely had a kind word for him. Their epic verbal battles usually ended in a draw. My uncle laboured in the nickel mines, a dirty, dangerous job that kept his family housed, clothed, and fed. Much later I learned that he was the one who had sent money to my parents in England after the Second World War to help them start their lives over in Canada. I wish I had known him better, but a heart attack and stroke cut him off in midlife while I was away growing into adulthood.

Aunt Stella was as tender as those two were thorny. She comforted me when I was angry and hurt, and she sheltered me when I ran away from home as a young adult, sulking at my mother's irrational outbursts and brutality. She never judged me, even when, as a child, I combed all the hair out of a doll dressed in a traditional Ukrainian costume she had sewn and embroidered. Sure she was annoyed, but she didn't hold grudges like my mother did. When

Aunt Stella died, I felt I had lost my soul mother, my guardian angel. For weeks after, I found myself crying at night as I lay in bed. I often dreamt of her.

That all ended the night she came to see me. She stood beside my bed, looking down at me with love and sympathy. "I am happy where I am, child, do not fret about me. All is well. There is no need to grieve." My eyes popped open and I watched her evaporate from my bedside, as ghosts are wont to do.

But on the Christmas Eve when I was nine, I lay on the couch in her living room and gazed at the tree hung with glowing icicles and dancing tinsel. There were no sounds but those of a sleeping house breathing, the air moving from my baba's room to the kitchen, from my aunt and uncle's room to Jean's room, finally floating back to where I lay. And then, around midnight I heard them, the fairy footsteps of reindeer on the roof. No, I didn't believe in Santa Claus, but I did believe in flying deer. I held my breath, my heart racing until their patter ceased and I knew they were gone. I fell into a sleep that night, deep and sound and dreamless.

The Christmas Tree

❄ Brenda Brindell ❄

A highlight of my childhood was our Christmas concerts at our one-room schoolhouse. The schoolhouse was located on a dirt road in a little community called Church Road, near Morell on Prince Edward Island. It was heated by a big potbellied, wood burning stove in the centre of the room. Each student had a desk, and the desks were in rows across the room. The youngest children sat at the front and the oldest at the back. The teacher's desk was in the centre at the front. The schoolhouse had beautiful windows, tall and narrow.

We never referred to the Christmas celebration as a concert but always as the Christmas Tree. Maybe because the tree was so lovely and so big and tall and played such an important role in our young lives. The tree seemed to take up the whole room in our tiny schoolhouse. Preparations for the Christmas Tree would start early in December. Our teacher, Mrs. James, would get out the old Christmas school books, with the pages tattered and torn at the edges, and with our dearly beloved Christmas plays written on those worn pages. The teacher would make the selection of the play the students would present at the Christmas Tree. She would also make a list of which students would play the parts. We were all excited to be given any part, as it was a great honour to perform in a play in front of our parents and other adults from the community.

The older kids would be given the longer parts, which took the most work to memorize. The younger kids were given the smaller parts, and sometimes we were asked just to sit on the stage or play a role as a walk-on. In any event, all roles were considered very important, and we sat dazzled with great anticipation waiting for the teacher's instructions. We were asked to rehearse and memorize our parts. At the end of each day, from the first week of December to the Christmas Tree performance, we had a special hour to rehearse. We packed up our books and scribblers and devoted a whole hour to our wonderful Christmas play.

Mrs. James also listed, in addition to the Christmas play roles, the other events during the Christmas Tree. There would be quizzes and math questions and spelling bees, appropriate to each age. All grades from one to nine would line up on the stage for the spelling bee, and as words were spelled incorrectly, those students would be asked to take their seat. When I was in grade two or three, I was still standing after several students in the higher grades had been asked to take their seats. What a proud moment.

As the dates in December advanced, we became more excited as the time approached to open the boxes kept in the white cupboard on the wall at the back of the classroom, and which contained our precious Christmas decorations. You would think it was full of Christmas gold. We held our breath as Mrs. James unlocked the cabinet. The first item to appear was our Christmas bell, made of red tissue paper in a honeycomb pattern. It was folded and held in place by a silver clip. When the teacher removed the clip and unfolded the bell, we were starstruck. It would take its place of honour in the centre of our stage, in the middle of the red and green ribbons, which we called stringers.

Amongst the other treasures were many handmade ornaments, including the tree angel dressed in silver and bought from the T. Eaton Company; shiny silver snowflakes and hearts, crafted from tinfoil; candy canes, cats and dogs, and tiny trees, all made of red or green wool and knitted by our mothers. There were Christmas stockings made of
cardboard and painted by the younger children in bright greens, reds, blues, and white. Other decorations ordered by Mrs. James from the T. Eaton catalogue included holiday wreaths created from wood and painted green with big red bows; butterfly, bird, and reindeer ornaments; glass bells in many colours; a teddy bear with a bowtie; and red and white poinsettias. Finally, there were white Christmas doves, serene and beautiful, even more so to us as they were store-bought.

The decorations were laid out carefully on a bench at the back of the classroom and there awaited the arrival of the Christmas tree, which was carefully selected from the bush across the road from the schoolhouse, and cut down by older boys with the help of a father or two. It was well over ten feet tall, regal, with perfect branches stretching out from the largest at the bottom to the smallest at the top.

When the tree was brought into the school during Christmas week, it was given a place of honour at the front of the classroom. We all helped decorate it and the tallest boy, with the help of the teacher, placed the Christmas star at the top of the tallest branch. When the decorating was finished, and even though there were no electric lights, as we had no electricity, it was a thing of beauty and wonderment. We all stared in amazement, quite proud of our contributions. When we left school late in the afternoon after the tree was decorated, it was dusk outside, and we could see the silhouette of the tree in the tall school windows.

As the night of the Christmas Tree approached, Mrs. James, with the help of her students, put the finishing touches on our stage. We made a curtain of old sheets and strung it on a wire around the stage. It had a pull cord and could be opened and closed for the acts of our play and other skits and presentations. We hung bells in the long, narrow windows and they, too, could be seen by anyone passing on the road. Pine branches with red ribbons were tied into a wreath and hung on the front door. The big potbellied wood stove, surrounded by wood, cast warm shadows and kept us cozy during our preparations and on the night of the Christmas Tree.

During one Christmas Tree there was no snow on the ground and we didn't need winter boots. We were able to wear our best shoes, and in those days they were called fine shoes. We were standing outside the schoolhouse in our Sunday best clothes, on frozen ground with no snow, admiring our fine shoes and the fact that we could wear them outside. I was with my sister, Lottie, my youngest brother, Albert, and our neighbour boy and classmate, Ray, watching the other parents and neighbours pull up in their old trucks and some in big Buick cars.

The Christmas Tree usually went very smoothly, and if an actor forgot words during the performance, the teacher was always at the side of the stage to give words of encouragement or to speak softly the forgotten lines. Prizes were awarded for the most words spelled correctly, and additional prizes for math, geography, and science quizzes. Our Christmas Tree was a time for entertainment, but also to show our parents that we were good students and learning properly under the careful direction of Mrs. James.

The big event of the evening was when a noisy roar and a clatter of boots and tin cans took place outside, and in through the back door from the direction of the chimney came Santa Claus. He had a fat belly, a big white beard, and a giant red coat with a massive black belt, and over his shoulder was slung a huge bag filled with gifts. He came into the room with a jolly "Ho Ho Ho!" Santa pulled gifts from his bag, all wrapped in shiny paper and colourful bows. Each student, from the youngest to the oldest, was asked to come forward, sit on Santa's knee, and receive his or her gift. The present was never handed out until Santa asked, "Have you been a good boy or girl this year?" I remember how shy the little ones were and how everyone laughed when the big boys were asked if they were good or bad during the past year.

One year, another ritual associated with the Christmas Tree attracted one of my older brothers who was still in school but old enough to go outside and get a drink from an older man's bottle. The special bottles that men kept in the trunks of their cars. My brother had a drink and came back into the classroom and used a bad word. It wasn't long before our teacher reminded him that she was in charge of this classroom and that there was no tolerance for his behaviour or bad language, and that if he continued to carry on in this manner, he would be asked to leave. It wasn't long before my brother settled down, gave his apologies to Mrs. James, and humbly took his seat.

The Christmas Tree finished with a homemade feast of sandwiches, biscuits with butter and jam, chocolate chip cookies, marshmallow bars, and holiday fruit cakes, light and dark, which in those days everyone loved. Big pans of chocolate cake with white icing, sugar cookies, gingerbread loafs, peanut-butter-fudge brownies, candy-cane-chip cookies, and cupcakes. Of course, there were piles of fudge, each mother trying to outdo the other with her best recipe. But the favourite sweet amongst the students was cookies covered outside with coconut and with a big maraschino cherry inside.

Such were the days of no electricity, no supermarket desserts, no excess of material possessions, and one gift for each child. A Christmas Tree remembered and dreamt about well into the cold winter.

I close my eyes and see the frozen ground, our fine shoes, the wreath on the door, the red bell hanging stately at centre-stage. I see the tree, topped with its star, through the tall, narrow windows.

What Shall We Do?

❄ Louise Burley ❄

It's the end of December and very cold today here in Lower Montague. Boomer Gallant, PEI's weatherman, says this deep freeze will continue right through the weekend. Close to shore under slow-moving swells, the Montague River is thickening like glossy wax. Further up, by what used to be the old Georgetown ferry wharf, there are long rectangular plates of dulling ice that look like the scales on a turtle's shell, grey-green. But in the middle of the river, the steely blue water, flashing with white caps, still races out toward the saltier expanse of St. Mary's Bay.

My dog, Sierra, walks more slowly in these frigid temperatures and looks baffled as the wind stings her eyes, but she still throws herself from her shoulder onto her back and rolls side to side on the icy bank.

Past the old wharf, where the river is still clear of ice, we saw a cluster of black ducks rise from the water, their wings whistling as they headed northeast out toward the bay.

Back in the shelter and comfort of our home, a farmhouse that has stood over 150 years against such weather, I load logs in the wood stove, but the cold surrounds us. And this old kitchen seems to be in perpetual winter twilight.

We got back here a few days ago after an all-night bus ride that left Montreal late Friday night. I spent the last part of the journey with a seven-year-old girl who begged me to join her, so I left my husband, Bill, sleeping and went up front to sit with her. I gathered that she had just made the switch from her father's house in northern New Brunswick back to her mother, who lives in Halifax.

She was a wistful little thing. Her mother, pale and grim, spoke to her daughter from time to time in a quietly enraged voice from a seat across the aisle. Now that I sat beside her, the little girl begged me to visit her in Halifax so that she and I might have a "play date." I wondered why she pleaded for the friendship of an old lady, a stranger she would never see again. "What shall we do?" she asked conspiratorially, as though I might have the perfect game up my sleeve. Her mother glared at her.

"Don't bother the lady, Deana."

Deana paddled her feet back and forth and lowered her head.

"Do you want to play twenty questions?" she whispered.

Bill continued to doze, his jaw slack, woken occasionally by his own violent snore. The little girl stared hard into my eyes: "You could come see me," she said urgently; her look was pleading and forlorn.

In Montreal, a world so different from the wide-open space of Lower Montague, my two grandchildren were anything but forlorn. Jake, the three-year-old, was bursting with joy. "Nana!" he shouted each day when we showed up at their place. He flew to me at a full run. "Where's Grampa Bill and Uncle Marty?" Our game every day was to play with two plastic polar bears, a big one named Jake and Little Bear. He seemed to prefer these two bears to the Duplo and car garage and tractors that filled the floor amidst the torn wrapping paper of Christmas morning.

For our game, Jake would put the two bears in the back of a yellow dump truck and race from one room to the next, swerving around corners and screeching to a halt, and then empty them on the floor. The key question was whether the bears would be allowed back into the truck or not. Often the truck was "parked." Shaking his head "no," Jake refused to transport the bears anywhere. "What shall we do?" the bears asked, in Nana's voice. All variations of the game returned to that one question, "What shall we do?" Jake would stand gazing downward with the slow delighted smile of a little god—the god of the yellow truck. Each day, as I struggled out of my coat and stomped the snow off my boots in their entryway, Jesse would run to me and say, "Let's play polar bears, Nana!"

Owen, my second grandchild, six weeks old, was dreamy and gazed both inward and outward with his dark blue eyes. Knowing nothing of winter, he waved his arms and pumped his legs as though he was trying to teach himself to climb or to swim. And he gasped for air when Jake pressed his head against his face. Always, Owen watched his mother Emma with intense interest, those dark eyes sliding toward her a beat after she moved, his whole being intent on bringing her into focus: "You are mine; you are *me*..." The rest of us carried him, rocked him, showed him the mirror and the lights on the Christmas tree, but Emma was his magnet.

For the most part he is a very contented baby, full of his own inner workings. He couldn't roll over yet, so he was often dumped unceremoniously on the couch or table, whatever was closest. More than once, someone almost stumbled over him on the floor, or sat on him as he lay on the couch, staring fixedly at the ceiling. Jake would rush to his baby brother and hug him, or lie beside him on the couch with his arm around him, still clutching one of the polar bears.

The night before Christmas Eve, we all bundled up and headed to Mont Royal, the mountain that towers over the city and gives Montreal its name. We crept past cars spinning their wheels or stuck in the deep snow. Apartment buildings were decked out in multicoloured lights, alternately gay and dreary. Tow trucks clanked down the narrow streets beeping their warnings.

But there was no one on the dark mountain—too cold. Emma carried Owen in a wide band against her chest with her coat partly buttoned up so that you could just make out his head below her scarf, and Jake rode on my son Liam's shoulders. Jake was so excited to be out in this cold winter night, his eyes wide with anticipation. We carried garlands of popcorn and cranberries that we had strung together in the kitchen that afternoon, and we also brought candles. We waded into the deep snow to a hemlock leaning into its own shadow. Then we draped the garlands, a present for the squirrels and birds, across the hemlock's branches and attached the candles. We lit them one by one with numb fingers and sang "Good King Wenceslas," "In the Bleak Midwinter," and "Angels We Have Heard on High." As we hit the "Glor-or-or-or-i-a" part, Jake sang loudly and bounced up and down on Liam's shoulders, his eyes shining. He looked at each of us as if to say, *here we are, and this is perfect.*

We had never done such a thing before. In the past, Liam, then Liam and Emma, and finally, Jake, too, always came to our house and shared in our way of doing Christmas. Now they had introduced a new tradition. In fact, I was aware that this was *their* Christmas, and that we were taken into their home as cherished guests. I was no longer the person who set the agenda. They tried to do the things that we had done in the past, but now there were small children, and by the time supper was over, the parents were ready to turn in. Owen would be up at the crack of dawn. By nine p.m. it was time to call it quits. We had planned to go to a candlelight Christmas Eve service as we always have in the past, but no one had the energy or inclination for it.

In spite of the advancing night, we did read out loud, as we have done other Christmas Eves: Emma read a funny piece about some "underprivileged" people who, besieged by Christmas do-gooders, got themselves hammered and behaved badly. My younger son, Martin, a student of philosophy, read from Camus' *The Plague,* and Liam read a beautiful poem by his father, my long-ago first husband, which made me ache for the distant past. I read an Emily Dickinson poem. Bill begged off—he was without the familiarity of his own library. He had been opposed to this Christmas trip to Montreal. He was too tired, he'd said, stressed to the point of collapse by endless problems at work. "Please just go without me," he'd said. In the end I had to strong-arm him, and he was a reluctant participant doing his best to be a good sport.

As we sat around Liam and Emma's apartment, I found myself longing for something that spoke of the mystery of divine presence. This seemed to be a Christmas without that, full of the delight of our grandchildren, but missing that one thing. I tried to listen to Martin make his way labouriously through an obscure passage of *The Plague,* but I thought of running away to join a convent the way I used to imagine running away to join the gypsies as a child.

A couple of weeks before, Martin had written to me about how Advent seemed to be characterized by missing—missing trains or planes. I replied that if missing planes were the deepest anguish of Advent there'd be a lot less for the fish to feed on. Dark words. I thought of those words now and realized that, in fact, missing was exactly what I felt.

There was the very real joy of family, but that one lovely elusive thing was absent—a thing you can't command, only wait for. And it seemed that nobody else was waiting. I smiled and smiled, and thought of my convent, the nuns singing Vespers in a quiet candlelit chapel, impersonal and devoted...

Bill, Martin, and I returned to our B&B, and I went straight to bed without a word. I figured that come Christmas morning I would pull myself together and be good old Nana once again. But I lay in bed unable to sleep. Bill and Martin were in the front room and I heard them murmuring...

But wait. Let me go back a few weeks. December is always busy—

of course, it is—one would feel inadequate if December just plodded by. Mere days before we left for Montreal, Bill and I went out to the Thornton Road in search of our Christmas tree. We walked through the icy mud, looking side to side at the scraggly spruce that flanked the road, and settled on a tall balsam fir with a series of skirts, a lovely lady tree, and brought her back to the house. Out came the old ornaments and the brown angel with her lace dress; half the lights no longer worked and the tree stand was pretty well busted, but we made do. We drank eggnog and visited neighbours. And in the last few days before we headed up to Montreal I went into high gear, making fruitcake and Christmas cookies, scouting out Christmas presents, and wrapping everything in shiny paper on the kitchen table, throwing a log into the wood stove every hour or so.

As well, I had this plan for Owen: I wanted to make him a mobile out of blown eggs. Each morning for about a week before we headed up to Montreal, I blew out two eggs and scrambled them for breakfast. Suddenly, the Montreal trip was upon us, and all I had were our other presents and a carton of hollow eggs. So I brought the markers with me and hoped that somehow I could assemble the mobile once we got there. At the B&B, I nagged Bill and Martin to help me decorate these eggs, but they were clearly indifferent. That mobile was not going to happen. Now it was Christmas Eve in Montreal, very late, and I was lying by myself in bed staring at the ceiling, bereft and inarticulate. I guess you could say I was waiting—I thought I was waiting for Bill to come to bed so I could sleep.

But at last I got up and went into the front room. In silence, Bill and Martin were trying to balance the mobile. They had already finished decorating the eggs: strong black designs with brilliant colours like stained glass. They pulled the threads this way and that. In silence, I moved toward them and began to help. They did not acknowledge my presence. We were all paying close attention to the task at hand. It was three in the morning.

There was no sound but the occasional faint clatter of hollow egg against hollow egg. At last, we succeeded in hanging it properly, and then all staggered off to bed for a few hours of unconsciousness.

The point is He—it—something came.

As the old gospel song says, "He may not come when you call him, but He's right on time." I didn't expect to find Christ in the assembling of a mobile. I thought that this year he would pass us by, like Santa missing a house. I was wrong. Something showed up in the silence when our resistance was down, and all we were doing was paying attention to the tying of string. It came to our midst when Bill felt awkward and trapped in Montreal, and Martin was exhausted by too many late nights drinking or studying. He came when I had given up on the possibility of anything more than empirical reality and had surrendered to the emptiness of waiting.

And then—the presence. Always there, yet also arriving, right on time.

With the arrival of this gift, I think of the lonely little girl on the bus. "What shall we do?" she asks. I think also of Jake's bears trapped beside the yellow truck wondering what to do. And I imagine Owen waving his arms at the egg mobile that floats above his head. His eyes shift to his mother bending over him. "What shall we do today, Owen?" she murmurs.

What shall we do when the presence, arrives, expected, unexpected? Pay attention, I guess. Love the moment. Say thanks. But also, listen carefully, just in case we hear the answer.

A Candle for Bucky

❄   Jocelyn Thorne   ❄

"Mom, you go on up and lay down for a while, I'll finish up here," Laura said as she turned on the tap and filled the sink with soapy water.

With a glance at the disarray on the counter where they had been making Christmas cookies, Audrey said, "I hate to leave you with this mess."

Turning around, a smile on her face, Laura spoke in her no-nonsense, schoolteacher voice. "Go lie down, Mom." And then, concern evident in her tone, "You'll want to be well-rested for to-night, right?" She referred to the impending arrival of Audrey's son, Norman, and his family.

"Okay, I guess I could use a quick nap," Audrey sighed, knowing there would be no use arguing with Laura.

"Wake me in an hour, though, okay?"

Audrey walked through the family room. As she started up the garland-strung staircase, her gaze fell on Laura's Christmas tree in the corner. It was eight feet tall, decorated with glittering purple ornaments and twinkling white lights. Audrey paused as she reflected on the colours. They were not at all "Christmas." These days anything went, apparently. The candles, however, were a nice old-fashioned touch, and even though they were electric, the imitation flames winked and danced in a pleasing simulation of the real thing. Laura was the exact opposite from her when it came to Christmas. She embraced the holiday wholeheartedly and neither the crowded malls nor the blatant commercialism deterred her. Every year Laura's house was decorated from top to bottom; she hosted the family dinner and thrived on the hours of preparation leading up to it with her baking and giftwrapping and decorating. It was all too much for Audrey, who supposed that when her two children were small, Christmas time at their house had been quiet and boring by comparison. It had been a very long time since Audrey had been inwardly enthusiastic about Christmas, though she'd done her best outwardly for the sake of her children. Sitting down on the bottom stair, Audrey fixed her gaze on one of the winking candles, and memories of another Christmas long ago came back to her.

In 1953 Audrey was eight years old and the third youngest of Frank and Rachel Harrington's seven children. Her family's nickname for her was "Cracker" because her father said she was like a little firecracker. She was often plotting mischief, mostly directed toward her two younger brothers, four-year-old Jack and two-year-old Bucky. She planned ways to get them in trouble or pulled spiteful pranks on them, which usually backfired and landed her in hot water.

Her family lived in the small fishing community of Northtown, where her father fished for a living. Theirs was a large family to feed, and times were often tough. Rachel was a resourceful woman and put in a large garden every year. The autumn saw the whole family involved in a flurry of activity, from salting their own fish to stocking the cellar with the fall harvest. They put up bottles of pickles and jams and cans of beef and chicken. When the cold blast of winter arrived, the Harringtons were prepared.

Every fall, her father would take the job of knitting heads for other local fishermen's lobster traps. The older children knitted heads along with him and all the money went toward Christmas. When Frank was paid, he and Rachel went into town to buy baking supplies and gifts for their family. Then, their mother sent them all to bed and she stayed up all night doing her Christmas baking, and in the morning the entire house was filled with wonderful smells. Her father went into the woods and brought back the biggest fir tree he could find; any bare spots, he drilled holes and filled with branches. The tree was always put in the front window of the parlour and everyone had a hand in the decorating. The children made string after string of popcorn and cranberries, which were carefully arranged on the tree along with an assortment of homemade paper ornaments. Lastly, their mother clipped the candles to the strongest branches. They were lit only once, on Christmas Eve.

The evening was spent in front of the tree, Rachel playing the organ and everyone singing carols. Afterward, the ceremony took place with Frank and Rachel lighting all the candles. Set off to one side, as a safety precaution, were two buckets of water. The lamps were turned down and with just the glow of the tree candles everyone would sing "Silent Night." Then the candles were extinguished for another year. That year, Christmas Eve morning brought with it the third winter storm of the month, snow and more snow, causing blizzard conditions and whiteouts. Audrey woke filled with excitement as she realized that tonight Santa was coming and she was finally going to get her doll. Throwing the blankets aside and oblivious to the shivering cold, she ran downstairs to the warm kitchen, where she knew her mom would be stirring a big pot of bubbling porridge. However, her sixteen-year-old sister, Evelyn, was the only one in the kitchen, standing in front of the old wood stove stirring the porridge.

"Where's Mom, Evy?" Audrey climbed up on the open oven door to get closer to the heat.

"Hi, Cracker. Bucky is really sick and Mom's with him. Dad's gone for the doctor."

For the past couple of weeks her youngest brother had been sick with a bad cough. A visit from the doctor and a round of medication had not alleviated his condition and he was increasingly ill.

"I thought the doctor already gave Bucky medicine to make him better."

"Well, I guess it didn't work."

Audrey jumped down from the oven door and raced up the stairs to her parents' bedroom. Poking her head in, she saw her mother sitting on the side of the bed, holding a cloth to Bucky's forehead.

"What's wrong with Bucky, Mom?"

"He's got a fever. Is there any sign of your father with the doctor?"

"Not yet."

"Go back downstairs and watch for them, okay?" Rachel turned away from the little boy on the bed and looked at Audrey. "I want you to look after Jack today, play some games with him to keep him occupied, okay, I'm counting on you."

Audrey crinkled up her nose. She hated it when she had to play with her little brothers, they were such a bother. At her mother's glare, though, Audrey gave a nod of her head and ran back down the stairs.

A half-hour later the stomp of heavy boots announced the arrival of her father and Dr. Wilson. The front door was flung open as they rushed in on a gush of cold air and wet snow.

"How is he?" Frank asked Evelyn as he and the doctor threw off their coats.

"Mom's still upstairs with him. She's waiting for you."

Hours later, Audrey wondered what was taking so long. Evy refused to play another game of Snakes and Ladders with her and none of her brothers wanted to either, except Jack. And she was bored playing with Jack. Her parents and the doctor had been with Bucky all day, hurrying in and out of the bedroom, a sense of urgency to their movements. Even in the snowstorm her Aunt Margie had come, as she always did on Christmas Eve. But she, too, had been up with Bucky since she arrived. It would soon be time to gather for Christmas carols and the ceremony. That was what Audrey loved the most about Christmas, even more than the gifts, watching the glowing candles cast flickering images on the walls and ceiling as they all sang "Silent Night."

"Audrey, Evelyn, Bobby, Jerry, Stevie, Jack, Bucky." Audrey intoned each name softly as she rearranged the Christmas boxes under the tree for the fifth time. Instead of Christmas stockings, each child decorated a shoebox, and on Christmas Eve the boxes were lined up under the tree where they waited to be filled with goodies from Santa. There! Her pink box, covered with hearts and flowers, first in line awaiting Santa's arrival, and the green and blue boxes for her two pesky brothers, at the very end.

"When are we lighting the candles, Evy?" she asked her sister for the umpteenth time. Putting her arms around Audrey's bony little shoulders, Evelyn hugged her close.

"Listen, Cracker, because Bucky is very very sick, I don't think we're going to sing or light the candles this year. So why don't you get ready and go to bed. That way, before you know it morning will be here and Santa, too."

"You mean we aren't having Christmas Eve just because Bucky's sick?" Audrey pulled away from Evelyn and stomped off toward the staircase. "That's not fair," she wailed and tromped up the stairs, chanting, "I hate him, I hate him."

Early the next morning Audrey woke filled with eager anticipation. "It's Christmas," she yelled joyfully as she scrambled out of bed and tugged the bedclothes off Evelyn, who groggily lifted her head at Audrey's shout. "Come on, Evy, let's see what Santa brought." She dashed out the door and raced toward the stairs. Evelyn's cry of "Wait, Cracker!" went unheeded.

Audrey ran into the parlour and straight to the line of boxes under the tree. Sure enough, they were filled with delightful treats, nuts, hard peppermints, oranges, apples, and a generous helping of colourful barley candy. Audrey saw the doll sitting on top of her box. Hair Bow Peggy. Grabbing her up with a shriek of delight, Audrey hugged her close and spun in circles. She stopped as Jack ran excitedly into the room, followed closely by their mother. Ignoring Jack, Audrey held her doll high. "Look, Mom, I got my dolly. Santa brought me Hair Bow Peggy."

"That's nice, Cracker," her mother said with a sad smile as she took a seat on the sofa. "Come here, Audrey, I want to tell you something."

Hearing the anguish in her voice, Audrey walked slowly, clutching her doll tightly in her arms. Rachel pulled her gently down beside her on the sofa.

"Honey, I have some very sad news. The angels came last night and took Bucky to heaven."

Seeing tears in her mother's eyes filled Audrey with apprehension. Her mom never cried. Confused and not clearly understanding what her mother was saying, she whispered, "What do you mean, Mom? Are they going to bring him back?"

"No, Audrey, Bucky is gone to live with the angels forever. He won't be coming back home."

Glancing over at the Christmas tree, Audrey noticed that Bucky's little blue Christmas box was missing. Looking back at her mother's face, she realized what she had done. In a strained little voice she murmured, "Mom, I think Santa took Bucky, not the angels."

"No, honey," Rachel said and hugged her close. "I told you, the angels came."

But Audrey knew better. She thought back to the day she had written her letter to Santa and clearly remembered what she had begged him for.

"Mom, make Bucky stop coughing," Audrey had said angrily as she looked up from the paper in front of her, a frown pulling her eyebrows low as she glared at her little brother.

"Audrey! Why don't you be nice to him for a change," her mother had replied as she plucked Bucky out of his highchair. "Can't you see he's not feeling well?" She sank down into the rocking chair and began to rock the red-faced little boy.

But Audrey's attention had already shifted back to the letter she was labouring over, for it had to be perfect. For weeks she had pored over the toy section of the Eaton's catalogue and every time she came to the page with the dolls, she stopped. There was the dolly she wished for with all her heart, curly black hair, pink pyjamas covered in red bows, and a large red bow in her hair. "I love you, Hair Bow Peggy," she whispered fervently. She scanned the letter one last time.

Dear Santa
I have been a good girl
I have only one thing on my list this year
A dolly with black curly hair and a big red bow.
She is in the Eaton's catalog on page 85
Thank you Santa
PS: I will give anything for this dolly. You can have
one of my little brothers if you want. But please please please
Bring me Hair Bow Peggy. Love Audrey

Audrey was jolted back to the present when her daughter touched her on the shoulder and spoke in a worried tone.

"Mom, what's wrong? You're crying."

That long-ago Christmas morning receded and Audrey took a deep breath. Getting slowly to her feet, she took Laura by the hand.

"I never told you about my little brother, Bucky, did I? His real name was Norman but we all called him Bucky and he died on Christmas Eve." Still holding her daughter's hand she led the way into the family room.

"Come sit and I'll tell you why your mother has never liked Christmas or the Christmas season. And afterwards, Laura, if it's all right with you I'd like to go to the church and light a candle for Bucky."

It was time to relieve the guilt she had carried all these years, time to unburden her heart with the telling of a secret that a little girl had carried from childhood into adulthood without ever breathing a word to anyone.

Christmas Mail

❄   Jessie Lees   ❄

My letter's in a black hole
no message back
I speculate
mail inefficiency
an unintended move
sickness, perhaps, or death

A lawyer's letter came
to say that Margaret died
more recently a cousin wrote
Ann wished to thank me
for my card, she said, but Ann
"does not know who you are"

I scratch another name
vow to remember
know that I am living at an edge
where two worlds often touch
and travellers move
in one direction

My friends now point the way
if not the end
making the strange familiar
giving that other world
a gentler look
because they' re there

raining carnations

❋ Steven Mayoff ❋

heart-jump of wings skipping across this salt river
   beating the silvered calm into white splinters

   then a wake fanning toward
     primordial shorelines

at rest the beak, head
and gangly
   neck form a question
     mark punctuating
       existence

   …

leaves flaming red and gold
curl into brown failed poems
   clinging desperately
   to gnarled limbs

   then into brittle shells
     eddying around trunk
      and root

rattling their last like a badly
 kept secret
   …

   salt water hardens
an iced-over cataract
  a blind gaze

   mocking grey emptiness above

before carnations
    rain their slow-motion magic
realism like crystalized tears blooming white

    blessing the nothingness
        of our lives

    ...

atop some frozen cliff (overlooking
    the marriage
        of two tides)

a sole pine raises its silver-needled
    menorah

star-lit with the oil of human
    mindfulness giving meaning
        to a finite

miracle and an infinite number
    of interpretations

    ...

shadows of constellations
    dot the blue blanketed
        rooftops
inside these wing-haunted midnights

smoking chimneys like breaths in repose
until sunrise brings
    a crow-gathering of
        string and twigs for the gifts
of transcendence

wreaths of nuts and dried berries halo
    all ecumenical doors

...

a cracking thaw summons back the heron's
clumsy wingspan

prehistoric lineage among the spring snowflakes
                    pushing through mud

a memory of raining carnations reflected in black
            water where a split in the ice
                    grins knowingly

A Christmas Reflection

❄ David D. Varis ❄

The Christianization and Europeanization of First Nations peoples, or colonization by another name, brought not only disease, dispossession, and displacement to our first inhabitants, but also Christmas.

Yet, after residential school children were snatched by the Indian Agents, the only gift they received was the privilege of spending Christmas with complete strangers. Requests by parents to bring their children home for the Christian celebration were swiftly met with "*no, it's against the rules*," delivered like the rawest of December winds, with no catchy carol. This Christmas tradition lasted over 150 years. These children's experience was the birth of something totally different.

After the government decided to close residential schools in the 1960s, with the last one closing its doors only in 1996, things were far from normal on the Reserve. Life on the *Rez*, as it was called, was just plain tough, day in and day out. But, then, there was Christmas. On the Rez, at least according to the Elders, Christmas was pretty much a day of smiling with anticipation, smiling at everyone else smiling, and smiling at one's gift—a pair of mittens, an orange, or a piece of hard candy that was hastily wrapped in God knows what. If one was fortunate to have the right connections to the outside world, used Christmas wrapping was a sign of wealth. No matter the veil, it was simply poverty dressed up in *happy to be alive*, which we all came to believe was the greatest gift one could receive, no matter the suffering.

I was a Westernized Scandinavian-Cree kid growing up in Winnipeg, a youngster who was sheltered from knowing his Aboriginal ancestry. Growing up *Indian* wasn't cool back then and you'd pay dearly if your heritage was revealed. We just didn't talk about that part of who we really were. Anyway, my brothers and I did okay. I have many pictures of me sitting on Santa's lap down at The Bay. You know the pictures, the ones conveniently placed in the Christmas theme postcard with all the festive characters dancing and prancing around you and Santa. I suppose this was to make Christmas special or, as we now call it, manipulative marketing. Yes, we did okay. Still, I used to wonder why Santa was so white, but also so red.

The world has changed since then. First Nations families celebrate Christmas like any other Canadian family. But, you know, we also celebrate the seasons, water, air, Mother Earth, all living things—the two-legged, four-legged, fish, birds, insects, trees and plants—and all non-living things—rocks, mountains, dust, sand, and mud. We honour our ancestors, children, and Elders, our gifts, strengths, and weaknesses, our path, the paths of others. We reverence the teachings, the sacredness of life, the ways of our peoples, the mysteries. We celebrate our resilience and humour, the giving to others, and the belief in the Creator, the one who has given us so much and everything we need to live the life that has been bestowed upon us.

When I go to a Pow Wow, sit in a sharing circle, participate in ceremony, help another person, balance my Medicine Wheel, or admire the trees and how they sway in the wind, I would have to say, it's like Christmas—a First Nations Christmas, every day of the year.

For Auld Lang Syne

❄ **Anne McCallum** ❄

And never brought to mind?
Should auld acquaintance be forgot,
And auld lang syne?
—Robert Burns, 1788

I have been involved in a love-hate affair with New Year's Eve (Hogmanay) since I left my native Scotland to make my life in Canada more than four decades ago. On the last day of the year, just three or four notes of "Auld Lang Syne" will bring tears to my eyes and start my lower lip trembling. The song has the power to pull me back to a time long past and a homeland long-ago abandoned. Add one glass of Glenfiddich too many, and my New Year's Eve celebrations might well descend into a morass of nostalgia.

For me, the countdown starts on the stroke of eight in Prince Edward Island—midnight in Scotland. At five minutes past the hour my phone rings and I answer to boisterous New Year's greetings from one of my many siblings, or the happy voices of my parents as they beam their good wishes to me across the Atlantic Ocean. Their words of affection, and mine, are expressed in the lowland Scots dialect that we grew up speaking in my hometown of Dumfries.

"Happy New Year, hen. How're 'ee gettin' oan?" they ask.

"Ah'm no bad but Ah miss hame somethin' terrible on Hogmanay," I invariably reply.

I love our lowland language but I have no opportunities to use it in Canada. On Hogmanay it always strikes me how much I miss that familiar way of talking, and hearing it makes me excessively sentimental. I also feel very proud, though, that people all over the world enjoy our old Scots words through the works of Robert Burns, or "Rabbie" as he's fondly known in Scotland. Burns's "Auld Lang Syne," sung at midnight every December 31 on both sides of the Atlantic, and in many other countries as well, is arguably the most widely known song in history. Burns is renowned, too, for his spirited narrative poem, "Tam O' Shanter"; for his expression of egalitarian ideals in "A Man's A Man For A' That"; and for hundreds of other compelling works that celebrate life, love, and the intrinsic worth of ordinary people.

Although Burns was born in Ayrshire, he spent the last eight years of his life writing and working in and around Dumfries. When he died in 1796, aged just thirty-seven, he was buried in St. Michael's churchyard there. Nearly a century later, the town erected a white marble statue of him on the High Street. Today, the sandstone house where he lived is a pilgrimage site for Burns enthusiasts who flock to Dumfries from far and wide. When I was coming of age in the late 1960s, I was surrounded by all things Burns—I competed in Burns poetry recitals; revered the ceremonial traditions of Burns clubs; and quoted Burns's poems to lend support to my left-leaning views. Inevitably, Rabbie became my supreme hero, and he is so, still—most especially on Hogmanay.

The language he used is based on an old form of English that has unique constructions and vocabulary in Scotland—it includes commanding expressions like "dinnae fash yersel" and "haud yer whisht," and evocative words like "dreich" and "teuchter." Many Canadians think Gaelic is the true tongue of the Scots, but Gaelic speakers mostly hail from the Highlands and Islands. In the south, where I lived for my first twenty-three years, few people knew any Gaelic, unless you count expressions like "sláinte mhath"—a toast for "good health," or the word "ceilidh"—a wild party where people fling themselves about in approximations of traditional dances. Some lowland place names do reflect Gaelic roots, it is true, but many centuries have passed since it was actually spoken there.

When I was growing up, our teachers forced us to replace our Scots words with the "Queen's English." We had to say "cry" not "greet," "clothes" not "claes," "girl" not "lassie," "know" not "ken." This often futile attempt to make us bilingual was to help us communicate properly in situations such as job interviews and medical consultations, or perhaps (in some families) for explaining dodgy behaviour to nosey police (pronounced POLiss). More than a few folk engaged in illicit behaviour, often related to items falling off the backs of lorries, and they found it useful to speak "proper" English so that the police would not treat them as uneducated riffraff.

But in the privacy of our wee draughty houses, where we told and retold family stories around glowing coal fires, or when we gathered in our local pub for a boisterous blether about Scottish Home Rule, we didn't hesitate to use the traditional expressions we'd learned from our parents—and they might well have been in Gaelic, so different were they from standard English.

Whenever I think back to my young life in Scotland, and the traditions that I learned there, I can't help but focus on the main event of every year—Hogmanay. It was much bigger than Christmas which we regarded as a party for the "weans." For adults, the mother of all celebrations began on December 31. And when I say "adults," I mean almost everyone who had stopped believing in Santa Claus. Scots youngsters grew up quickly then. In the 1960s we could leave high school at fifteen if we were so inclined, and could legally marry when we turned sixteen. By then we were certainly considered old enough to celebrate the New Year, adult-style, and we did.

Our preparations for the two-day party always began at first light on Hogmanay day. After we had cleared away the breakfast porridge bowls, my mother commandeered us would-be adults to clean the entire house. She called this "a guid muckin oot" which suggests that we lived like pigs, but nothing could be further from the truth. Then, like now, she'd be up at dawn every day vacuuming immaculate carpets and scrubbing gleaming floors. Yet, in her view, "if ye didnae make the hoose spotless on Hogmanay it wouldnae be clean enough a' the next year." Her idea of spotless was when "ye could eat yer dinner aff" whatever was being cleaned, so we had our work cut out for us.

While my sisters and I polished chairs and tables and sideboards until we could see our faces in them, my mother centred herself in our tiny kitchen. First, she prepared a vast pot of Scotch broth to line our stomachs for the excesses that lay ahead. Everything went into that soup—a wee bit o' boiling beef, barley and split peas, dried beans, leeks and carrots and turnips (or tumshies), and, finally, the parsley. While the simmering soup spread its aroma all over the house, my mum baked thick rounds of butter-rich shortbread, made mincemeat tarts, and whipped up sponge cakes to be spread later with cream. She'd send me and my sister, Rose, to the nearby shops to fetch a three-day supply of Mother's Pride plain bread because they'd be closed until January 3. Plain bread is tall with a dense texture and a tough crust. It came wrapped in tartan wax paper (and still does). There were seven of us in the house then, so you can imagine the mound of red plaid packages we wobbled back with on our bikes.

Later in the afternoon, my father, home from work as early as possible, would give out "wee halfs" of whisky and chunks of my mother's rich fruit cake to workers who came looking for "their New Year." Sometimes it was the milkman, or it was the "scaffies" (men who collected the rubbish). It's the coalman I recall most clearly. This strapping fellow could carry a hundredweight sack of coal on his back from his lorry parked on the street to our bunker behind the house. A thick leather vest was all that cushioned his spine from the sharpness of the coal. His cap only partly protected his ginger curls from the dust that covered his whole body. When I think of him now, I see startling blue eyes and a roguish smile beaming through the soot on his face as he gratefully accepted his wee glass of cheer from my dad.

Early on Hogmanay night, everybody who was old enough, or almost, went to the pub for a few wee drinks. If we chose an old-fashioned place, like the Hole in the Wa' on the High Street (said to have been frequented nearly two hundred years earlier by Rabbie himself), the piano-accordion would be going strong and a boisterous singsong under way. It wasn't really possible to dance there because bodies were squeezed into every available inch of space, but we swayed back and forth in unison as we belted out drinking songs like "I Belong Tae Glasgow" or crooned sentimental classics like "Annie Laurie" and "The Northern Lights of Auld Aberdeen." And when everyone's feelings of national pride were near to bursting, the band would strike up the first notes of "Flower O' Scotland" and the entire pub would break into the chorus of that anthem-song made so famous by The Corries. Every right arm would be held high as our voices rang loud and proud—*O Flower o Scotland / When will we see your like again? / That fought and died for / Yer wee bit hill and glen / That stood against him / Proud Edward's army / And sent him homewards, Tae think again*—I can hear it still.

The pubs closed early then, at ten p.m., in fact, even on Hogmanay, and publicans derived sadistic satisfaction from following the letter of the law. After the barman's five-minute warning, "Drink up, lads and lassies. Have ye nae hames tae gan tae the night?", the staff opened all the windows and doors no matter how bitter the weather, and set about collecting every glass, full or empty, with a zeal that bordered on the evangelical. The revellers who had felt so welcomed just minutes earlier had to gulp down their half-finished drinks before they were unceremoniously ousted onto the streets. By eleven p.m. on Hogmanay everybody was either safely aboard a double-decker bus heading home or they were continuing the party out on the cobbled High Street around Burns's Statue.

Our family tradition—that is, my mother's unopposed version—dictated that we had to be in "oor ain hoose weel afore midnight in plenty o' time tae see the New Year in." So home we'd rollick, my sisters and friends and I, with our arms linked and our coats wide open to show off our skinny-rib tops and tight miniskirts. We'd sing something modern like "Norwegian Wood" or "I Can't Get No Satisfaction" as we sauntered from the bus stop round to our house. Looking back, I see that our lives were being shaped by two contradictory influences—The Beatles and The Corries, Mick Jagger and Rabbie Burns, bold new freedoms and proud cultural traditions. On Hogmanay, though, the power of the past was much more potent than the promise of the future.

By the time we arrived home, my parents would have already turned on our black-and-white TV to enjoy the stirring strains of "Donald Where's Yer Troosers?" by Andy Stewart, the exuberant host of The White Heather Club. Our mum and dad loved this show and we knew better than to criticize its cheerful cheesiness. As our toes tapped in time with the kilted dancers, we scoffed steaming bowls of Scotch broth served with thick slices of plain bread to dip in. And to keep us merry while we waited for "The Bells," we supped tall cans of Tennent's Lager, colourful cans that sported photos of "lager lovelies" with names like Linda or Jean.

One or two "lovelies" later, we'd hear the band striking the first notes of "Auld Lang Syne." This was our cue to leap to our feet and grab the hands of the two people on either side of us as we broke into a vigorous rendition of Burns's most famous song, while moving in and out in a lopsided circle around the coffee table, trying not to trip into the open coal fire. We sang the final chorus with our hands crossed over our chests and when the hilarity eventually died down, we breathlessly kissed and wished each other a Happy New Year. Then we sat down well back from the table so my father would have enough space to pour us all a "wee whisky" to welcome the future.

It's probably evident by now that in lowland Scotland many things are described as "wee"; a "wee half" or a "wee minute." It is inter-changeable with "small" but has other meanings, too. When alcohol is involved, "wee" translates as "big." It can mean "many" as when my mother would say, "ah think ah'll away and bake a wee scone." In that case, she meant about three dozen scones. Or it can soften the impact of a Scottish insult, as in "He's a right wee scunner, is he no?"

A scunner is a person who is really off-putting in manner or ap-pearance. He is the opposite of the ideal Hogmanay first-footer who is tall, dark, and handsome. The term "first-footer" describes the first visitor who crosses your threshold after midnight on Hog-manay. He (it's always a "he") brings luck to your house; he also arrives with drink, food, and, when I was growing up, lumps of coal as symbols of prosperity and warmth for the coming year. One of my much older cousins usually first-footed us. Billy was short and stocky with wiry hair that stuck up unflatteringly and he had a pudgy face, but he was a hilarious storyteller so we forgave him his physical imperfections. Every Hogmanay he took immense delight in recalling and embellishing past New Years' embarrass-ments, of which there were many:

"Can ye mind the year ye couldnae fin yer false teeth, Rosie?" Billy's brown eyes would dance as he directed this question to my mother, who always tried to look shamefaced; then he'd take a long slow swallow of his whisky to give us time to focus our attention. That's when my dad would chime in:

"The silly bugger forgot tae take her teeth oot afore she went tae bed. She spent the whole nicht lyin' on top o' them. It was only when Ah spied the teeth marks on her arse the next mornin' that Ah figured it oot!"

"Whit aboot the year oor daft cousin Mick fae England couldnae mind whaur he left his car and it took them twa days tae fin it, whit was left o' it that is…?" And so it would continue, with each story outdoing the one before until our raucous chatter was interrupted by a new round of well-wishers chapping at our front door.

That was usually the cue for those of us who wanted to visit nearby friends and family to make our exit. After sharing kisses and handshakes with the newcomers who were joining the remaining revellers at our house, we'd set off around the corner, joking and jostling, to our Aunty Betty's place. She was a witty Glaswegian with a real gift of the gab. Her irreverent humour promised to keep us entertained for half the night.

The next afternoon, New Year's Day, after we'd slept off the indulgences of the night before, we'd get our second wind and visit my Aunty Margaret's. With luck, her husband, Lindsay, would be at home and feeling lively enough to play some reels on his red accordion. If not, we'd slip into the dark bar of the old Newton Hotel where my grandfather and his cronies loved to gather for a wee half and a blether. It didn't matter where we went as long as we shared the festive spirit with everyone we cared for. The carousing continued throughout that day and sometimes into the next, until all our significant others had been wished a Happy New Year or until our bodies started to rebel, whichever came first.

For me, the end usually came sooner than later. The year I was seventeen was my lowest point ever. Against my mother's better judgement, she let me accompany some older friends to the Hogmanay street party at the Midsteeple—that's the historic sandstone building and bell tower at the opposite end of the High Street from Burns Statue. Her permission came with two conditions—that I not drink anything "oot 'o ither folk's bottles" and that I get back in time to appear at my grandfather's house where our extended family was gathering after midnight. I broke my promises on both counts. When the Midsteeple bells rang out among the crowds gathered at the town centre, bottles of whisky and vodka and rum were passed around with gay abandon and everybody shared Hogmanay drinks and lingering kisses with friends and strangers alike—including me.

The next thing I recall is waking up a few hours later, in my bed, to the sound of my mother's wrath: "Ye're drunk, ye stupid lassie, and ye missed yer Papa's pairty," she fumed. I tried to turn my back and she tried to stop me. That's when I rolled down onto the floor and grazed my forehead slightly on the nearby dresser. It wasn't a serious injury by any means, but I blamed it for the terrible thumping in my skull the next morning. I thought my mother would feel mortified for causing me such agony, and she later told me that she was very sorry that it happened. But at the time all she said was "Ye've naebody tae blame but yersel," and although I hated to admit it, I knew she was right. I knew, too, that neither of us would ever live it down. It would go on to become part of our Hogmanay lore for many years to come.

In the four decades since I moved to Canada, I have faithfully visited my old country at least once a year, but I've celebrated a Scottish Hogmanay there only twice. After we moved to PEI in 1977, my Canadian husband and I started our own traditions. We stay at home every December 31 to prepare food for the New Year's Day party that we throw for friends and neighbours, and now some of our children's acquaintances and partners. Vast trays of veggie lasagne, steaming pots of garlic mussels, and mounds of black-bottom cupcakes replace the delicacies of my mother's kitchen. Some of us drink our share of whisky and beer, to be sure, but we also serve bowls of fresh fruit punch and flagons of non-alcoholic cider pressed from our own apple harvest.

Our more energetic guests come early to enjoy skiing and snow-shoeing on the trails we've built in our rolling woods and fields. And then, after a potluck feast that includes everything from sushi to tourtière, we play guitars and sing tunes together from *Rise Up Singing* — old classics like "Norwegian Wood" that I once considered cutting-edge.

Our January 1 gathering is a wonderful way to celebrate everything we have on this beautiful Island, and to look forward with joy to the New Year ahead—at least that's what I tell myself as soon as Hogmanay is over. It might be a different story next December 31, if I've had one glass of Glenfiddich too many, and the sentimental strains of Rabbie's "Auld Lang Syne" start me pining for a time long gone and a country I've never truly abandoned.

New Year's Rhyming

※   David Helwig   ※

Exterior: village, night; a moon
half-lights a frozen stretch of lawn;
snow drifts beneath the trees that twist
contorted branches in a waste
of angular calligraphy
as winter triumphs where a sky
of lurid almost-glowing cloud
enlightens snowy fields, a road
as nebulous as one in dreams.
So one year ends, another comes.

Interior: bedroom, night; a pair
lie parallel and breathe cold air
as history's blind-eyed cameras creep
close to the bed in which we sleep,
our bodies bent, insistent, curled
two into one against the world.
Closeup: the lined and aging skin,
the eyelids flicker, dreams within
the house of bone, the intrepid brain.

Most mornings I'll wake up again,
rise to cross off a numbered square,
yesterday fled beyond repair.
As memory calls back the lost,
the complex multifarious past,
a new today begins to be,
recovered from infinity.
By revolution of the spheres
entangled with rotation, years
subdivide into solar days
of holy and unholy joys.

A gradual neurologic loss
will breed a slowed and clumsy pace,
diseases various assault,
threatening to call a sudden halt,
but soon enough enough's been said
about this growing old and dead;
in spite of all let rhyming give
a glitter-gloss to how we live,
a cosmic rule for how to play,
nor let disease define the day.

Headline: Rome's church declares no wings
are found on angels, rather rings
of disembodied shimmer pass
through those observed, like light in glass.
Oh much beshimmered heart, sing out
your next line in the vexed debate
between flesh known and soul supposed,
and praise whatever's to be praised.

Exterior: village, day; I'll write
some couplets of the dog's delight,
how half-immersed in drifts she bounds
across the snowy field, astounds
us watching her go leap and stretch
into the woods in hopes to catch
sight of a fleeing rabbit, fox;
her gaiety cheers our winter walks.

Exterior: village, dusk; the year
will last till midnight, disappear.
The black calligraphy of trees
stands amid ice and snow as these
octosyllabic lines are sent
to those with whom life's hours were spent,
a page or two of dancing rhyme
riding electrons into time,
tumbling toward the final coast,
to sum it up, offer a toast:
all stoics to austerity,
satirists to asperity,
hard poets to complexity,
parliaments to prolixity,
Tom Eliot to Macavity,
seducers to depravity,
comedians to levity,
survivors to longevity.

Remember, going off to bed,
the greatest words of the great dead,
sing hallelujah or the blues,
and so to sleep by ones and twos.

CONTRIBUTORS

Renée Blanchette has been an educator in Charlottetown for twenty-five years. Enriched by the dual perspective of her French and English families, she has been writing poetry and short stories for years but has only recently begun to publish. Her chapbook, *On a Blue Colander*, was well-received in May 2014. Her ambition is to write the cultural stories of Islanders and their environment in candid, refreshing, and generous detail.

Brenda Brindell was born and raised on PEI and spent a great deal of her adult life living and working in Toronto. She retired to Panmure Island, where she wrote, gardened, and lived with her beloved husband, Murray Hill, and their cat Mia. Murray has since passed but continues to be an inspiration for her writing as is the lovely novel of prose poetry by Elizabeth Smart, *By Grand Central Station I Sat Down and Wept.*

Susan Buchanan is an award-winning author who decided to "get serious" about her writing when she turned fifty. Since then, she has written almost daily. She thanks her writing group for making her a better writer. Currently at work on a self-published poetry book, each fall she coordinates and hosts a one-day writing workshop for women. You can find her on Facebook.

Louise Burley was born in 1949 on PEI. Her family moved to Pennsylvania when she was young, but they came back to PEI every summer. In her twenties she worked as a reporter and freelance writer on PEI. She then moved to Halifax, where she spent over thirty years teaching part-time at various universities. She and her husband live in Lower Montague, PEI. They have two sons.

Sue Campbell lives and writes in Summerside, PEI. As well as stories and articles, she has published two books, *Dear Me,* in 2005, which won the 2005 Woman of Excellence Award, and *Two Bricks Short, My Journey With Cancer,* both published by Changing Tides. Sue has lived all across Canada and came home to Summerside in 1995. She always said, "When I grow up, I want to be a writer, for that is what I love to do." Growing up took a long time.

Margie Carmichael is a musician, entertainer, and writer. Her song, "Red Dirt Road," is a contemporary unofficial PEI anthem; one of her parodies, "Grenades and Spam," was aired on BBC Radio; her play, *Raining Cats and Daughters*, was produced by Mulgrave Road Theatre; her collection of short stories in collaboration with visual artist Dale MacNevin, *and my name is...Stories From the Quilt*, was published by Acorn Press. Margie is working on a fantasy novel. She lives in Pisquid with her husband, Michael Scotto.

Carolyn Charron is a transplanted Islander with short stories published in *The Saturday Evening Post, Fabula Argentea*, and *Enchanted Conversations*, among others. She writes all forms of speculative fiction and reads slush for the Hugo Award–nominated *Apex Magazine*. She is currently at work on her third novel, a magic-realism tale based on the Acadian Expulsion. She lives in Toronto with her husband and children.

Michael Conway was born and raised in Charlottetown. He enrolled in the Canadian Army at seventeen and served throughout Canada as well as in postings in Germany, the Middle East, and Cyprus. He enjoyed a second career in Charlottetown Police Services Telecommunications Section, retiring in 2013. In May 2014 he graduated from the University of Prince Edward Island with a Bachelor of Integrated Studies Degree and is currently working towards a Master of Arts in Island Studies.

Orysia Dawydiak is an award-winning writer of fiction and nonfiction. Her first novel, *House of Bears*, was published in 2009. *Kira's Secret*, the first of a young readers' series that takes place on Canada's Atlantic coast, was one of the books chosen to represent Prince Edward Island writers as PEI celebrated the pre-Confederation meetings 150 years ago. The second book, *Kira's Quest*, was published in 2015.

Catherine Edward lives in Belfast, PEI. Her award-winning book, *The Brow of Dawn— One Woman's Journey With MS,* was published by Acorn Press. She was a contributor to *Northern Lights—An Anthology of Contemporary Christian writing in Canada*, and to the anthology, *A Closet Full of Dresses.* She was one of forty-nine contributing writers to Canada CODE, the Vancouver Cultural Olympiad. She and Michael have three children and seven grandchildren.

Sarah Glassford is an Ontario-born Islander-by-Choice who holds a PhD in Canadian History. In 2012 she moved to Charlottetown to teach history at the University of Prince Edward Island. Although she has enjoyed creative writing since she was nine years old, this story (which grew out of her research on the PEI Women's Institutes during the First World War) marks her first venture into historical fiction.

Kathleen Hamilton is the author of *Sex After Baby: Why There is None*, published by Acorn Press. She is also an accomplished stage actress and a multiple-award-winning playwright, screenwriter, and poet. Her plays are *Shameless Hussies* and *Blonde Moments*. Kathleen's current project is a coming-of-age memoir entitled *High Flying Bird*.

Elaine Breault Hammond was born in Manitoba. After marriage, she moved with her family to many provinces and states, but PEI, where she started writing (instead of teaching), is her favourite. She published three books with Ragweed Press and was listed in *Who's Who in Canada* for her many writing awards. She published a fourth novel with Acorn Press. A fifth is in the works.

David Helwig was born in Toronto in 1938. He attended the University of Toronto and the University of Liverpool and in 1962 he began to teach at Queen's University. In 1980, he gave up teaching and became a full-time freelance writer. He has published fifteen books of poetry. Currently he lives in an old house in the village of Eldon in Prince Edward Island. His most recent book is *Clyde*, a novel.

Beth E. Janzen's fiction has appeared in *Riptides: New Island Fiction* and in *Galleon III*. Her poetry has been published in journals such as *The Antigonish Review*, *Grain*, and *The Malahat Review*. Her book of poetry, *The Enchanted House* (Acorn), was nominated for a PEI Book Award in 2008.

Glenna Jenkins' PEI roots hale back to 1830. Her short stories appeared in *Jilted Angels, A Collection of Short Stories*, published by Broad Street Press, and *Riptides: New Island Fiction*, from Acorn Press. Her first novel, *Somewhere I Belong*, based on a true story, was released in November 2014, also by Acorn Press. The Canadian Children's Book Centre selected this YA novel for its 2015 list of Best Books for Kids and Teens, and gave it a Star Rating, signifying "titles of exceptional calibre."

Sam Jensen has lived on the Island his whole life and at twenty-two is a student at the University of Prince Edward Island. This is his first published work, but he has been writing fiction for years and hopes to continue to do so in the future.

Louise Lalonde is a screenwriter and digital media producer. She has written, directed, and produced several short films and documentaries, and is working diligently towards writing and producing her first feature film. Louise runs an annual series of workshops, the PEI Screenwriters' Bootcamp, and has recently begun producing audio books by Atlantic Canadian authors.

Diana Lariviere has a history of interacting with people and hearing their stories. Born and raised in rural Quebec to a family involved in tourism, she met people from all walks of life. Her career in human resources and as a chartered arbitrator honed her skill as a technical writer. Diana now writes unique marriage ceremonies for clients and focuses her vivid imagination on storytelling. She lives in PEI with her husband and two dogs.

Jessie Lees writes that when she and her husband came to Canada from Scotland with three very young children, Christmas was a time of wonderment. Later, as a mathematics teacher, she felt delight when students came carolling. Later still, the season was linked to loss. Now, joys of life and realities of death are interwoven in a textured image of Christmas. Family and friends are still foreground figures.

T. N. MacCallum is the recipient of the 2014 Lucy Maud Montgomery Writing for Children Award. In 2013 she was shortlisted for the Maritime Electric Short Story Awards. Her writing has appeared in various Canadian journals and anthologies. She is the author of a collection of short fiction and is currently writing her first novel.

Philip Macdonald is a sixth-generation Islander who, because of his CNR Station Agent father, lived in communities around the Island and created fond memories of boyhood days in Tignish. Since his retirement from teaching he has taken up creative writing and published material in *The Voice for Island Seniors, Riptides: New Island Fiction*, and *RED: The Island Story Book*. He received an Honourable Mention Award in the 2014 Island Literary Awards.

Margôt Maddison-MacFadyen lives in PEI. She has published poems, short stories, and essays in journals such as the *Newfoundland Quarterly, Canadian Stories,* and *Bermuda Journal of Archaeology and Maritime History*, a long poem in *Women Remember the '60s and '70s*, and a book chapter in *Critical Insights: The Slave Narrative*. A co-editor of *A Gathering of TWiGS*, 2014 PEI Book Award recipient for poetry, she has won fiction and poetry prizes in the Island Literary Awards. She is a PhD candidate at Memorial University of Newfoundland.

Steven Mayoff lives in West Prince, PEI. He has published fiction and poetry in literary journals across Canada and the US and in Ireland, France, and Algeria. His story collection, *Fatted Calf Blues* (Turnstone Press 2009), won a PEI Book Award in 2010. His novel, *Our Lady Of Steerage,* was published in May 2015 by Bunim & Bannigan Ltd. He is currently completing a poetry collection, *Red Planet Postcards.*

David McCabe worked in four provinces as a teacher, school principal, and school superintendent. After forty-three years, he escaped the witless trap of political bureaucracies and quickly stumbled into the sticky web of poetry. He writes to discover surprising things about the world and himself. And to encourage graduate students in education to think more carefully about their students' learning needs, and to create more inspired careers for themselves. David resides in Stratford, PEI, with his wife Joanne.

Anne McCallum grew up in Scotland. After completing her English degree in Aberdeen, she wrote for the *Aylmer Reporter* near Ottawa. She has lived in Hazel Grove, PEI, since 1977. Highlights of her writing career include four years as a farm reporter, thirteen years as Managing Editor of *Common Ground; The News and Views of PEI Women*, and a decade as *Alumni Magazine* Editor/Communications Coordinator at UPEI. Now she is slowly strengthening her voice as a creative writer.

Liam McKenna is a writer and illustrator. His work can be found at oldsoulscomic.com, where he publishes cartoons with no consistency whatsoever, as well as in occasional publication on PEI and on the Internet. A lifelong Montreal Canadiens fan, Liam also contributes to the sports blog habseyesontheprize.com. He lives in Charlottetown with his wife, Holly, son, Elliot, and two goofy cats.

Ruth Mischler was born and educated in Switzerland, and moved to a farm on PEI thirty years ago, where she raised four children on her own. Writing poetry and short stories since the turn of the century, she has won several awards. She loves words, eagles, and hawks with their ability to grab her mind and fly it like a kite.

Dianne Hicks Morrow is PEI's current Poet Laureate, and a recipient of the Award for Distinguished Contribution to the Literary Arts on PEI. Her second poetry collection, *What Really Happened Is This,* won the 2012 PEI Book Award. Her non-fiction publications include *Kindred Spirits: Relationships that Spark the Soul* and a forthcoming memoir, *Fixing Up The Farmhouse: Forty Years of Living, Loving, and Lamenting* where a version of "Angel Missing" also appears—both from Acorn Press. She has given readings and workshops across Canada, and in Tasmania and Mexico. Several of her Seniors College classes still meet as independent writing groups.

Malcolm Murray is a philosopher, fiction writer, and playwright. His stories have appeared in *Fiction Fix* (2010), *Riptides* (2012), and *Galleon* (2015). His produced plays include *The Abettor* (2013) and *Art of Posing* (2014). His philosophy books include *The Moral Wager* (2007) and *The Atheist's Primer* (2010). He lives with his wife and a few other species.

Liza Oliver is originally from Newfoundland but has called PEI home for twenty years. She has written and performed monologues, and co-written and performed a play. In 2010 she was the recipient of an Island Literary Award for her fiction. Liza has dabbled in many forms of writing, and is currently completing a novel. She often draws from life's experiences to enrich her writing, finding joy and humour in almost everything.

Shaun Patterson, author and artist, makes his home in Charlottetown with his wife, Christina, and his dog, Rosco. Shaun is a learning manager with Holland College, as well as an illustrator and a musician in the local band, O'Leary. Shaun has written numerous children's books including *Fairies on My Island* and *The Pup From Away*.

Julie Pellissier-Lush, bestselling author of *My Mi'kmaq Mother*, was born in Summerside, PEI, in 1970. She grew up all over Eastern Canada and spent a number of years in Winnipeg, Manitoba, before coming home. She writes, acts, and does photography to preserve the history and culture of the Mi'kmaq for future generations. She lives in PEI with her husband, Rick, her five children, and her new granddaughter, Miah.

Dorothy Perkyns was a teacher in England before coming to Canada in 1969. She began writing in the early 1970s, publishing magazine articles and broadcasting on CBC radio. She is the author of seven young-adult novels. Her work has been approved for use in schools and nominated for a number of awards. *Rachel's Revolution* won the Bilson Award, a national award for historical fiction for young people.

Sylvia Poirier grew up on her family's farm in Miscouche. She had a long career in nursing education, followed by ten years as Registrar of Holland College. Now retired, Sylvia delights in her grandchildren and dabbles in gardening, hooking, painting, and politics.

Lee Ellen Pottie leads an active life as partner, mom, mamie, writer, photographer, painter, teacher/mentor, student, marketing coordinator, and editor for a company in the Yukon. She is still working on a poetry manuscript about Vincent Van Gogh, his letters, paintings, and life. Lee Ellen and her partner live in The Bird House where they garden, walk their collie, Théo, and babysit the grandchildren.

Sally Russell, originally American, came to Canada in 2005, and PEI in 2012, with her English husband. She has written five books on Georgia history, nature, and storytelling, published by the University of Georgia and Mercer University Presses. PEI feels like home with its red fields, farming, and folk who will tell you a story as an answer to almost any question.

Mersedeh Sayafi was born in Tehran, Iran, in 1995 and moved to Charlottetown with her family in 2010. She graduated from Colonel Gray High School with an International Baccalaureate diploma in 2013. Currently, she is an undergraduate student, studying Biology, at the University of Prince Edward Island. Mersedeh has had an active role in her community through volunteering, and shows an interest in writing as well as acting in plays.

Don Scott grew up in a coal-mining town in Cape Breton and has lived on PEI since 1964. During a two-year hiatus from university he worked as a coal miner, and as a meteorological technician with a ten-month adventure on Sable Island. After graduation from Mount Allison and McGill Universities, he worked at various positions in the Prince Edward Island Provincial Library Service. Always a storyteller, recounting incidents in Cape Breton and his later experiences, he is keeping a self-promise to record them.

Jeanette Scott grew up in rural Prince Edward Island at a time when it was common to see young people skating on local ponds. After a career as a teacher and an education consultant, she is now retired. She enjoys travelling, gardening, making music, and writing. She also derives vicarious pleasure from being a spectator of skating.

Laurel Smyth's early career in children's theatre honed her skills as a writer of plays, poetry, TV scripts, and fiction. Her work has been published in anthologies and magazines, and performed on stage, film, television, and radio. Laurel has received grants from the PEI Council of the Arts for writing and theatre work, and prizes from the Island Literary Awards, Theatre PEI Playwriting Competition, and PEI Theatre Festival. She now concentrates on her collection of short stories and stage plays. And on being Grandma Lolo, the greatest reward of all.

Richard Snow and his wife Wendy live in the century-old farmhouse she grew up in, on the edge of Malpeque Bay. He loves equally the tranquility of a shaded hammock in the summer breeze and the allure of the open road. Richard considers himself fortunate to be surrounded by the talented and encouraging circle of PEI authors and editors, including a constantly challenging and supportive writing group. *Kennebecasis* is from a work in progress about the open roads of his life.

J. J. Steinfeld lives in Charlottetown, where he patiently waits for Godot's arrival and a phone call from Kafka. While waiting, he has published sixteen books, including novels, *Our Hero in the Cradle of Confederation* and *Word Burials*; short story collections, *Dancing at the Club Holocaust, Should the Word Hell Be Capitalized?, Anton Chekhov Was Never in Charlottetown, Would You Hide Me?, A Glass Shard and Memory,* and *Madhouses in Heaven, Castles in Hell*; and poetry collections, *An Affection for Precipices, Misshapenness,* and *Identity Dreams and Memory Sounds*.

Helena Sullivan was born and raised in Sherwood, PEI. Her favourite pastime is reading and writing short stories. She is proud to have survived raising five teenagers, who finally left the nest, allowing her to enjoy her husband, her dog, and a tidy home. She is also proud to have won third prize (2009) and first prize (2010) in the PEI Literary Awards and first prize in the *Eastern Graphic*'s Adult Essay Contest, December 2010.

Jocelyn Thorne is an uprooted Islander, born and raised in Alberton, and now living in Saint John, NB. A retired bookkeeper, she dreams and longs for the red clay, sandy shores, and salty sea air of home. After retirement, she decided to pursue a lifelong dream of writing, has coauthored a story for *Red: the Island Story Book* magazine, and is working on a second novel. Her other interests include history, genealogy, reading, and travelling.

David D. Varis, a Scandinavian Cree, is an educator, poet, storyteller, photographer, and visual artist. He is the founding member of the Aboriginal Writers Circle of Prince Edward Island and created the first Aboriginal stage production for the Charlottetown Fringe Festival. His published works are principally in the field of addictions; but he always welcomes opportunities to explore and present on the experiences of First Nation peoples of Canada.

Florence Vos immigrated to Canada as a young elementary school teacher. She had teaching positions in Ontario, British Columbia, Yukon, and NWT. Her husband was in the RCMP. They chose to come to PEI when they left the North, and were happy to be able to raise their three children on the Island. Until she joined the writing group fostered by the Seniors College of PEI, the only writing Florence had done was letters to friends and family.

Paul Vreeland's poetry and prose have won several Island Literary Awards, and his work has appeared in Canadian journals such as *Grain Magazine*, *CV2*, and *The Toronto Quarterly*. He has published two chapbooks, *Hydrostone Quartet* and *Mother-in-Law Suite*, and "Smoked Herring and the Talking Dog," a short story based on his Haiti experiences, appeared in *The Caribbean Writer*. Torn between writing and photography (three-time "best in show" winner in the PEI annual photo club show), he maintains a blog at artsconflicted.wordpress.com.

Sean Wiebe lives in Charlottetown and is an associate professor of education at the University of Prince Edward Island. For the last three years he has been researching the connections among critical thinking and writing and arts-based methodologies. A portfolio of his work can be accessed at upei.academia.edu/SeanWiebe.